Immigrants and Nationalists

IMMIGRANTS AND NATIONALISTS

ETHNIC CONFLICT AND ACCOMMODATION IN CATALONIA, THE BASQUE COUNTRY, LATVIA, AND ESTONIA

GERSHON SHAFIR

STATE UNIVERSITY OF NEW YORK PRESS

Published by
State University of New York Press, Albany

For information, address State University of New York Press,
Stte University Plaza, Albany, N.Y. 12246

Production by M. R. Mulholland
Marketing by Dana E. Yanulavich

Library of Congress Cataloging in Publication Data

Shafir, Gershon.
    Immigrants and nationalists : ethnic conflict and accommodation in
  Catalonia, the Basque Country, Latvia, and Estonia / Gershon Shafir.
       p.   cm.
    Includes bibliographical references and index.
    ISBN 0-7914-2673-4 (acid-free paper). — ISBN 0-7914-2674-2 (pbk.
  : acid-free paper)
      1. Nationalism—Case studies.   2. Ethnicity—Case studies.
  3. Immigrants—Case studies.   4. Xenophobia—Case studies.
  I. Title.
  JC 11.S484   1995
  305.8—dc20   94-46187
                                       CIP

Inheritors of the rhetoric of the homeland,
into which we fit like a glove,
although just yesterday,
it seemed too tight.

—Julia Hartwig

The nations that form the subject of history are no mere products of nature, but of world history...

—Otto Hintze

CONTENTS

MAPS

TABLES

Acronyms

AP	Alianza Popular [Popular Alliance]
CDRP	Current Digest of the Russian Press
CDS	Centro Democrático y Social [Democratic and Social Center]
CDSP	Current Digest of the Soviet Press
CNT	Confederación Nacional del Trabajo [National Confederation of Labor]
CPSU	Communist Party of the Soviet Union
CSCE	Commission on Security and Cooperation in Europe
EA	Eusko Alkartasuna [Basque Solidarity]
EE	Euskadiko Ezkerra [Basque Country Left]
EIU	The Economist Intelligence Unit
ECP	Estonian Communist Party
ESSR	Estonian Soviet Socialist Republic
ETA	Euskadi ta Askatasuna [Freedom for the Basque Country]
HB	Herri Batasuna [People United]
IU	Izquierda Unida [United Left]
LCP	Latvian Communist Party
PCE	Partido Comunista de Euskadi
PCE	Partido Comunista de España
PDC/CiU	Pacte Democràtic per Catalunya/Convergència i Unió
PSUC/IC	Partit Socialista Unificat de Catalunya/Iniciativa per Catalunya
PNV	Partido Nacionalista Vasco [Basque Nationalist Party]
PP	Partido Popular
PSC	Parti dels Socialistes de Catalunya [Party of Catalan Socialists]
PSOE	Partido Socialista Obrero Español [Spanish Socialist Workers Party]
PSE	Partido Socialista de Euskadi [Basque Socialist Party]
RSSFR	Russian Soviet Socialist Federal Republic
SSR	Soviet Socialist Republic
UCELC	United Council of Estonian Labor Collectives [formerly United Council of Production Collectives]

UCD-CC   Unión de Centro Democrático-Centristes de Catalunya
UGT   Unión General de Trabajadores [General Union of
          Workers]

PREFACE

Nationalism in its wide ranging manifestations, from benign to sinister, has always been a source of fascination as well as concern to me. The barriers placed by nationalists in the way of the waves of global immigration has brought home its vast influence yet again. An empirical study of nationalism, ethnicity, and immigration and their interaction seemed necessary to sort out the different aspects and limitations. Comparative and historical sociology go a long way toward providing the tools for this task.

I chose to study nationalism in developed regions because of the challenge they posed to existing theoretical wisdom and because they seemed to have a number of potentially benign inclusionary aspects. In the autumn of 1988, when I first read about the formation of the Popular Front movements in the then Latvian SSR and Estonian SSR of the USSR, I planned to compare Catalonia with Latvia and Estonia. Later that year, when I read Diez Medrano's dissertation I recognized that there is another type of nationalism in developed regions, every bit as exclusionary as some of the less savory types of nationalism, and included the Basque case in the study.

Anybody familiar with the work of Juan Diez Medrano on the genesis and character of Catalan and Basque nationalism and of Kit Woolard on Catalan society and language will notice the profound impact they had on my thinking. Many of my thanks go them for their warm personal support and for putting at my disposal unpublished versions of their work. It is a pleasure to thank my student Lynne Hanney, who helped me collect sources when I started this project. I gratefully acknowledge the helped given to me by Ana Devic with some of the Russian sources. This might be the first time Edis Bevan and the other "mailmen" of the Balt-L computer network are thanked for their contribution to a research project, but probably not the last time. And I would like to thank Andy Scull for being the thoughtful and dependable colleague he consistently has been to me. Carlos Waisman gave me very useful suggestions on an earlier version of the manuscript which helped give this work its present emphases.

Chapters from earlier versions of this study were presented at
different forums: at the Second International Conference of the International Society for the Study of European Ideas on European
Nationalism: Toward 1992, in Leuven, Belgium, in September 1990;
at the 62nd Conference of the Pacific Sociological Association in
Irvine in March, 1991; at the Gaspar de Portolà Catalan Studies
Program of the University of California, Berkeley, in April 1991; and
at the Convention of the Hungarian Sociological Association on
Hungary in the World: Central European Societies from the Perspective of Comparative Social Analysis, in Budapest on June 24–28,
1991.

1

INTRODUCTION

Contemporary migration waves pose a clear challenge to the European conception of the nation-state as the political framework of a culturally homogenous citizenry. In fact, the presentation of the nation-state as the spontaneous corollary of commonality of language, historical continuity, common descent, and shared religion or religious tradition has usually been based on the expurgation from the collective memory of the actual homogenization of the nation, through the transcendence or suppression of local and super-national identities by a centralizing state. But global factors once again increase the heterogeneity of nation-states. The growing number of migrants and their descendants, having forsaken one nation-state but not yet merged into another, therefore, pose legal and cultural anomalies.

Although immigration is hardly a new phenomenon, in the past few decades the rate of migration has accelerated considerably over previous periods and more countries are affected by global migration than before. In the era of reconstruction after the Second World War, many Western European employers, with the assistance and active involvement of their governments, set up organized schemes for the recruitment, control, and regulation of temporary migrant workers from lesser developed countries.[1] When the same governments, at a time of economic recession and with the global dispersal of investments, sought to slow or stem the tide of immigration they discovered that global forces of change had overtaken them. By the 1990s, the marketization of many of the command economies, the disappearance of old empires, the redrawing of boundaries, and the consequent national conflicts added their huddled masses of immigrants and refugees to the earlier "guestworkers," many of whom also elected to remain in their host societies and raise their families there. The new international migration waves are part of a transnational transformation that is reordering many societies and their politics around the globe. Increased immigration will undoubtedly continue into the developed societies and transform their demographic compositions and social structures and, by increasing their heterogeneity, lead to a crisis and reevaluation of their collective identities.

My aim, in this study, is to examine *the variation in the reception of masses of immigrants* in developed states or regions that, at the same time, are also known as possessing distinct cultures and nationalist movements of their own. Immigrants to developed regions pose only a limited threat of economic competition and, therefore, rarely jeopardize the economic well-being of its relatively prosperous people. Furthermore, these immigrants associate the culture of their host societies with their high level of economic development. Conferring high prestige on the culture of their adopted societies, the immigrants are usually willing to be integrated into their customs and culture, learn their language, and intermarry with their inhabitants. These immigrants are not likely to "denationalize" their new societies or significantly dilute their culture and its manifestations. Nevertheless, even in developed states or regions there are nationalist protests against the threat that large-scale immigration seems to pose to the region's economic well-being or cultural identity.

A special case of immigration involves migration from one national territory to another without, however, requiring immigration from one state to another. *Internal migration* usually takes the form of movement from the countryside or small towns to cities as part of the process of industrialization that in some cases favors one region over others within a multiethnic state. There is an obvious difference between the two kinds of migrants in that international immigrants cross political borders and, therefore, are subject to state regulation through naturalization and the acquisition of citizenship whereas internal migrants are by and large free to come and go.

The current emphasis among students of immigration, however, is less on the division between citizen and noncitizen immigrants and more on the variety of intermediary statuses and additional changes required for the immigrants' successful integration. Hammar, for example, locates between citizens and foreigners a new status group of "denizens" who, though not naturalized have attained a secure resident status due to length of stay or other ties.[2] Others point out that substantial citizenship does not follow automatically from formal citizenship (or in T. H. Marshall's distinction, possession of political citizenship does not have to afford access to full civil or social citizenship rights)[3] nor does it protect against widespread discrimination on the basis of ethnic, national, or gender difference.[4] Under conditions of migration within a multiethnic state, therefore, the vulnerability due to nationalist hostility might exist in spite of inalienable political citizenship rights.

Instead of singularly focusing on issues related to the access of immigrants to citizenship we will be better served by inquiring how sharply and rigidly the line of demarcation is drawn between them and the native born. Where the insistence on the cultural homogeneity of the nation is strong, political citizenship will be less valuable and other vulnerabilities are more likely to accompany the lack of or limitations on citizenship. Conversely, where the division between hosts and immigrants is ambiguous or muted and a multiplicity of cultures is tolerated, the potential for the integration of immigrants is enhanced. Theories of immigrant-host relations that examine the preconditions for assimilation and segregation will allow us to place the question of citizenship within this broader framework of cultural and structural relations.

Though differential access to citizenship denotes a crucial difference between international and internal immigrants and has to be examined on its own right, many of the other economic and cultural characteristics of migration are shared by the two types of migrants. The subject of this study will be internal but inter-national migration to developed regions because it directs us to focus on the broader parameters of immigrant-host relations of which the willingness to grant political citizenship is but one manifestation.

To examine immigrant-host relations and their variations I will place in a comparative framework four developed regions at opposite ends of Europe: Catalonia and the Basque provinces (known together as Euskadi) in Spain and the Republics of Latvia and Estonia on the Baltic shore of the former Soviet Union. Starting at different historical moments, these regions became economically more developed than the state of which they are, or were, part of as indicated by per capita incomes above the national average. Though Euskadi lost ground since the mid 1970s it still is—as are the other three—a relatively developed industrialized region. The four regions also possess distinctive cultural attributes that potentially set them apart from Spain and Russia, and later the USSR, respectively. The special combination of economic development and cultural distinctiveness sustained in all four significant national movements that have been intermittently active for over a century and left a distinct imprint on their history.

The cases under study also share a demographic condition. As developed regions that are part of less-developed states they lacked the political power to stem or prevent the arrival of internal immigrants.

These regions, like so many southern Californias, attracted immigrant workers or cadres from other, less developed, parts of Spain and the USSR, respectively. As a result, the percentage of the native born has declined in the Basque country to 67.5 percent, in Catalonia to 63.7 percent, in Estonia to 61.5 percent, and in Latvia it became as low as 52 percent of the total population.[5] Furthermore, in the urban population, particularly in capital cities such as Barcelona, Bilbao, Riga, and Tallinn, the concentration of immigrants is even heavier.[6]

Immigrants relocate to other prosperous areas and states as well, but the populations of the regions in this study are relatively small: 1.5 million in Estonia; 2.6 million in Latvia; 2.3 million in the three Basque provinces; and 6.1 million in Catalonia. Because of the size of the population and their inability to control the influx, immigration carries a special onus for the nationalists of these regions. The process of "demographic denationalization" seems to threaten the professed uniqueness of their ethnic or cultural identity, and migration has served in three of these regions as a rallying cry for the nationalist movements. The clear exception is Catalonia, where immigration has not generated sustained opposition or served as the trigger of its nationalism. While Catalans sought to assimilate Andalusians, Murcians, and Castilians, the hostile attitude toward the Russian, Ukrainian, and Belorussian residents of the Baltic republics was expressed through the speedy adoption of restrictive electoral and language laws by the first relatively freely elected republican Supreme Councils (i.e., Parliaments) under *glasnost*.[7] After independence, these exclusionary policies were incorporated into citizenship laws, though in Latvia in a more extreme fashion than in Estonia. The Estonians, with a legacy of a liberal minority policy in the interwar years and less massive Soviet intervention than in neighboring Latvia, still seem to be unsure of their ultimate approach toward the immigrants. In the Basque country, the relationship to Spanish immigrants had undergone significant change: in the last decade of the nineteenth century, Sabino Arana, the founder of Basque nationalism, agitated to have them expelled, but since the 1960s the many factions of the, otherwise extremist, ETA adopted a more accomodationist perspective toward immigrants, though one of dubious coherence. Basque nationalism, therefore, is somewhere in between the Catalan integrationist view and the exclusionary Baltic one.

I would like to reiterate that the attitude of the immigrants toward integration cannot explain the divergence in the nationalists' positions toward them. In all four regions, there exist many distinct and separate indicators of the willingness of the majority of the immigrants, though far from all, to integrate into their new societies, and in this respect they are not different from most immigrants to other well-developed regions. The imbalance between the immigrants' readiness and the measure of the nationalist opposition indicates that the causes of antiimmigrant hostility are usually found among the hosts. My goal in this study will be to locate and present the factors that explain this variation in host societies and evaluate its consequences.

The intersection of migration and nationalist and ethnic conflict within the structure and ethos of the modern nation-state also demands a theoretical effort to join the literatures on immigration and nationalism that, so far, have addressed these areas of research as separate concerns.[8] My theoretical aim in this study is to juxtapose *theories of immigrant-host relations*, which examine the conditions and patterns of conflict and accommodation within immigration societies, with *theories of nationalism*, which seek to understand the origins and dynamics of nationalist sentiments and movements in developed regions.

The extent of the willingness to integrate immigrants is, in large part, a reflection of the task set by the nationalists for themselves that, itself, is the product of the conditions under which nationalism emerged and is being reproduced. The major split seems to be between nationalists who view their task as defensive, that is, the protection of their nation from the ravages of external, usually modernizing, political, cultural, and economic forces, and those who believe that they are well positioned to ride the forces of modernization to advance their nation's fortunes. Immigrants usually arrive as a direct result of the regions' industrialization and, therefore, become emblematic of modernity. Opposition to the winds of modernity eo ipso entails fear of immigrants just as sympathy to modernity reduces the potential of anxiety vis-à-vis immigrants.

I will label the defensive form of nationalism, which simultaneously favors excluding immigrants or viewing them as a separate ethnic minority, *corporate nationalism*, and the modernizing one, which also tends toward the assimilation of immigrants or is ready to tolerate multiple cultures, *hegemonic nationalism*.[9] As the Basque case—where a transition from a rigidly corporate to a less coherent but clearly hegemonic conception of the nation—demonstrates, these attitudes are not fixed in an immutable conception of the nation. Similarly, the opposite shift from granting the most far-reaching cultural autonomy to minorities in independent Estonia in the inter-war years to a more restrictive policy toward Slavic immigrants after the restoration of their independence in 1991, points to the decisive influence of the changing conditions under which nationalists operate.

Hostility toward immigrants in relatively developed regions is rooted neither in the threat of "denationalization" nor in economic competition but, I wish to argue, in the danger they pose to the *way of life and privileges* of traditional and to the *privileged position* of modern political, economic, and cultural *elites* already unsettled by the uneven pattern of development that set their regions at a variance with the state of which it is a part. These threatened elites conse-quently transform regional cultural distinctions into nationalist sentiments and the latter into antiimmigration movements.

The extent of the readiness to grant political citizenship and collective cultural and linguistic rights to immigrants and view them as contributing to the dominant national group's own culture is strongly influenced by the intensity of the host societies' own struggle for democracy. Nationalists in each of the four region have struggled not just for autonomy or independence but were also at the forefront of the battles to overthrow authoritarian regimes: Primo de Rivera's and Franco's dictatorships in Catalonia and the Basque provinces, Czarism and Soviet authoritarianism in the Baltic republics. Where the struggles for independence and democracy coincided and were sufficiently drawn out, the gap between host and immigrants usually lessened.

Conversely, hostility toward immigrants, whether taking the form of xenophobia, discrimination, or the restriction of access to civil, political, and social citizenship rights jeopardizes the immigrant populations as well as the stability and democracy of the host society. There was, and continues to be, a close association between economic modernization, in-migration, national aspirations, and the struggle for democracy in these regions. In the long run it is doubtful whether democratic societies, which are based on the political equality of their citizens, will be able to remain stable if they are composed of citizens and a significant portion of denizens and foreigners.

I will now present the theories of immigration to be followed by a theory of nationalism in developed regions. Then, I will examine the limitations of our theory of nationalism in developed regions for the study of issues relevant to immigration. The final section will pose the question of immigrant-host relations in the theoretical terms proposed in this Introduction. In Chapter 2 I will argue for the comparability of the cases under study, and Chapters 3, 4, and 5 will be devoted to detailed studies of nationalism and the relevant issues of immigration in Catalonia, the Basque country, and the Baltic republics of Estonia and Latvia, respectively. The sixth chapter will present the conclusions of this study.

Immigrants and Hosts

The study of immigrant-host relations may be divided into three fairly distinct theoretical frameworks: push and pull or assimilation, structural inequality or segmentation, and multiculturalism. The first of these theories—a theory of social mobility and assimilation—originated in the quintessential immigration society: the United States, between the 1920s and the mid 1960s as a reflection of the experience of the largest wave of immigrants to it. The second one—a theory of segmentation—evolved in response to migration to both the United States and western Europe, in the years following the Second World War. Finally, multiculturalism,the most recent of the theories, has emerged in Canada, Australia, Great Britain, and Sweden in the early 1970s and surfaced in the United States more recently.

Push-and-pull theories viewed immigration as a mechanism for restoring economic disequilibrium between societies at different levels of development. Potential migrants were pushed out of their unrewarding agrarian societies and pulled by a modernizing society's promise of available jobs, higher income, and social mobility. This liberal, or laissez-faire, perspective is associated with the Chicago School of sociology, and expressed in the assimilation theory developed by its foremost proponent, Robert Park.[10]

Although newcomers often live under wretched conditions and struggle to find their way in the mazes of a new culture, Park posited a cycle of host-immigrant relations that leads from initial contact to competition, and from conflict to accommodation and, finally, assimilation. By assimilation he essentially meant the fading of ethnic differences and the disappearance of ethnic groups in the process of the Americanization of individual immigrants. Although cultural differences and racial characteristics determine the length of assimilation and, where differences between immigrants and hosts are bigger, might prolong this process, he expected all immigrants to eventually reach the final destination of assimilation.

A more complex, and open-ended, version of assimilation is found in Milton Gordon's work. He distinguished seven stages of assimilation, spawning from cultural to structural, to marital, to identificational, to attitudinal, to receptional, and finally, to civic assimilation. Though Gordon might have been carried away in breaking down the process of assimilation into so many constituent units and others might arrange the stages in a different order, he, nevertheless, established some important relationships between the more important subtypes. He contended that cultural assimilation, or acculturation, though the first attained upon immigrant-host contact, does not necessarily lead to structural assimilation. Only once structural assimilation, or "large scale entry into cliques, clubs, and institutions of host society," takes place, Gordon concluded, will "all of the other types of assimilation...naturally follow."[11]

For the purposes of this study, I will be satisfied with the more modest distinction between two stages in the incorporation of immigrants into their adopted society. I will refer to Gordon's structural assimilation by the term *integration*, that is, structural incorporation into local economic, political, and other organizations, and to all other aspects of incorporation by the term *assimilation*, that is cultural incorporation through, for example, learning the local language and marrying local spouses.

As part of their larger dilemma of assimilation-separation, most immigrants face in their adopted land a linguistic dilemma: their native language ties them to their old society whereas their new society speaks another language. Inglehart and Woodward presented a theory that fits in with the assimilationist approach. They set out two conditions under which a language exerts a strong assimilative influence on the speakers of other tongues in a multilingual situation: it has to be the language of a prosperous country and no barriers should exist to its acquisition. In the absence of such barriers the path of social mobility is open to bilingual members of linguistic minority groups.[12] The prevalence of each of these two conditions encourages linguistic assimilation and their coincidence makes it a likely outcome, whereas the absence of each, or both, will contribute to the continued separation of the groups from one another and to linguistic diversity.

The push-and-pull theory expects social mobility and entry into the manifold institutions of the host society to lead, in most cases, to a gradual assimilation of the immigrants. Though usually called an *assimilation theory* it could therefore, with equal justice, be termed the *mobility theory* of host-immigrant relations.

The second set of theories argues that the result of immigration is not the reduction of inequality but its maintenance or even enhancement. The neo-Marxist theories, for example in Castels and Kosack's and Portes and Walton's versions,[13] still view immigration as a result of the unevenness of the world economy but approach it with the tools of political economy. In this view, cheap labor is the key to profit appropriation by capitalist entrepreneurs in the developed world, while the departure of immigrant workers simultaneously removes the pressure for socioeconomic change on the dominant classes of the lesser developed regions. Immigration, in short, is an integral part of the capitalist system's worldwide inequality and interregional domination. Consequently, within the developed economies immigrants are channelled into sectors of the labor market where incomes are lower. Immigrant workers cannot attain the social mobility expected by push-and-pull theory and remain segregated in the lower segments of the market or in ethnic enclaves. The ethnicization of the lower segments of the working class and the establishment of permanent barriers to occupational mobility and cultural assimilation makes their exclusion long lasting.

The most recent, and still not very well defined, of the theories of host-immigrant relations, is multiculturalism. The adoption of self-styled multiculturalist policies by the governments of the typical immigration countries of Australia and Canada in the early 1970s resulted from the replacement of quota system with universal immigration policies in the former and the desire to limit the ethnic appeal and range of demands of francophone Quebeçois in the latter. Sweden and Great Britain also espoused multiculturalist policies by extending their already established approach of integrating the working class into society through the extension of social citizenship rights to immigrants. In the Netherlands multiculturalism rests on the precedent of religious tolerance and the establishment of confessional economic, political, and cultural institutions.[14] In short, the origins of multiculturalism are diverse though its aims in different countries seem to be similar.

In contrast to both push-and-pull and segmentation theories that describe spontaneous phenomena, multiculturalism is a governmental policy and in some places also emerged as a social movement. Multiculturalist policies use tax money to set up, for example, ethnic schools and cultural institutions, research institutions for writing ethnic histories, ethnic radio stations, but also of diversifying school curricula in public schools, and so on. In some cases the policy includes institutional watchdogs to guard against discrimination of individual immigrants in employment and housing. Nevertheless, multiculturalism addresses inequality on a narrow front only. Its proponents attack direct discrimination while ignoring the larger economic dynamic that placed the immigrants at the lower rungs of the developed economy in the first place. Multiculturalists usually accept the political practices of the host state as a common, public framework for all residents.

The goal of multiculturalism, simply stated, is to allow and facilitate each ethnic group's right to develop its own culture and values within the context of the founding majority's political framework while diversifying the majority's culture and including as an integral part the contributions made by immigrants. Both immigrants and hosts, in this view, have to traverse part of way to meet each other. In Castles and Miller's words: "immigrants are not forced to conform to a dominant cultural or linguistic model but rather can maintain their native languages and cultural life if they choose to do so. The diversity produced by immigration is seen as an enrichment rather than as a threat to the predominant culture."[15]

Diversity is viewed as a value in itself, but advocates of multiculturalism qualify it in two ways. First, insofar as diversity is justified in the name of greater democracy, they reject religious and legal practices in the immigrants' cultures that are incompatible with human rights—such as those that violate gender equality—accepted in the host societies. Second, they warn against the danger of treating culture as preset and fixed values. After all, viewing culture in an "essentialist" fashion might stifle the development of cultural change, for example, the combination of cultural elements from the immigrant and host cultures, and thus slow the process of integration and ultimately assimilation of the children of immigrants.[16]

It seems that multiculturalism represents the uncertainty typical to an interregnum, the era when it is not yet known whether the post-Second World War migrants will assimilate or remain in restricted segments of the economy and evolve the permanent features of an ethnic minority. The statistical and anecdotal evidence presented from Catalonia and the Basque country points to signs of social mobility and occupational integration among Spanish immigrants, but also to continued residential and cultural separation. In short, the jury is still out on the fate of the post-1945 immigrants; it is not clear how far will their integration proceed, and if it does whether it will lead to assimilation, as was the case with most immigrants who arrived before the Second World War.

Multiculturalist policies in Sweden, like almost everywhere where they are being tried out, are based on the expectation that the immigrants affected by them will eventually be integrated into Swedish society although only with the passing of a number of generations.[17] In Australia, high levels of intermarriage between children of immigrants and native-born Australians also indicate the temporary span of multicultural practices.[18] The British sociologist John Rex states this expectation most clearly:

> it is wrong to suggest that European societies will move from being monocultural to being permanently multicultural. Indeed I do not think that they should be. What is likely to happen over three or four generations is that some members of the minorities will voluntarily enter the mainstream and that, as they do, they may well modify the shared culture of the society. What will remain will be the symbolic ethnicity which is common among those descended from European immigrant groups in the United States.[19]

If multiculturalist aims correspond to a temporary stage, then their vagueness, for which this approach is criticized so frequently, might be one of its main assets. This ambiguity allows multiculturalism to cohabit with either assimilation or segmentation, though permanent compromise between these views is unlikely. The evolution of multiculturalism into a permanent quota system, for example, cannot be squared with the civic conception of individual rights. Pervasive occupational and residential segmentation will also severely limit the chances of multiculturalist accommodation.

Another way to recognize the novelty of multiculturalism and the greater flexibility it affords to interethnic relations is to compare it with an alternative approach, the offspring of an earlier era that evolved as part of the theory and practice of nationalism for national groups that found themselves under conditions where self-determination was impossible. With the victory of the principle of self-determination in the wake of the First World War, the Hapsburg and Ottoman Empires were broken into nation-states and the national groups that were too small or too dispersed, and therefore did not gain a territory of their own, were placed under the protection of the League of Nation's *national minority* system. Though the league's covenant did not address the issue of minorities, it signed specific treaties with the successor states under which the latter agreed to guarantee the rights of their national minorities to enjoy equal civil rights, the right to establish at their own expense cultural and welfare institutions and schools, the right to practice their religion and use their language in private and public, and so forth.[20]

In contrast to the League of Nations' haphazard system of treaties that, therefore, did not lead to the creation of customary international law, the United Nations adopted a new approach. Although its charter again ignores minorities and emphasizes the protection of individual human rights, Article 27 of its International Covenant on Civil and Political Rights (known as the *Political Covenant*) from 1966 states that "in those states in which ethnic, religious or linguistic minorities exist, persons belonging to such minorities shall not be denied the right, in community with the other members of the group, to enjoy their own culture, to profess and practice their own religion, or to use their own language."[21]

This declaration still suffers from four obvious weaknesses: it does not define what a minority is, it guarantees the rights of individuals and not groups, the rights it seeks to protect are presented only in a negative fashion, and finally, it implicitly refers only to citizens and thus excludes foreigners and stateless people from its purview.[22] Even the 1992 Declaration on the Rights of Persons Belonging to National or Ethnic, Religious and Linguistic Minorities settles only one of these ambiguities by restating minority rights in positive terms. At the same time, the declaration does not resolve clearly any of the other ambiguities, though it refers alternatively to "persons belonging to minorities" and to "minorities." This treaty, in Lerner's view, "is not innovative" and "on the whole...is...mild." He concludes that "the international community is not ready to embody rules regarding minorities in an obligatory treaty."[23]

At a time when traditional minorities enjoy only "a rudimentary regime for the protection of minorities,"[24] Wolfrum points out, "new minorities," such as migrant workers, trading diasporas, and Russians who remained outside Russia in the process of the USSR's break up, came into being. Do the "new minorities," he asks, enjoy even the partially developed rights guaranteed to the old minorities? A United Nations memorandum from 1949 defines minorities as groups "which have long formed a group different from the main population," such as groups that had a state of their own or were living in a part of their own state that lost jurisdiction over their area of residence.[25] The Slavic populations of Latvia and Estonia are neither a classical old nor a typical new minority. They indeed lived in part of the USSR that used to be and now is again independent Latvia and Estonia. But the presence of most Russians and Ukrainians in the Latvian and Estonian SSR is relatively recent, they immigrated after the annexation of the region to the USSR and, consequently, hardly constitute a historical national minority. Furthermore, they are concentrated only in some regions of the Baltic republics, most are dispersed in many cities and towns. Consequently, they might be considered either a minority or a group of immigrants. A multiculturalist approach, therefore, might serve as an alternative to their recognition as a national minority.

The relevant question is, What would the differences be between considering the Russian and Ukrainian residents of Latvia and Estonia a national minority or an ethnic group with blurred boundaries within a multicultural society?

Territorially concentrated national minorities and political institutions are more distinct and stabler than immigrant groups made of mostly dispersed individuals. The recognition of a group as a national minority, which often predates the modern state, accepts the society's permanent cultural and national fragmentation whereas multiculturalism seeks to fashion a new national culture made up of many diverse strands and is usually contemplated for a limited duration. The protection of minorities seeks unity in spite of diversity, multiculturalism pursues unity through diversity.

In the Baltic context, Russians and Ukrainians might evolve either into a permanent national minority or, given the indications many of them gave of their readiness to identify with the new Baltic states, become integrated into them depending, in large part, on the policy adopted by the Estonian and Latvian authorities toward them.

Immigrants and stateless people, as our survey of national minority protection has shown, rarely have the rights that national minorities may claim, in large part because they are not citizens of that state.[26] Granting citizenship to the majority of the Slavic inhabitants in Estonia and Latvia will go a long way toward dampening their hostility toward their hosts, but only in combination with a multiculturalist approach is it likely to lead to the integration of the Russian-speakers over time. Granting secure minority rights to the Slavic populations to establish their own cultural institutions is likely to lower the level of suspicion and conflict but will simultaneously enhance the separation between the groups. The potential for conflict will be the highest if the Russians, Ukrainians, and Belorussians will become recognized as a permanent Russian-speaking minority without being granted rights of citizenship. Such approach enhances the very dangers that the official recognition, protection, and cultivation of cultural and national distinctiveness of a group, by granting it minority rights, seeks to avoid; it might lead to expressions of peripheral nationalism and irredentist aspirations.

One more facet of multiculturalism ties it not into the theoretical frameworks of host-immigrant relations but to the process of globalization. Although it is customary to point to the ways in which globalization reduces differences between societies far apart, it has another side. Globalization also enhances specialization and with it the occupational, regional, and technological *diversification* of modern industrial societies. Multiculturalism might be one of the approaches that successfully expresses the diversity of developed societies already cross-cut by the requirements of a complex or, in Emile Durkheim's terms, organic division of labor and organic solidarity.

Though multiculturalist tolerance is most likely to work as a facilitator during periods of uncertainty, it probably also expresses a diminished aspiration for the homogeneity of industrial societies and the recognition of the potential benefits of cultural heterogeneity for expediting the absorption of outside influences in an increasingly more cosmopolitan world. Multiculturalism, if so, is a step beyond the liberal goal of "pluralism," though along the same route, and it entails both the recognition of diversity of immigration societies and the weakening of the purported goal of nation-states to homogenize their populations.

Hegemonic and Corporate Nationalism

Attitudes to immigrants in the modern era are frequently articulated by nationalist movements or justified by reference to nationalist sentiments. Examining immigration reception by nationalists in relatively developed regions requires that we consider the relationship of nationalism and development in general.

Influential theories of nationalism, both neo-Marxist approaches derived from Trotsky's writings and liberal perspectives, view it as a response to the *uneven pattern of development* in the modern era. The pressure of the early developers' rapid economic and military buildup on their less modernized neighbors, argue Hechter and Nairn, led to the subjugation of some of the latter, put others at the risk of becoming colonies of the former, and therefore compelled many of them to try to catch up.[27] Nationalism proved to be the most potent mobilizing ideology for the sacrifices required by modernization at a neck-breaking speed and for the creation of a solidarity that overrides traditional infra- and supranational divisions as well as competing modern class divisions. Nationalism is a unique synthesis of economics, culture, and politics; namely, politicized culture in pursuit of economic development. This creative synthesis is focused on the attainment of an independent state uniquely equipped to protect and promote the economy and raise the status of a given culture.

Liberal versions of uneven development, for example, Ernest Gellner's work, also hold that the unequal and gradual spread of industrialization created or enhanced gaps of development between the regions it penetrated and by "engender[ing] very sharp and painful and conspicuous inequality"[28] between them became one of the causes of nationalist dissension. Nationalism, in both neo-Marxist and liberal theories of uneven development, is the reaction of suffering regions and social groups; and their protests against the misfortune, or injustice, of unequal growth is also a strategy for rectifying it through massive interclass mobilization and accelerated development.

According to Tom Nairn, however, nationalist movements may also emerge in small regions with relatively scant populations that are more prosperous, due to their rapid capitalist development, than the rest of the state of which they are a part. The aim of nationalist movements in well developed regions is "to free their own strong development from what they had come to perceive as the backwardness around them—from some larger, politically dominant power whose stagnation or archaism had become an obstacle to their further progress."[29]

In 1979, another version of the same explanation was developed by Peter Gourevitch. Movements of "peripheral nationalism," in this view, emerge in ethnically distinct regions that are economically dynamic but play a limited role in the leadership of the state's central political institutions. This lack of congruence may result either from the ability of the periphery to improve its economic position or from the faltering of the state's original core.[30] The examples Nairn provides are Belgium in decaying mercantile Netherlands,[31] the Czech-speaking Bohemians in the parasitic Austro-Hungarian Empire, the Basque and Catalan regions in a backward former imperial Spain, and Scotland in Great Britain.[32] Gourevitch lists most of the same cases and adds Quebec in Canada. The very first systematic study of nationalist movements from developed regions is Juan Diez Medrano's comparative study of Catalonia and the Basque country.[33]

When we add to Nairn's, Gourevitch's, and Diez Medrano's lists contemporary examples: the breakup of the USSR ignited by Estonia, Latvia, and Lithuania, where per capita income was higher than in other parts of the USSR, and of Yugoslavia by Slovenia and Croatia, which are more developed than Serbia and the other three republics that used to make up Yugoslavia, and the more developed Czech districts rapid consent to Slovakia's hasty demands of independence, we are led to acknowledge that, contrary to existing views, an important terrain of nationalist upheaval and political transformation is the developed region of the less developed state. Nationalism of relatively developed regions contributes a sizeable share of nationalist movements and constitutes many of the most current ones.

Nairn's and Gourevitch's perspectives further accentuate Hechter's emphasis on the nationalist concern with the instrumental role played by the state vis-à-vis the economy. Nationalist separatism, whether in underdeveloped or developed regions, is rooted in the diminished value of the state for further economic development.[34] The fateful, and fitful, shifts of Ukrainian public opinion between the retention of close ties with Russia and independence since 1991 is a fine illustration of this instrumental relationship. It also explains why for some two centuries Catalans were content to accept the hegemony of the Spanish state and why in the early 1960s so many Balts were proud of the economic development their republics attained within the USSR.

In examining the impact of uneven development on the legitimating ideas adopted by early and late modernizers, or developed and developing societies, Nairn observes the preference of the former for the universalist framework of the Enlightenment and of the latter for the particularism of Romanticism. The Enlightenment idea of "an even and progressive development of material civilization and mass culture...both outwards and downwards" to be diffused by commercial capitalism and the copying of the early developers' institutions was typical of the elites of societies that enjoyed the advantages of unevenness and, therefore, were convinced that progress was identified with their traits and virtues.[35]

Many peripheric elites, however, were filled with anxiety because they experienced the predominance of the early modernizers as foreign domination and invasion. To stand up to this tidal wave, without modern economic and political institutions, these elites sought to mobilize the one resource they possessed—their masses—through a Romantic culture of distinctiveness.[36] Though Nairn's theory of nationalism in developed regions is not very extensive, there is little doubt that he considers them as belonging in the same category with early developers and, therefore, as proponents of Enlightenment universalism.

The distinction drawn between the Enlightenment and Romantic fountainheads of nationalism leads to alternative criteria of membership in the nation. In reproducing one of the most celebrated distinctions in the study of nationalism, Liah Greenfeld distinguishes between types of "criteria of membership in the national collective, which may be either 'civic', that is, identical with citizenship, or 'ethnic.' In the former case, nationality is at least in principle open and voluntaristic; it can and sometimes must be acquired. In the latter, it is believed to be inherent—one can neither acquire it if one does not have it, nor change it if one does; it has nothing to do with individual will, but constitutes a genetic characteristic."[37] This categorization lays the foundation for two types of host-immigrant relations. Where the criterion of membership is *civic*, that is, based on individual rights of participation in the political life of the community in disregard of the variation in the cultural attributes of the individuals concerned, the integration of foreigners should be easier than where the criteria of membership in the community is *ethnic*, that is, based on putative origins and deeply anchored cultural markers.

In a study focused specifically on the relationship between nationalism and citizenship Rogers Brubaker clarifies the alternative legal frameworks that articulate the distinction presented by Greenfeld. In all societies, he points out, citizenship is bestowed on children of citizens on the basis of the legal principle of jus sanguinis (right of blood). In Germany, this is the only criterion for citizenship and, consequently, immigrants and even their descendants do not automatically become citizens.

But in other societies, such as France, this principle is complemented by another. Jus soli (right of the soil) accords persons born on the state's territory its citizenship. Though not an immigration society, France is nevertheless an assimilationist one: until recently it automatically naturalized the children of its immigrants, at birth if one parent was born in France or at age 18 when both parents are foreign born.[38] In Brubaker's view, the reason for the differential legal bases of citizenship in Germany and France reflects the historical legacy of the formation of the French nation by the state, which preceded it, and the ethno-cultural basis of the German nation, which preceded the state. He points out that although German and French citizenship and naturalization laws have undergone changes, the revised versions do not depart from these "deeply rooted habits of national self-understanding."[39]

I will tie, in the present work, the criteria of citizenship or membership in the nation, presented in Greenfeld's and Brubaker's works, directly to immigration reception, on the basis of Hechter's, Gellner's, Nairn's, and Gourevich's theories of nationalism, by designating the nationalism of host societies that offer a measure of integration to immigrants and favor further modernization as *hegemonic nationalism* and the nationalism in societies in which opposition to immigrants and their integration is exhibited and accompanied by a fear of modernization as *corporate nationalism*.

The hegemonic conception of society is usually rooted in confidence in the continuous process of economic expansion and attendant cultural hegemony, typical to the Enlightenment, which underwrites the possibility of social expansion through the absorption of newcomers. Conversely, the corporate view of society is derived from viewing outside forces as a threat against which protection is required. In relatively developed regions, it is anticipated that nationalist sentiments and movements will possess a hegemonic dimension, that is the intellectual and moral authority to lead all the social strata in the region at critical historical junctures.[40] This hegemonic influence will limit the ability of the foes of integration to mobilize wide support for their unease with and opposition to the inclusionary attitude. The political predominance of nationalist parties and the attraction of their region's cultural prestige—the former toward other parties, the latter vis-à-vis immigrants—are two sides of the same coin, the coin of hegemonic leadership.

Concomitantly, the willingness of immigrants to voluntarily loosen or abandon some aspects of their native culture and be absorbed into the population of the host society is a likely response in relatively developed regions where a higher standard of living and high cultural prestige reinforce each other. Individual members of the immigrant group are likely to feel that their interests are best served, as Inglehart and Woodward would expect, by acquiescing in the cultural hegemony of the host society, even at the risk of submerging their previous identity in the latter's language and culture.[41] In relatively developed regions the linguistic tug-of-war of immigrants and hosts is frequently resolved through the compromise of bilingualism: the learning of the new tongue by the younger members of the first generation of the immigrants in addition to their old language (and by members of the second generation, frequently in lieu of their parents' ancestral language), due to the attractions of social mobility it promises.

Conversely, the fear of the early modernizers' predominance and "denationalization" due to migration from less developed regions merge in late developers and developing regions and lead to a defensive conception of the nation. The beleaguered nation is inward looking, and its concern with "survival" leads to the erection of protective walls around its culture and domain and foreigners are seen as diluting its uniqueness. Full democratization would require the political integration of ethnically different newcomers and, therefore, is rarely sought.

In times of economic recession, the same logic that led to self-confidence in continuous economic expansion, social mobility and hence to a readiness, typical to hegemonic nationalism in developed regions, to assimilate immigrants is likely to steer in the opposite direction. Immigrants at such times might be seen as a threat to prosperity and national identity and exclusionary measures will be called for. But recession, a single section of the capitalist economic cycle, is likely to lead only to a *temporary reversal* in the inclusionary sentiment toward immigrants.

I the next section I will present the conditions under which the nationalist movements of relatively developed regions will adopt not hegemonic but corporate views of their society and, therefore, will express *permanent opposition* to the integration of immigrants. Conversely, I will present two situations in which potential conflict between immigrants and hosts is attenuated by shared interests or presence of third parties that override potential antagonism between them.

The Contexts and Limits of Hegemonic Nationalism

Nairn's theory, like so many other theories of nationalism, suffers from overgeneralization. As was already pointed out by Diez Medrano, assuming an aspiration for economic modernization behind all nationalist movements in relatively developed regions is mistaken.[42] Developed regions have spun not only movements of modernizing nationalism as in Catalonia, Latvia, and Estonia but, on occasion, such as in the Basque provinces in the late nineteenth and early twentieth centuries, a nationalist movement that was opposed to large-scale industrialization and its modern consequences tout court.

This form of defensiveness is the product of *traditional elites*, sometimes including the religious hierarchy, that derive their privilege from a corporate system of power distribution or religious status order and, therefore, are threatened by modernization and the creation of new economic strata, the universalization of civil rights, and cultural homogenization. Such elite strata are usually the product of continued diversity, typical to empires, or the medieval system of corporate privilege. Unable to translate their customary political advantage into modern economic assets, they are unable to spearhead the drive for modernization. With a lack of effective modern resources, traditional elite strata are likely to adopt a "defensive nationalism."[43] To shield their region from the forces of modernity they seek to mobilize their followers with highly charged traditional cultural appeals usually of a religious sort.

We need to keep in mind the balance between pro- and antimodernist nationalism. Overall, most antimodernist nationalists operate in underdeveloped regions. Antimodernist nationalism in developed peripheral regions is relatively rare. Where corporate nationalism makes its appearance, this will be part of its attempt "to modernize" its premodern political privileges, arrangements, and traditions. When nationalist movements that are more likely to appear in underdeveloped regions make their appearance in a relatively developed region, they carry many discordant and odd elements with them into the modern era. The traditional leaders of such movements frequently adopt extreme language, and sometimes programs, because not only are their status and privilege threatened by a competing modern elite stratum but also their *whole way of life* without which they cannot imagine their existence.

The study of Basque nationalism and its hostility toward Spanish immigrants will allow me to confront one of the most frequently invoked perspectives to the study of relations between culturally distinct groups that span its own view of nationalism—the theory of *primordial nationalism*. Primordialist explanations are especially prevalent in the analysis of the intense, and sometimes violent, nationalist sentiments in postcommunist Eastern Europe and Central Asia and also of the rising hostility toward immigrants in Western Europe. I find it important, therefore, to examine the uses and limits of primordialist theory in the context of this study.

Primordial attachments were defined by Clifford Geertz as the "'givens'...[of] congruities of blood, speech, custom, and so on, [that] are seen to have an ineffable, and at times overpowering, coerciveness in and of themselves."[44] The loyalty they command is seen as "flow[ing] more from a sense of natural—some would say spiritual—affinity than from social interaction"[45] and are "rooted in the non-rational foundations of the personality."[46]

The significance of these ties is their "absolute import," which sets them apart from and in tension with other types of social interaction that are aimed at the formation of a dynamic modern state based on civic loyalties. This distinction is similar in some ways to Greenfeld's typology of nationalist movements and their criteria of inclusion-exclusion; that is, the civic and ethnic types. But Greenfeld locates the origins of primordial sentiments in the frustrated status aspirations of déclassé intellectuals, whereas Geertz views primordial loyalties as having belonged to the prepolitical masses who, in the process of political mobilization, are called to act upon them. This is a telling disagreement, and it points to the complexities that lie behind the seemingly simple concept of primordial sentiments and loyalties.

It seems to me that, despite Geertz, the invocation of primordial identity is not an atavistic reaction to modernization. The very notion of primordial loyalty seems to be an anachronism: it is a politicized, and therefore, in part modern, form of identity that invariably uses the tools of its despised modern nemeses and that could not have existed before the "age of nationalism." Primordialist nationalism, then, does not signal lack of modernization but rather an extreme response to a certain kind of modernization, an "unbalanced" form, which develops one sector of society at the expense of another and usually does so at breakneck speed. The Janus face of nationalism,[47] especially exaggerated in situations of "combined and uneven development"—to apply a term, developed by Trotsky for his theory of revolution, to the study of nationalism—also makes possible the invocation or attempted re-creation of past glories and the slowing down of the dynamic of modernization.[48] Primordial loyalties are incongruous: their paradox is that insofar as their adherents struggle against the modern world they also have to use modern instruments, national identities and institutions being some of them, in their struggle.

Within this paradoxical struggle, immigrants appear a relatively easy, one-dimensional, target. Because immigrants are always associated with, and emblematic of, the process of modernization that brings them to the region, opponents of modernization can focus on them as adversaries and, therefore, seek to curtail their arrival, rights, and influence. We shall see all these ambiguities and contradictions, but also a strong antiimmigrant sentiment, in examining antimodern Basque nationalism, which is singled out just as much by its primordial character as by the fact that it was born in one of the most highly industrialized regions of Spain, rather than in one of its underdeveloped provinces.

Whereas traditional elites evolve a defensive, corporate, nationalism in opposition to economic modernization and the extension of democratic institution, a strata of *modern elites* might deploy it against administrative centralization by a larger political unit. *Political imperialism*—a term I will associate with the political process of empire construction while I reserve the term *colonialism* for economic exploitation of a subjugated region—played an important role in the birth and, consequently, in the fortunes of the nationalist sentiments of Latvian and Estonian elites and influenced the thinking of their Catalan and Basque counterparts.

In part the reason is that, given their geopolitical location, all four regions in this study were suspectable to imperial designs. Catalonia and the Basque provinces were contiguous to Spain, and Estonia and Latvia to the Russian Empire and later the USSR and, therefore, were incorporated by them not as colonial outposts but rather as part of their own territorial expansion. The strategic location of the Basque country, on one of the few passable roads from France into Spain, and of Lithuania, Latvia, and Estonia along a major route from Central Europe toward Leningrad or St. Petersburg (one of the three routes of Hitler's 1941 invasion)[49] made their possession particularly valuable. But their territorial incorporation was also part of the larger dialectic of imperialism and state formation—a political process sui generis.

The paradox of early state formation is that in many ways it resembles empire building: the agglomeration of peripheral regions through conquest or annexation by a successful core region in spite of occasional resistance by the local inhabitants. All the current Western European states are the result of this process of expansion that lent them their present geographical boundaries.[50] The difference between state and empire building is found in the ability of the expanding political unit to acquire legitimacy. This distinction is captured well by Lustick:

> If, after several generations, the indigenous population of the newly acquired territories ascribes legitimacy to the central

political authority exercised over it, the acquisition will be deemed to be the kind of state-building conducive to the emergence of a nation-state—i.e. "national expansion." If, after several generations, the indigenous population is still prone to consider the political authority exercised over it from the expansive core as illegitimate, then an "empire" has been formed.[51]

Where expansion was accepted as legitimate, local elites were coopted through a wider network of rewards and privileges into the state-building effort and acted as intermediaries between the central authority and the populace, which, on its part, was gradually offered increased participation in political life.[52]

In contrast, when the strata of the eponymous elite are excluded from the new political framework because they were deemed inferior or inassimilable or when attempts were undertaken to replace their members with a new elite that directly depended on the external power, the expanding state will be perceived not as subsuming its newly acquired region but as intruding into it and, therefore, as illegitimate. Such conflict will lead to opposing views on the immigration of part of the larger political unit's own elite into the newly acquired region. The modern immigrant elite will be regarded as part of its state-building and modernizing effort by the central authority and by the eponymous elites of the annexed region, an attempt to subjugate them to a foreign power. Such view of the Soviet state was typical to the Baltic elites and an important source of the Baltic nationalist movements's separatism and, simultaneously, their opposition to the incorporation of Slavic immigrants into their societies.

Another reason for viewing incorporation into a larger state as illegitimate is that the top strata in developed regions do not have much to gain from such process and have much to lose from it. Elites of annexed regions, as Nairn correctly indicates, rarely can prevent the imposition of political mechanisms that will decelerate and retard their economic progress and potentially interfere with their cultural life, by a less developed state. An even stronger indication of a region's vulnerability is the failure of its native-born elites to prevent the entry and establishment of a competing foreign elite that threatens their *privileged status* in their very own region.

Immigration under conditions of political imperialism, as was the case in most of the USSR's non-Russian republics, led not to the more typical form of *horizontal stratification* of hosts and immigrants but to the creation of two societies, one immigrant the other native born, through *vertical segmentation*. Integration of two societies, each with its own elite, as in Latvia and Estonia, is much more difficult than integration through the social mobility of the immigrants from lower to higher social echelons, as is the case in Catalonia, and through their mixing in the contemporary Basque country.

Although vertical segmentation poses a greater danger than horizontal stratification to elites, it is even harsher in a traditional than in a modern setting. Traditional elite strata are doubly threatened: by displacement and by modernity. The modern elite strata, which rises as a result of rapid industrialization, deprives its traditional counterparts of their privileges as well as of their position as the guardians and embodiments of a tightly organized way of life, without which they lose their usefulness. The elite stratum becomes déclassé and passé at once and hence, as was the case with the Basque notables, will show unremitting hostility toward the forces of modernity and the immigrants they bring to the region.

Vertical segmentation also poses a direct threat to the privileged status of the eponymous elites but not to their way of life. The scope of activity of the native-born modern elites is narrowed but not eliminated. Consequently, a more mixed approach is likely to evolve: the desire to deprive the immigrant population's own elite from its status combined with some readiness to integrate part of the immigrants into the host society; that is, a combination of corporate and hegemonic elements that makes the adoption of a coherent policy toward the immigrants impossible. This is the current situation of host-immigrant relations in Latvia and Estonia though in the former the corporate elements are much stronger than in the former.

Finally, there are political conditions in which the expression of corporate nationalism will be limited and accommodation with minorities and immigrants sought, due to shared interests or presence of third parties that override potential antagonisms. The predominance of a German nobility in Latvia and Estonia until the end of the First World War, similarly to many other Eastern European states, required Estonian and Latvian nationalists to seek the assistance the ruling Russian authorities in attaining their aims that, consequently, remained limited to political and cultural autonomy within a reformed Russia. It also reduced the element of conflict with the minorities within their societies.

Similarly, common interests, such as the *campaigns for democracy* and, sometimes, for social justice and socialism, will bring the native born and immigrants together. The opposition to Franco's dictatorship in Spain and to Stalin and the USSR's Communist Party's repressive single-party regime earned the sympathy of Spaniards and Russians, respectively, both outside and inside these regions.

Repression of both peripheral nationalist and social rights by authoritarian regimes bent on centralization and the upholding of their own regional privileges, on many occasions, unified groups and classes that otherwise would have been locked into an ethnic conflict of their own. Where regional and prodemocracy struggles coexist, political decentralization and sometimes even regional independence are accepted as an integral part of the process of democratization and increase the civic dimension of the nationalist movement. The Catalan experience clearly illustrates the strengthening of the hegemony the civic character of a nationalist movement in the context of determined opposition to tyranny. The Baltic Popular Fronts support for *perestroika* also led to cooperation between Baltic nationalists and immigrants but, ultimately, the disintegration of the USSR was so rapid that the struggle for democracy within it remained too short to significantly increase the hegemonic and civic dimension of Latvian and Estonian nationalist aspirations.

Immigration and Nationalism: Summary of Propositions

The object of this study is to examine the status of internal immigrants in larger states's relatively developed peripheries that are inhabited by a distinct nationality. I will employ in this study three theories of immigrant-host relationships: *assimilation*, which expects immigrants to seek social mobility through cultural and structural assimilation; *segmentation*, which views immigrants and their descendants and hosts as permanently divided economically and culturally; and *multiculturalism*, perched uneasily between the previous two, which accepts the legitimacy of cultural diversity created by immigration but views it as existing within a common sphere of public and political life and with the, often hidden, assumption that the goal of the immigrants' descendants' assimilation is delayed but not abandoned. I will juxtapose these theories of immigration with an amended version of Nairn's and Gourevich's theory of nationalism in relatively developed regions to examine which of the immigrant-host theories accounts best for the cases under study.

I will connect the discussion of nationalism with immigrant-host relationships by distinguishing between hegemonic and corporate nationalisms. The sustained expansion of the economy of developed regions requires the extension of the insufficient native-born labor force. The appeal of the well-developed economy accords the regional culture a higher prestige and equips the nationalist elites with considerable moral influence—a political and cultural *hegemony*—that they exert on other political parties and on the immigrants to their region. The latter will be even more strongly attracted to the nationalist movement when it struggles not only against a laggard state, which slows down its further development, but also against its anti-democratic character. This model seems to describe Catalonia fairly accurately.

Where modernization threatens the traditional or modern elite strata by bringing an alternative elite associated with the central state, as part of a process of political imperialism or state building, to the region and in this fashion rob the elites of the region from their predominant position, the latter are likely to adopt exclusionary policies against the immigrants. In both cases, a vertical segmentation evolves, diving the host society into two hostile societies and the native elites are likely to evolve a *corporate* view of their societies that requires the protection of their societies from outside intervention.

If the elite threatened is traditional its opposition will be even stronger and uncompromising because not only its privilege but its entire traditional way of life is under jeopardy. Where a native-born modern elite is endangered by competition with a foreign elite the threat is lesser and it will adopt a *mixture of corporate and hegemonic nationalist policies* toward immigrants. The first wave of the nationalist movements of the Basque region, between its emergence in the 1890s and the end of the Franco era, was an example of the former type of nationalism. The nationalist movements of the Baltic republics that led it to independence from the USSR was of the latter.

Though ethnic and civic elements of membership coexist, in varying degrees, in the thinking and practices of every nationalist movement, hegemonic movements emphasize civic membership criteria at the expense of ethnic markers and are open to integration and *assimilation* of newcomers, whereas corporate nationalists rate ethnic membership criteria as paramount and treat immigrants as permanent outsiders thus leading to a *segmentation* of hosts and immigrants.

Finally, I will examine in the appropriate cases under study the potential and actual place of *multiculturalism* in the societies under study. I will be examining multiculturalism in two contexts.

First, multiculturalism will be studied as an alternative to either assimilation or permanent ethnicization of immigrants that results from their separation from the native-born. In both the Basque Country and Catalonia there are growing indications of a multiculturalist approach side by side with an assimilationist ambition. But whereas in Catalonia multiculturalism is expressed through acceptance of cultural diversity, in ways typical to other societies where it was adopted as an official policy, in the Basque Country it fills in the void left by the weakness of the Basque language and culture.

Second, multiculturalism can be an alternative to an official policy of turning immigrants into national minorities, which recognizes cultural divisions as permanent and is always potentially under the threat of minority irredentism. In Latvia, and to a lesser extent in Estonia, the predominant tendency is for treating Russians and other Slavs as a permanent national minority though there are also some indications of a readiness to integrate some portion of them.

In this dual context, it seems that multiculturalist policies might increase potential participation in, and lower the threshold of identification with, the host society instead of accepting or encouraging its permanent divisions.

2

SIMILARITIES BETWEEN THE REGIONS

Although comparative work cannot assume the regional specialist's level of expertise, by suggesting new questions and answers or by investing old ones with new relevance, comparisons may yield benefits that case studies do not. Comparative study can reap such gains only if the cases it compares are chosen on the basis of sufficient commonality. Spain and the Soviet Union are located at opposite ends of the European continent and their histories seem to be divergent, but I will demonstrate in this chapter that the comparison I am undertaking is warranted not only by structural similarities among Catalonia, the Basque country, Estonia, and Latvia in their relationship to Spain and the USSR, respectively, but also by some unexpected similarities between the USSR and Spain. The most relevant resemblance concerns the disjunction between state and nation formation evident in both cases.

The Soviet Union had an important anachronistic streak in its origins. In contradistinction to the Hapsburg and Ottoman empires, which were dismembered upon their defeat in the First World War, the Romanov empire was given a new lease on life in a transformed form by the communist revolution. The USSR in fact was strong enough to acquire new territories after the Second World War. As a result, the Soviet Union remained a multiethnic state, organized as a centralized federation of fifty-three ethnic homelands, of which fifteen were union republics, twenty autonomous republics, eight autonomous oblasts, and ten autonomous okrugs.

In contrast, we tend to think of Spain, a state that was formed in the fifteenth century, as a unified nation-state. But although Spain became a state early, it started its nation formation relatively late and left it as an "unfinished agenda." Spain then is an old state, but as Juan Linz pointed out just in the early 1970s, "Spain today is a state for all Spaniards, a nation-state for a large part of the population, and only a state but not a nation for important minorities."[1] In consequence of this regional fragmentation Linz concluded that "Spain's problems resemble those of some Eastern European countries."[2] Since 1983, Spain followed a policy of regional devolution that made it resemble the former USSR in some respect. Now Spain is organized into seventeen "autonomous communities," of which the majority are hardly distinguishable from one another, but some, first and foremost Catalonia and Euskadi (which is made up of the three Basque provinces of Guipúzcoa, Alava, and Vizcaya) and in some respects the forth Basque province of Navarra, are distinct from the Castilian heartland.

The diverging paces of state building and nation formation in Spain and the Romanov empire have been the result of extended periods of external expansion carried out at the expense of the consolidation of territories acquired earlier. After the Reconquista, according to William A. Douglass, instead of expanding the centralizing drive, which was undertaken earlier in Castile, into outlying

MAP 2.1

Catalonia and the Basque Country in Spain

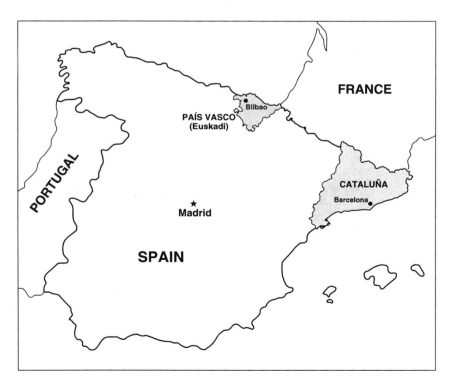

areas and successfully unifying the helter-skelter administrative arrangements of its provinces and in the process assimilating its diverse ethnic groups, the Spanish monarchy embarked on overseas colonial adventures.[3] Colonial prizes were offered as new opportunities, and "there was a tendency for the subordinated ethnic groups," especially among Basques, "to become the handmaidens of colonial enterprise." Catalonia, on its part, made extensive use of the colonies as captive markets for its products.

Nation formation, consequently, remained the "unfinished agenda" of the Spanish state. In the eighteenth century, when Cuba and the Philippines, Spain's last overseas colonial possessions, were lost the Catalans and Basques have not yet been made into "Spaniards." In Douglass's view, ethnic nationalism in some regions of Spain, France, and Britain is "the recrudescence of unresolved sixteenth and seventeenth century issues" that without the distraction of colonialism would probably have been settled earlier.[4]

This pattern was repeated, with some variations in the Romanov empire. Whereas Spanish expansion took place in overseas colonies, the Romanovs made additions to their empire by a dual process: "incorporating powerholders into the state apparatus in its central regions, but employing the classic methods of indirect rule through partly autonomous intermediaries in peripheral areas."[5] Romanov expansion and colonization were accelerated in the past three centuries, at a time when the external borders of most Western European states, including Bourbon Spain, had already been fixed.

Belated nation formation in Bourbon Spain and Romanov Russia allowed, to varying degrees, the continuous retention of histories, cultures, and social structures in Catalonia, the Basque country, Estonia, and Latvia that were distinct from those of the predominant nationality of their respective states. The peripheral groups's markers of collective identity were never the once and for all self-evident symbols of the nation as the primordial perspective would have it. The centrality of their national characteristics ebbed and flowed: at times they were relegated to the domain of private life or forgotten, at other times they were moved to the heart of public life where they were invested with new significance as part of the response to the modern political, economic, and cultural influences of their mega-states. The checkered fortune of these markers, that is, the reversal of the importance of peripheral religion, language, and political autonomy, demonstrates that state building is the setting in which nations and ethnic groups are born and die.

The focus of the relationship between central state building and peripheral nation formation in Catalonia, the Basque provinces, Latvia, and Estonia were three characteristics—cultural distinctiveness, relatively early and quick economic development that put them ahead of Spain and Russia-USSR, respectively, and their status as magnets for immigration—that allow us to compare these regions in a fruitful way. I will illustrate the importance of the state building context for their nation formation in the rest of this chapter and return to the issues presented here in the subsequent chapters as they become relevant to the nationalist movements and to the assimilation of immigrants in the regions under study.

Distinct Cultures

The two most important "cultural infrastructures" that had served as bases for national differentiation and modern demands of autonomy in Europe are language and religion. Of the two, Orridge pointed out, "*Language* has been by far the most common basis of autonomist nationalisms in Europe."[6]

Two fracture lines divide most Europeans into speakers of Romance, Germanic, and Slavic languages, and leave only a few fault zones of unrelated languages in the continent's linguistic geography. The populations of the four regions under study possess such distinct languages. The Basque language, Euskera, is not an Indo-European language and, in fact, no relationship has been established with certainty between Euskera and any other known language. The most likely explanation for Euskera's uniqueness implies its antiquity: it seems to be one of the very few remaining pre-Indo-European languages on the continent.[7] It is a polysynthetic tongue in which language elements are joined in composite words that function as sentences do in Indo-European languages, but the constituent elements have no meaning apart from the sentence. Latvian belongs to the Baltic subfamily of Indo-European languages and Estonian to the small, and mostly extinct, group of Finno-Ugric languages. Catalan is the only one of the four that is related to a major European language family: it is a Romance language, and as such a descendent of Latin, but resembles French more than Spanish as it developed in close association with the Provençal tongue since the eleventh century. Almost all speakers of Catalan and the majority of Latvians and Estonians are bilingual and , in addition to their native tongue, also speak Spanish or Russian. Although most Euskera speakers are

MAP 2.2

Estonian S.S.R. and Latvian S.S.R. in the U.S.S.R.

literate in Spanish, the majority of Basques know Spanish but not Euskera. Most Catalans, but also many members of the other groups under study speak another major European language.

Though languages are a major foundation of collective identity, their relationship to nationhood had to await the results of two sets of homogenizing processes: linguistic and political. First, most national languages were created in the early modern, and in some places only in the recent, era through the choice of one idiom out a number of possible regional dialects. For example, there are eight known dialects of Euskera. "Literary Latvian is based on the middle one of three variants,"[8] and Estonian, on the dialect spoken in the northern part of the province.[9] In addition, the grammar and orthography of the dialect chosen required standardization.

Second, a close bond, with clear public and political significance, needed to be forged between language and nationhood. Because a multitude of factors played a role in determining the strength of this connection, many "mis-matches" ensued. The major defining characteristic of Catalan distinctiveness is the Catalan language; nevertheless the province of Valencia and the Balearic Islands, which also speak Catalan, had not evolved separatist tendencies and Catalan nationalism did not develop a political doctrine of the Països Catalans to justify the incorporation of these regions willy-nilly into its vision. Catalan nationalist leaders learned to accommodate the paradox of Catalan speakers who required no commensurate political rights. And, Basque nationalism "at its inception...was more powerful among those sectors of the population who did not speak Euskera."[10]

The second cultural infrastructure of European ethnicity and nationality is *religion*. But throughout most of Europe the new secular solidarity of the citizens actually replaced traditional religious faith. Only occasionally (more frequently in the south of the content and in the Middle East) were national identities sustained by religious affiliations, usually where religious affiliations stood in for another, suppressed, cultural distinction. Although local dialects, as we have seen, were frequently broadened into national languages and served as the cultural glue of the new nation, a real wonder of reinterpretation was the opposite process; namely, the one that narrowed of the scope and lowered the sight of universalist religions to the plane of nations.

Catholicism was accepted, in absence of another marker, as a symbol of national identity, especially when it could be deployed in contradistinction to Protestantism, as in Quebec and Ireland, or Orthodoxy, as in Lithuania and Poland. In an even more radical departure from the universalist premise of Catholicism particular religious fervor could also be viewed as the mark of the true nation, such as in the Basque country where devotion was used to differentiate Basque Catholics, who supposedly enjoyed a better prospect of salvation, from Spanish Catholics. At the same time, the strongest foothold of the most extreme Catholic doctrine, the Integralist position that replaced loyalty to the king with the Kingship of Christ, was in Navarra, the most "Spanish" and antinationalist Basque province, which sided with Franco's unitary Spanish nationalism against the provinces of Vizcaya and Guipúzcoa, the strongholds of Basque nationalism. No such association of religion and nationality surfaced in Estonia and Latvia, which are both Protestant and, therefore, could easily have distinguished themselves from their neighbors on religious grounds. The reason was that Latvian and Estonian Lutheran churches had been affiliated with the dominant German Balts, who for long also supplied the church's upper echelons, and relied on it as part of their ruling apparatus.[11]

Comparing the national loyalties of members of different religions who belong to the same ethnic group demonstrates that the importance of religion itself varied with the respective region's political and economic conditions. Catholic Latgalians were more easily Russified than their fellow Lutheran Latvians, since the social structure of Letgalia remained similar to Russia's, while Lutheran Latvians enjoyed the benefits of economic modernization earlier.

Neither linguistic not religious homogeneity predict the intensity of national consciousness. Divergence between political and economic homogeneity frequently tied a region to a linguistically or religious different state or province or separated it from a culturally similar one. Cultural homogeneity competes with other forces in commanding collective loyalty and serving as the basis of national sentiment.

Level of Development

Catalonia, the Basque provinces, Latvia, and Estonia were the most developed regions of Spain and the former USSR, respectively. Of the four regions under study, however, two followed chronological trajectories that differed from the others. The Basque provinces lost their relatively developed position in Spain in the aftermath of the 1973 economic crisis, though in 1985 Alava, Guipúzcoa, and Vizcaya still were in third, eleventh, and fourteenth place in terms of their development among the fifty-two provinces of Spain. The third of the Baltic republics, Lithuania, was a late developer in comparison with the other four regions: it had still been an agricultural country when it was annexed by the USSR and was industrialized only under Soviet auspices to reach the development level of its Baltic neighbors in the 1960s. Consequently, it did not experience the same rate of in-migration as its Baltic neighbors.

Spain's "only two industrial nuclei" from the second half of the nineteenth century until the 1960s were Catalonia (mostly in the province of Barcelona) and the Basque country (above all in the province of Vizcaya and its capital Bilbao).[12] In Douglass's words: "the Basque Country and Catalonia constitute the womb and apogee of industrial development on the Iberian peninsula....Throughout most of the twentieth century the two regions have consistently enjoyed the highest per capita income in Spain."[13]

The major industries in Catalonia were cottons and woolen textiles, dating back to the end of the eighteenth century.[14] Although for Spaniards Barcelona was a second Lancastershire, it was, in fact, dominated by small firms and geared for exports to the protected markets of the Spanish empire. In the 1870s, a second center of rapid

TABLE 2.1

Spanish Provinces with Highest Disposable per Capita Income,
in 1977 and 1985, in Pesetas

Province	1977		1985	
	Income	Rank	Income	Rank
Madrid	306,646	1	887,536	1
Baleares	255,601	7	867,997	2
Alava	291,683	2	812,381	3
Barcelona	287,413	3	810,316	4
Gerona	269,798	6	799,513	5
Lérida	219,406	16	693,465	9
Navarra	239,576	9	690,401	10
Guipúzcoa	277,907	5	684,090	11
Tarragona	245,085	8	676,644	13
Vizcaya	279,505	4	673,106	14

Source: Banco de Bilbao, *Renta nacional de España y su distribución provincial* (Bilbao: 1985), p. 88. Reprinted by permission of the publisher.

economic development evolved on the coast of the Basque country. There, the old iron industry, based on the mines of Vizcaya, received a boost by supplying a growing British demand for low-phosphorus iron ore. Subsequently mining led to the formation of shipbuilding and heavy metallurgical industries. The first modern corporations, the railway companies and the mixed banks of Spain, were also established in the Basque provinces.[15] In Castile, the influence of towns remained overshadowed by the agriculturalists well into the Franco regime although Madrid was, and is, Spain's political, administrative, financial, military, and ecclesiastical center.[16]

The Basque regions and Catalonia have retained their advanced industrial and high-income status relative to Spain's other regions into the second wave of industrialization, which commenced with the 1959 Stabilization Plan. The renewal of rapid Spanish economic development found the Basque provinces and Catalonia, this time with the addition of Madrid, once again at the top of the list of rapidly developing regions, though the large early differences between the relative economic development of Spanish regions have diminished. Table 2.1, comparing disposable income per capita in Spain's provinces, demonstrates the results of the prominent place of the Catalan and Basque provinces in the Spanish economy. The three Basque regions occupy first place, and Barcelona, in which the overwhelming majority of the Catalan population is concentrated, is in fourth place. Even the least industrial of the Basque provinces, Navarra, finds itself among the highest income regions when compared with Spain's other regions.

After the 1973 steep oil price hikes and the worldwide economic downturn, development slowed down throughout Spain, causing special hardship and, it seems, permanent damage to the heavily specialized and export-oriented industrial production of the Basque region (see Table 2.2). The major shift in the relative ranking of Spanish provinces occurred in Guipúzcoa and Vizcaya, the old industrial regions of the Basque country, which slid from first and second place in 1967 to eleventh and fourteenth place in 1985. Official unemployment rate in the Basque provinces rose from 1 percent in 1973 to 11.2 percent in 1980, and during those years, 11 percent of the jobs in the region were lost.[17] Euskadi, therefore, should not be classified with the well-developed regions of Spain in the past decade, although it is still among the relatively prosperous regions.

Madrid and the Balearic Islands now top the list of highest income provinces in Spain and the respective positions of provinces within the Catalan and Basque regions was also slightly altered. In

TABLE 2.2

Spanish Provinces with Highest Disposable per Capita Income,
in 1967, in Pesetas

Province	Income	Rank
Guipúzcoa	57,154	1
Vizcaya	54,545	2
Alava	53,028	3
Barcelona	52,377	4
Madrid	51,623	5
Navarra	47,266	6

Source: Banco de Bilbao, *Renta nacional de España y su distribución
provincial* (Bilbao: 1967), p. 29. Reprinted by permission of the publisher.

1985, one region of the Basque country, Alava, and the heartland of the
Catalonia, Barcelona, maintained their positions from 1967 among the
top group. Of the other three provinces of Catalonia, Gerona's position
had not changed meaningfully, whereas Lerida, its agricultural region,
and Tarragona, which has a mix of developed and less developed
industries, had just about changed places, thus preserving Catalonia's
relative position in the Spanish distribution of regional incomes.

The "essential point of departure" for the social and economic
development of Latvia and Estonia was the emancipation of their
serfs. Serfdom was abolished in Estonia in 1816, in Courland in 1817,
and in Livonia in 1819. Emancipation in most of the Baltic region
took place two full generations before being implemented in the
Great Russian center of the empire by Alexander II's famous decree of
universal emancipation (which also included the Lithuanian lands) of
1861.[18] Freedom initially remained a mixed blessing because it was
not accompanied by land reform or even by freedom of travel. But by
the end of the 1840s Baltic peasants were permitted to buy land; in
the mid-1860s their freedom of mobility was legalized and urbanization and occupational differentiation spread.[19]

The freed serfs enjoyed another benefit available to few peasants
in the rest of the empire. Beginning in 1819, new legislation was
enacted to "open...the way for the establishment of an elementary
educational system that spread literacy among the Baltic peasants
several generations earlier than elsewhere in the empire (with the
exception of Finland)."[20] Estonian and Latvian peasants were already

the beneficiaries of the sporadic educational efforts of the Moravian Brethren, the Lutheran clergy, and Catherine II, but from then on were able to become literate and receive elementary education in the rural schools. Rapid urbanization also allowed access to technical schools and to the University of Dorpat (Tartu). The 1897 census found that whereas only 30 percent of the residents of European Russia were literate, 95 percent of in the province of Estland and 92 percent in Livonia were literate.[21]

The location of the Baltic provinces on the short strategic route between the empire's capital and its more developed western neighbors, the freedom of its inhabitants, and their relatively advanced educational level fueled the region's rapid development. Latvian and Estonian development commenced during Tzarist times, which propelled the country into being "one of the most developed parts of the empire."[22] Agricultural modernization was affected in part by Baltic German landowners and in the northern part of Baltic provinces by the agricultural societies and cooperatives of the new Estonian farmers and renters.[23] But the most crucial modernizing step, the construction of "a significant railroad network and large industrial concerns," was the work of Russian, Baltic German, and foreign German investors.[24]

The fortunes of Baltic industrial development were checkered in the first half of the twentieth century. Latvian and Estonian industries suffered from the evacuation of machinery into central Russia during the First World War, the loss of their Russian export market after independence, and the great economic crisis between the wars. The products of a modern agriculture, especially the high-quality meat products, remained the basis of Baltic exports to Germany and Great Britain. However, the flourishing Estonian textile industry, oil-shale production, and the Latvian metal goods industry demonstrated that, though war and independence had set back industrialization, the gains of the past were not lost but through adjustments were retained and expanded.[25]

"Prior to their inclusion in the Soviet Union in 1940," according to Bohnet and Penkaitis, "the Baltic states were at a more advanced stage of economic development and enjoyed a higher standard of living than that prevailing in the Soviet Union."[26] Educational levels in 1939 were also significantly higher in the Baltics than in Russia or the USSR, with the exception of Georgia. The number of individuals, over the age of 10, with secondary and higher education was 176 out 1,000 in Latvia, 165 in Georgia, 161 in Estonia, 128 in Armenia, followed by 120 in the Ukraine and 109 in Russia. In 1970, the gaps were smaller but similar proportions obtained: 554 in Georgia, 517 in Latvia, 516 in Armenia, and 506 in Estonia, but only 489 in Russia.[27]

The factors that singled out the Baltics in the late Tzarist period, such as a favorable location on the coastline and proximity to other urban centers, the advantage of early development, the availability of an educated, though by Russian standards small, labor force, and the "very substantial physical infrastructure which had not been destroyed during the [Second World] War,"[28] impelled the Soviet leadership to again intensify industrial development in Latvia and Estonia after the re-annexation of the Baltics. This policy of continued development allowed Latvia and Estonia to sustain their economic lead even within the USSR.[29]

It is a consensus of the observers that in the 1980s "the standard of living in most [particulars] is higher in the Baltic region than in the RSFSR (Russian Soviet Federal Soviet Republic)." The Baltic republics also enjoyed a higher personal income per capita then many of the other twelve Republics of the USSR (see Table 2.3). Among the Baltic states, Estonia was ahead, "followed closely by Latvia,"[30] and the per capita personal income in the republics not mentioned in this table were below the 100 percent. This advantage continued into the 1980s, as demonstrated in Table 2.4. The Estonian and Latvian advantage was manifested in higher gross industrial and agricultural production per capita and higher consumption of most basic foodstuffs, consumer durables, and new housing construction than their counterparts in the Russian SFSR.[31]

TABLE 2.3

Soviet Republics with Highest Personal Income per Capita
in 1960 and 1970 in Percentages

Republic	1960	1970	Rank
Estonia	129.0	133.2	1
Latvia	124.9	125.1	2
Lithuania	107.8	117.7	3
RSFSR	107.8	108.0	4
Ukraine	94.5	97.1	5

Source: McAuley 1979, Table 5.1, p. 109. Reprinted by permission of the University of Wisconsin Press.

TABLE 2.4

National Income per Capita for the RSFSR and the Baltic Republics
in 1984 in Current Rubles

Republic	1984
Estonia	2,534
Latvia	2,598
Lithuania	2,128
RSFSR	2,184

Source: Bohnet and Penkaitis 1988, p. 36 (based on the republics' statistical
yearbooks). Reprinted by permission of the Journal of Baltic Studies.

The overdevelopment of the Baltic economies was relative to the
Soviet Union's level of development. As such they suffered from the
same ailments as the economy of the USSR and were not on par with
Western economies. As in their first period of independence, when the
Russian economic hinterland and markets were lost to Baltic producers
and "the whole economy was eventually remodeled to meet the needs
of the Western European market,"[32] the economy is being restructured.
The second adjustment is likely to be more painful than it was between the wars because of the considerable technological and organizational gap between former communist and market-based economies
that grew up in the post-Second World War years, but the Baltic
Republics already gave indications of being better able to catch up with
the West after a period of modernization than most of the lesser
developed economies of the new states of the former Soviet Union.

Internal Migration

Religious and linguistic distinctiveness were coincidental to
levels of economic development, but the latter was closely tied with
migratory patterns. The political integration of regions with high
levels of economic development into a larger, less developed political
unit generated massive in-migration in the four cases.

We have detailed Spanish census data on internal migration for
the period starting in 1900 (see Table 2.5). Catalonia and the Basque
provinces experienced two major periods of in-migration: 1910–1930 in
the former,[33] 1880–1900 in the latter, and the 1950–1960s in both.
Though the numbers available for the pre-1900 period are less precise,
all the indicators point to massive in-migration into the Basque littoral.

TABLE 2.5

Net In-Migration into Catalonia and the Basque country, 1900–1981

Years	Catalonia	Basque Provinces
1901–1910	33,669	-6,005
1911–1920	224,302	19,878
1921–1930	321,995	25,809
1931–1940	110,123	11,270
1941–1950	256,718	25,758
1951–1960	439,782	152,226
1961–1970	720,808	256,190
1971–1975	227,141	64,213
1975–1981	39,231	-40,821

Source: Del Campo and Navarro López 1987, Table 21.1 p. 86. Catalonia
includes the following provinces: Barcelona, Gerona, Lérida, Tarragona; the
Basque provinces are Alava, Guipúzcoa, Vizcaya. (The original table
mistakenly switched the numbers for the years 1941–1950 and 1951–1960 for
Catalonia.) Reprinted by permission of Ariel Publishers.

The population of the Basque provinces increased dramatically
between 1877 and 1900, from 190,000 to 310,000, making it the
province with the highest population increase in Spain (48 percent as
compared with 24 percent in Barcelona). The population of the
Basque industrial zone increased from 74,000 in 1877 to 162,000 in
1897, and the mining and industrial region of Vizcaya absorbed 86
percent of the increase of the province, raising the percentage of
people born in other parts of Spain and other Basque provinces from
13.7 percent in 1877 to 26.4 percent by 1900 (it stayed stationary
afterward).[34] In Bilbao, Vizcaya's largest industrial city, the percentage
of Vizcayans declined to 35 percent, as the percent of migrants from
other Basque provinces rose to 16 percent, and of migrants from other
Spanish regions to 49 percent.[35]

In just two decades, the 1950s and 1960s, an influx of 1,160,540
migrants to Catalonia and 408,416 into the smaller Basque country
completed the radical restructuring of their populations. As a result
of these massive internal migration waves the percentage of the
population born in these provinces has diminished to 63.76 percent
in Catalonia and to 67.47 percent in the Basque provinces (excluding
Navarra, where it was 80.52 percent) by 1981. The number of native
born in Catalonia that year was 4,006,071 and of the migrants
2,158,935, and in the three Basque provinces there were 1,624,704

native born and 696,843 migrants.[36] The actual size of the native-born Catalan and Basque population in their respective provinces is even smaller if we take into account the fact that many of those born in these provinces are the children of previous internal immigrants. For example, if we discount from the overall population of the Basque regions the 11 percent of the population whose father and mother were born outside the region and the 8 percent of the population who had one parent born outside the region, second generation Basques make up only 51 percent of the inhabitants.[37]

The combined population of the three Baltic states was always small and is only around 8 million. Their populations were diminished as a consequence of staggering losses during both World Wars and as part of their forcible incorporation into the USSR. During this period, Latvia alone lost over one quarter of its population due to military deaths, executions, deportation of peasants, cultural leaders, and members of the two Latvian divisions of the German Army, border corrections, guerilla warfare, and flight of refugees.[38] At the same time, we need to distinguish between losses inflicted by the alternating German and Soviet authorities against the will of the native populations, and the extermination of 95 percent, the highest percentage for all of Europe, of the 250,000 Jews of Lithuania, Latvia, and Estonia, "a considerable number of [whom]—if not the majority—were massacred by or with the active assistance of Lithuanians...Latvians and Estonians" who served as volunteers in the Nazi militia and police[39] and, therefore, cannot be lumped and listed together with the Baltic losses, as is customarily done in demographic studies of the Baltics.

The effects of immigration have been felt particularly strongly in Latvia and Estonia because of some of their distinct demographic characteristics. The birth rate of native Latvians and Estonians, as of others in highly urbanized and industrialized Western European countries with high levels of education such as the Netherlands and France, were the lowest in the USSR. The same dynamic affected Russians who migrated to the Baltic republics of the USSR: their birth rate rapidly fell below that of the eponymous populations. This low birth rate is combined with a significantly high death rate, due to the relatively high percentage of old people in the Baltic population, to produce a declining rate of natural increase that, in Latvia, is already one of the lowest in the world. Additional contributing factors to low natural increase are the late marriage age, a divorce rate over 50 percent, and the highest accident caused fatality rate in the USSR due in large part to a high incidence of alcoholism, even by

Soviet standards.[40] These demographic trends are not novel; they were present in Tzarist times, and the marriage patterns of Latvia seem to date back at least to the seventeenth century.[41] Both Latvia and Estonia already experienced low fertility rates before the First World War, and in Estonia these fell below replacement level before the Second World War.[42] Natural increase rose in the early 1970s to a yearly average of over 12 per 1,000 in Latvia and over 7 in Estonia but by 1979 dropped steadily in Latvia to 2.8 and in Estonia to 3.8.[43]

Developed regions with low rates of natural increase, in which almost all the working-age population, including a very high percentage of women, is already in the labor force or in school, have been fertile grounds for high rates of mechanical increase (difference between immigration and emigration) in their populations.[44] Latvia and Estonia have experienced the effects of internal migration of Russians, Ukrainians, and Belorussians into their republics after their annexation to the USSR.

As the numbers in Table 2.6 indicate, in 1989 Latvians made up only 52 percent of the population in their republic and were near to losing their majority. Estonians were steadily losing ground, too, down to 61.5 percent of the residents of their republic. Although immigration into Latvia and Estonia continued throughout the Soviet period, its rate was in decline: the number of average annual immigrants into Latvia dwindled from 14,364 between 1959 and 1970, to 11,556 between 1970 and 1979, and to 9,802 in the 1979–1987 period. The numbers for the same intervals in Estonia were 8,409, 6,667, and 6,322 respectively. Even the continuation of this number of immigrants, however, would have made Latvians a minority in their republic in the early 1990s and the Estonians some time later.

There is considerable disagreement as to how much weight may properly be assigned to the attraction posed by higher standards of living to potential immigrants in a country like the USSR, in which the movement of people was bureaucratically controlled. Many observers maintain that immigration into the Baltic republics was in fact a form of colonization, a politically motivated process aimed at the reduction of the eponymous nationalities' share in the population to make its political control easier. The willingness of the Soviet authorities to import into the region both the raw materials of heavy industry and the labor power required to process it even though a very high percentage of the goods were intended for export into the other parts of the USSR seemed to indicate a conscious design.[45] "At times, colonization," argue Misiunas and Taagepera, "seems to have become a goal in itself rather than a means of industrialization."[46]

TABLE 2.6

Population (in millions) and Ethnicity of the Baltic Republics, 1945–1989

Year	Population			Percentage Belonging to the Eponymous Nationality		
	Estonia	Latvia	Lithuania	Estonia	Latvia	Lithuania
1945	0.854	1.400	2.400	88.2	75.5	80.6
1950	1.097	1.944	2.570	76	63	75
1960	1.209	2.113	2.756	74.1	61.7	79.4
1970	1.356	2.364	3.128	68.2	56.8	80.1
1980	1.474	2.529	3.420	64.5	53.5	80.1
1985	1.530	2.604	3.570	63.1	52.6	78.7
1989				61.5	52.0	79.6

Source: Misiunas and Taagepera 1983, Table 1, pp. 272–73. The data for
January 1985 is estimated by Misiunas and Taagepera 1989, Table 2, p. 71.
Reprinted by permission of the University of California Press. Data for 1989
is based on preliminary unpublished results of the 1989 census, in Schroeder
1990, Table 1, p. 45.

Others, however, do not see in the industrialization of Estonia, and by
extension that of Latvia, "a purposeful, centrally directed technique
of Russification."[47]

Demographers, who study not just the Baltics but the USSR as a
whole or study the USSR in comparative frameworks, tend to the
conclusion that "despite assertions of fundamental differences
between migration in Soviet and market-economy societies, existing
generalizations concerning migration processes for Western countries
describe quite well much of the recent Soviet experience."[48] For
example, Lewis and Rowland point out that Russian immigration to
Latvia is more extensive than into Lithuania even though both people
were hostile to the annexation of their states to the USSR.[49] They
argue that the rate of Russian immigration into a Soviet republic was
directly correlated to its level of modernization, was inversely related
to the rate of growth of its native labor force, and inversely but less
strongly associated with its level of education.[50]

Studies that break down the immigration flows by period offer a
proper balance between these contradictory views and by considerably refining them offer overall support to the economic incentive
perspective. The majority of the immigrants into Estonia, in Parming's study of the pre-1970 period, arrived involuntarily.[51] Russian
sources also report that between 1945 and 1949 thousands of tech-

nical specialists were sent to Latvia.[52] The period of reconstruction in the wake of the Second World War allowed the use of organizational and administrative methods for migration regulation. Subsequently, concludes Zaslavskaya, such methods failed to provide the required results and "since the early 1970s greater reliance came to be put on economic methods."[53] The reason for the change seems to be part of a larger pattern: much of the immigration from the rest of Europe in the sixteenth to the nineteenth centuries led immigrants to less developed regions of countries or the world, whereas in more recent times the direction of migration was reversed and immigrants sought out the more advanced economies of the world or their country. Immigration destination correlated closely with the attractiveness of the higher standard of living in the Baltics, and given their "Western" standards of living by Soviet standards, there was little need to use economic incentives to increase immigration.[54] The dynamic of migration to the Baltic resembles such movements in other parts of the world, not the least the Spanish migration to Catalonia, Vizcaya, and Guipúzcoa, to seem exceptional.

Comparative studies can attempt in J. S. Mill's view either to provide causal explanations for agreement (similarity) or difference. In the former case, a circumstance common to two or more cases (when other circumstances between the cases are relatively different) coincides with a similar outcome in them and, therefore, is recognized as its cause. In the latter case, a difference between circumstances in two or more cases (when otherwise the cases are relatively similar) is correlated with different results in them and, therefore, is recognized as their cause.[55] I will employ the second method—the method of difference—in this study because it seems to better fit historical comparisons in which the awareness of the differences even between similar cases is unavoidable. This method affords less sweeping causal explanations than its alternative, but is more discerning. In this chapter I presented the commonality of the cases under study. In Chapters 3, 4, and 5, I will examine their unique configurations against this common background with the aim of suggesting "new problems of interpretation and point[ing] to discrete patterns of causation."[56]

My aim in this study is sociological and not historical, and therefore my presentation will not follow a strict chronological logic. My focus is the relationship between immigration and nationalist movements and where, as in Estonia and Latvia, the years 1920–1940 were a period of nation-building but not of immigration whereas the period 1945–1989 witnessed massive immigration but only limited nationalist activity, I had no reason to examine them in detail. In Catalonia and the Basque country I ignored much of the Civil War and the Franco period for the same reasons. The eras dominated by the interaction of nationalists and immigrants form the chronological focus of my study; conversely, I treat the intermediary lulls only in passing.

3

Hegemonic Nationalism in Catalonia

Hegemony and Autonomy

Catalonia was a politically and territorially unified region, as well as the hub of a sprawling mercantile empire, between the twelfth and the fourteenth centuries. Vicens Vives observed that in its heyday Catalonia was on par with Venice and Genoa in its involvement in the spice traffic and the trade between the Mediterranean and Flanders, as well as in commerce, finance, and shipping in general.[1]

Though united with the kingdom of Aragon through marriage in the twelfth century, Catalonia kept its status as an autonomous principality. Catalonia possessed, as did Valencia and Aragon, one of the most advanced constitutional orders of late medieval Europe based, according to J. H. Elliot, on a powerful Parliament "which shared the legislative powers with the Crown and [was] well buttressed by laws and institutions which derived from a long tradition of political liberty."[2] Even when Aragon and Castile were united, Catalonia maintained its Corts, the Parliament that represented its estates, and a standing committee, the Diputació, its *fueros* (corporate privileges of regional autonomy), and retained control over the level of taxes paid to the king.[3]

The kingdom of Castile was much different: its "social organization was geared to the needs of crusading warfare" and its Parliament was too weak to stand up to an energetic king.[4] After the union of the crowns of Aragon and Castile, Catalonia registered a long period of decline, due to shifting trading routes from the Mediterranean to the Atlantic, piracy, and recurring famines and plagues. Consequently, during most of the Hapsburg era, Catalonia played little if any role in Spanish and Spanish imperial affairs. At the same time, the desire for autonomy remained strong, and in the 1460s Catalans rose against their Aragonese king. They rose again at the end of the Thirty Years War, and yet again in the Spanish Succession

War, against their Castilian rulers. These rebellions and civil war, which resulted from internal social conflicts that were sharpened by the economic decline, exposed the principality of Catalonia in the 1460s and 1640s to the peril of becoming a French protectorate.[5]

The conquest of Grenada in 1492 from the Muslims and the annexation of Navarra in 1515 unified the territory of Spain under one king but not its political framework. A major drive to place Spain on unified constitutional foundations was made possible only after the Spanish Succession War of 1702–1715, which, ironically, confirmed Spain's declining position in Europe.[6] The Bourbon king, Philip V, defeated rebellious Catalonia and conquered Barcelona. In 1714, he abolished the regional *fueros* and the quasi-independent status of Catalonia, Valencia, and Aragon and subjected them to his central authority. Among Spain's regions only the Basque provinces, which supported the Bourbons, were allowed to retain their *fueros*.

Not only was the Catalan Corts absorbed into the Spanish Cortes, but in 1716 a radical program, the Nueva Planta, was promulgated with the aim of suppressing Catalan political and linguistic distinctiveness. The plan forbade the use of Catalan in administration and the courts but, at the same time, expressly respected Catalan property and family law, and in consequence, Catalonia retained its separate civil and mercantile law and internal jurisprudence. Though "the success of the New Plan...was never complete,"[7] by and large Catalonia became just another part of Spain, divided into four provinces that were linked to Madrid rather than to one another.

In the eighteenth century, "for the first time in its history" Catalonia was fully integrated into Spain and Spanish affairs.[8] Catalonia's integration into Spain, however, led to a new phase of economic expansion and prosperity, and "Catalans revealed themselves to be fully conscious of the advantages offered by the Spanish system and proved completely loyal subjects of the Crown."[9] Although from the fifteenth century to the early eighteenth century Catalans repeatedly rose to defend their medieval fueros against the modernizing Absolutism, after 1716 Catalan relationship with Spain entered a peaceful stage that was to last until Catalonia's industrialization in the nineteenth century changed the view of its proper association with Madrid yet again.

Most of the nineteenth century and the first half of the twentieth century was a period of two intertwined changes in Spain: a political conflict between liberal reformers and religious traditionalists, which was ushered in by the French Revolution and the

MAP 3.1

Catalonia

Napoleonic conquest, and industrialization, in competition with England.[10]

The political struggle produced two civil wars, two republics, two dictatorships, and many military *pronunciamientos*. When the Bourbon monarchy was finally replaced by the Second Republic, its short life was characterized by deepening social conflict, a slide into a brutal Civil War, and subsequently, into Franco's fascist dictatorship. These conflicts played and replayed the themes of the French Revolution and, often in a caricaturelike way, its drama.

The reason for this protracted political and social conflict was that the Spanish monarchy and Church were more robust than their

French counterparts and the forces of modernity were much shallower though their militancy and ideas were just as far-reaching as those of French reformers and revolutionaries. An example of the contradictions engendered by this time warp was the establishment of universal male suffrage already in 1890, only to be subverted through the system of municipal *caciques*. The *caciques* allocated the seats and spoils between the two dynastic parties—the Liberals and Conservatives—and effectively denied representation to republican parties.[11] Yet other demonstrations of the peculiarity of Spanish politics was the belated arrival of a mass-based socialist party, in spite of the great social inequalities that characterized the country, and the survival of the militant champions of the ancien régime, the Carlists, into the 1870s and of the anarcho-syndicalists into the 1930s.[12]

The same type of unevenness was manifested in Spain's industrialization. The Castilian political core that created the Spanish state in the late fifteenth century remained preindustrial. Spanish politics, in Vilar's telltale words, were dominated "by classes whose origins, psychology, and shared interest predated the Industrial Revolution. The landowning aristocracy, old and new, heirs of the *hidalgos* and *letrados*, waiting for careers in the army, the university, or Parliament, speculators in a capitalism still commercial or financial—these are the social types who alternated in power in Madrid."[13] Conversely, industrialization in Spain started on the country's geographical perimeters. First, in the beginning of the nineteenth century, in Catalonia, which was joined by another nucleus of industry in two of the Basque provinces, Vizcaya and Guipúzcoa, in the second half of the century.

Consequently, the measure of unity accomplished by the political centralizers and based on the earlier and supposedly hallowed forms of territorial integrity was imperilled by the new, heterogeneous economic geography of industrialization. The inability of the nationwide dynastic parties to absorb regional interests left a constant thorn in the side of the body politic and contributed to the instability of the regime.[14] The demands of the Catalan industrialists (I will examine their Basque counterparts in the next chapter) were frequently at odds with the worldview and interests of the political elites of Madrid, which were united by their antibourgeois animosity. Given this mismatch, "from 1835 on, Catalonia became the region in which all the major problems were fought out with the greatest intensity."[15]

The origins of Catalan industrialization are found in its mild feudal system, which encouraged the consolidation of large plots and investment to increase productivity and, coupled with Catalonia's seashore location and the availability of Spain's captive Latin American colonies, fostered a market-oriented viniculture as well as a commercial network and mentality. The relative prosperity of the province fostered the development of a wool cloth industry that produced for the Spanish market and transformed the Barcelona region into a second Lancastershire by the end of the eighteenth century.[16] Textiles, initially, were produced though a putting out system that benefited both city and countryside, and by the middle of the century, when wool was complemented with cotton imported from the United States via Cuba, textile production was mechanized. Wool and cotton textiles remained the paramount product of Catalan industry until the Civil War.[17]

The Catalan bourgeoisie, led by the textile manufactures, in the word's of Pierre Vilar's classic study of Catalan history, "was animated by one coherent thought, to construct a nation *by and for industry*." Initially the Catalan manufacturers' frame of reference was "the *Spanish* nation."[18] They sought to convince Spain that its future lay with Catalonia. Hence, for most of the nineteenth century, *national market* and *national industry* meant "Spanish market and industry" for them.[19] The aim of the captains of Catalan industry was not just to capture the lackluster Spanish markets but to become the new mold, if not the new core, of Spain; that is, to identify the economic outlook of the state with their own.

This Catalan ambition was disappointed again and again. In the rest of preindustrial Spain, Catalan demands for "national market" sounded like a Catalan plot for monopoly or a demand that Spain finance Catalan prosperity.[20] The failure of the Progressive liberals' transitional government and short-lived First Federal Republic, which was supported by the Catalan bourgeoisie and supportive of its goals, revealed the extent of the latter's isolation in agrarian and traditional Spain.[21] When this experiment ended with the Bourbon Restoration of 1874 a great disillusionment set in among the Catalan industrial bourgeoisie.[22] An even greater setback was the loss of Spain's last colonial possessions—Cuba, Puerto Rico, and the Philippines—to the United States in 1898. This was regarded as a veritable disaster by Catalan industrialists, and under its blow their *espanolista* federalism was transformed into particularist Catalan nationalism.

An early, and still unfocused, publication of Catalanism was Valentí Almirall's *Lo Catalanisme*, written halfway between the failure of the First Republic and the colonial debacle of 1898. The contingency of Catalan nationalism, and its instrumental character, is captured in the speech delivered by a Catalan representative to the Cortes: "If instead of the colonial disaster, Spain had been victorious, if its colonial power had grown, if it had made the effects of a more extensive economic development felt in the internal life of the nation, if the Spaniard felt himself fortunate to belong to this nation—or to this state if you prefer—would you have seen this movement of protest from which 'Catalan solidarity' has finally emerged, arise on the foundation that I have described? Surely not."[23]

The Catalan industrial bourgeoisie began refocusing its sight from Madrid to Barcelona and from the elusive goal of becoming the national bourgeoisie to forging an autonomous regional block in the narrow, but more secure, little "fatherland."[24] It was felt that Catalan interests would be better served by a decentralized political order that delegated decisions that affected Catalonia to local authorities. This Catalan nationalism, in Solé-Tura's view, was a frustrated and redirected revolution by a bourgeoisie that failed to remake Spain in its image in order to impose itself on all of Spain.[25]

This Catalan industrial bourgeoisie was inspired by a Catalan cultural renaissance, started in the 1830s by a small circle of upper middle class poets and litterateurs whose aims were "almost exclusively aesthetic."[26] The aim of the *renaixença* was to revive the Catalan language, which had been overshadowed and then replaced by Spanish as the language of culture in the sixteenth century and as the language of public life in the eighteenth century. Catalan did not, however, undergo complete diglossiation: it continued to be used in addition to private life for correspondence and commercial bookkeeping and for worship in the Montserrat Abbey. The broader cultural inspiration behind the cultural revival movement was European Romanticism, and it led to the rebirth of vernacular Catalan poetry and literature and the historiography of the Middle Ages, which focused on Catalan grandeur and identity.[27] The "core value" of Catalan identity was established then, and remained since, the Catalan language.[28]

The prosperity of Catalan industry and agriculture, both based on the use and growth of local resources, enhanced regional self-confidence and catalyzed the *renaixença*.[29] Both strands of nationalism were entwined in the labors of Carles Aribau: the author of the renaissance's first great Catalan language poem, *Oda la Pàtria* of 1833 and, in Spanish, the history of the textile industry, which he composed as an employee representing the organization of Catalan manufacturers.[30] The poetry contests of the Flower Games in the 1860s contributed a great deal to the penetration of the movement into a wide spectrum of educated Catalans. This broader intelligentsia undertook the protection of what survived of Catalan autonomy—its distinct civil law and judicial system—and sought to reverse the ongoing attempts to enforce Castilianization in schools and the courts.

The politicization of Catalan nationalism was aided by some of the structural characteristics of the regional industry. Catalan industry was hampered by being made up of relatively small-scale woolen and cotton textile enterprises, and thus exposed to the competition of superior British textiles, and by its inability to sustain the second industrial revolution of steel, steam, and railroad.[31]

Not surprisingly, Catalan industrialists voiced contradictory desires: they sought, like English manufacturers before them, the abolition of tariffs on grain from the United States and Russia to lower the production costs of their labor force and increase the purchasing power of the Spanish market, but at the same time, they also demanded the imposition of high tariffs on English textiles to prevent competition with their enterprises. Castilian grain producing landowners, on their part, sought cheap textiles and protection for their grain. The compromise solution was high trade protection for both grain and textiles, but because of the contrary interests of the Castilian and Catalan elites, Castilian concessions in the form of tariff protection were never secure and needed to be rewon periodically.[32] Already in 1820, a Catalan spokesman expressed this combination of dynamism and frailty in the textile industry: "internal freedom is what we need. Free trade from abroad would be a mortal blow to our factories."[33]

To make the picture complete, an additional feature of Catalan industry needs to be mentioned. Catalonia's modern social structure, especially in Barcelona, also generated a self-conscious and militant anarchist and later syndicalist, and a much smaller socialist, working class ready to do battle for the protection of its interests. The need to contend with their workers moderated the demands of Catalan industrialists from the Spanish state. At times—for example in 1919 in response to intense labor militancy, in September 1923 in welcoming the military dictatorship of Primo de Rivera,[34] and again during part of the Second Republic—Catalan industrialists were willing to conspire with the Spanish state against other Catalan classes and institutions.

The espousal of the nationalist aim of political and administrative decentralization in the form of regional autonomy did not mean the total abandonment of the Catalan industrialists' old goals.

In fact, after the loss of the overseas colonies, Spanish tariff protection and the growth of its internal market assumed even greater importance. The Catalan nationalist movement, consequently, expressed the contradictory status of the Catalan bourgeoisie within the Spanish state as the leader of Spain's earliest and one of its fastest modernizing regions, while only a peripherial group vis-à-vis Castilian political power in need of both its tariff and police protection to prosper. Being ahead and on the sidelines at the same time created a seesaw pattern of political expression: an aspiration to become the bourgeoisie of all of Spain combined with the desire to attain regional autonomy. As a result of its dependence, Catalan nationalism remained a movement seeking home rule, that is, regional autonomy: the satisfaction of Catalan demands within Spain, not independence from Spain.

The great leader of the first generation of Catalan nationalism was Almirall's disciple Enric Prat de la Riba. Prat formulated the first nationalist program in a series of resolutions from 1892, known as the *Bases of Manresa*, in which he called for "home rule for a Catalan-speaking state with posts reserved for born or nationalized Catalans."[35] He expected that modernization under the guidance of a fully autonomous regional government would lead simultaneously to social harmony and the preservation of Catalan traditions.[36] In the first decade of this century, the most powerful and effective body of Catalan nationalism, the conservative Lliga Regionalista, was created by Prat, who led it in Barcelona, together with Cambó, the head of the Catalan textile manufacturer's association, who represented it in Madrid.[37] The Lliga was the first modern cohesive political party in Spain, the child of the most industrial and modern of its provinces.

For a span of about two years (1906 to 1908), the Lliga successfully organized and dominated the first nationalist coalition—the Solidaridad Catalana. The coalition included a wide spectrum of parties, from the Republicans to the Carlists, and won the overwhelming majority of the locally elected Cortes representatives in 1907. This unlikely coalition came together in defense of the constitutional liberties and judicial rights that served as the foundation of all the parties' relatively unhindered existence; that is, in defense of the formal democracy of the Restoration from the threats of the military.[38] The ability of the Catalan nationalist organization to become the axis of the parties' cooperation was already indicative of its future preponderance.

Though the coalition rapidly disintegrated, in 1913 the Lliga won its first concession from the Madrid government, the unification of the preexisting powers of the four provinces in a single body, the Mancomunitat. The Mancomunitat, under Prat's energetic leadership, combined a program of social and economic reforms, aimed at improved regional communications, with "renationalization": the revival and protection of Catalan culture by financing the historical and philological research of the Institute of Catalan Studies as well as museums, libraries, and so forth. Though this homogenizing geographical achievement partially reversed the impact of the breaking up of Catalonia into four separate provinces, it fell short of the desired autonomy.[39]

The Lliga failed to gain further concessions from the Madrid government because both Spanish dynastic parties were struggling "to complete the centralizing mission of absolute monarchy" and, therefore, were opposed in principle to devolution of authority. To gain the cooperation of the Madrid government, Catalan nationalists had to present their conservative and constitutional visage, which, under the social conservatives Prat and Cambó, they were easily able to do.

However, the meaning of conservatism was different in Madrid and in Barcelona. The conservatism of the Spanish government was political, social, and economic; that of the Catalan manufacturers was social, but neither political nor economic. Because of this yawning abyss between the core and the periphery, not even Castilian conservatives could grant Catalan conservatives the autonomy they wished for. The establishment of the Mancomunitat was interpreted by the Maura government that granted it as a reform of local administration, whereas for Catalan nationalists it served as a recognition of their nationhood.[40]

Spanish liberalism was also committed to a centralized Spain and, therefore, was equally burdened with "a regional problem it was incapable of solving."[41] In spite of its limited character, the Mancomunitat legislation had a calamitous effect on Spanish liberalism. The Liberal Party split permanently in its result, demonstrating Catalanism's contribution "to the decomposition of the Spanish polity."[42] To make an impression on the government in Madrid and ride the wave of local pressure, the conservative nationalists of Catalonia sought on occasion to ally themselves with the urban lower classes. Because the latter supported Republicanism, Catalan nationalists became tainted with revolutionary schemes. Only a Republican and socially progressive government in Madrid could have consented to the recognition of Catalonia's distinct nationhood and grant it political devolution but such government would have been seen as a threat by the socially conservative Catalan manufacturers.

This contradiction, as Carr insightfully points out, points to similarities between Catalonia and Ireland, between Parnell and Cambó. The latter, like the former, "was a politician who faced two ways: a social conservative who played with revolutionary threats but detested revolution."[43] We already touched upon the similarity between Catalan industrialization and the English pattern; in the political sphere, however, Catalonia resembled Ireland. Being England and Ireland rolled in one was the consequence of Spain's uneven development. Ultimately, this unevenness, which defeated the drive to harmonize Spanish interests with Catalan demands, also doomed bourgeois Catalan nationalism's autonomist aspirations.

The very limited accomplishments of the conservative Lliga's moderate tactics left the door open for a more radical nationalism to seek broader Catalan autonomy in a Republican Spain. Gradually, in place of the short-lived coalition of the Solidaridad Catalana, around the fulcrum of the conservative bourgeois Lliga, a more permanent and broader based Catalan nationalism emerged under petty bourgeois intellectual leadership and with conditional working class support. The growth of this petty bourgeois nationalism coincided with the demise of the corrupt *caciquismo* that allowed the traditional elites of Spain to subvert the constitutional monarchy's parliamentary system under the Second Republic. An expanded Catalan nationalist organization stood poised to receive the influx of the masses.

One would expect that Catalan nationalist demands of autonomy and linguistic revival would have little attraction for workers, many of whom were immigrants to Catalonia from other parts of Spain and supported political parties or trade unions concerned with bread and butter issues or revolutionary social and political visions. In fact, a significant part of the working class and the lower layers of the society in Barcelona were attracted to the rabble-rousing revolutionary and violently anticlerical and antibourgeois rhetoric of Lerroux, the Radical Republican Party's leader. His all-Spanish Republicanism and hostility to Catalanism combined with his appeal to workers made him into the bête noir of the Lliga between the beginning of the century and the First World War when his organization went into decline. The term *lerrouxismo* has ever since been preserved in Catalonia as a derogatory epithet for divisive political conflict that plays into the hands of the Spanish authorities.[44] Conflict between classes seemed to preclude regionally based coalitions.

The Partido Socialista Obrero Español (PSOE), the gradualist socialist party and its trade union, the Unión General de Trabajadores (UGT), also made only limited inroads among the workers of Barcelona. The majority of the industrial workers of Catalonia gave their support to revolutionary anarcho-syndicalism, and the head-quarter of its trade union—the Confederación Nacional del Trabajo (CNT)—was located in Barcelona. Anarchism usually appealed to new rural recruits to industry and retained its strength in Barcelona because of the paternalistic industrialists' uncompromising opposition to trade unions of any kind.[45] And yet there were parallels between the position of nationalists and anarcho-syndicalists in Catalonia. The apolitical attitude of Catalan anarchists, in Balcells's view, was not just a reflection of Bakunin's well-known influence in Spain but an expression of their lack of trust in the Spanish state, which they saw as removed from the workers' real concerns. Anarchism, he concludes, was but "a workers' variant of Catalan particularism."[46] Furthermore, anarchism was just as jealous of group liberties as of individual free-doms, and consequently, there was no inherent contradiction between regional autonomy and social reform or revolution.[47]

The indifference and, sometimes, anti-Catalan stance of much of the working class of Barcelona was to change during the 1920s. The bond between nationalist ideals and social programs was pro-vided by the new leadership of Catalan nationalism, which hailed from the radical members of the Catalan petty bourgeoisie. The common programmatic foundation was supplied by Federal Republi-canism with a social conscience. The leader of the radical wave of Catalan nationalism was Francesc Macià, an army colonel, who stood simultaneously for Catalanism, republicanism, and socialism. Never-theless, "it required," according to Susan DiGiacomo, "a political event of major proportions to bring the Catalan opposition and the working class opposition together: the dictatorship of Miguel Primo de Rivera."[48]

The Primo de Rivera dictatorship brought together workers and Catalan nationalists because he combined national and social oppres-sion. His regime abolished the Mancomunitat, thus alienating Catalan nationalists, and in spite of his verbal sympathies for mild social reform, Primo de Rivera essentially sought to "save society, not to reform it."[49] By arresting anarchists agitators he demonstrated that he was the enemy of the workers. Against such opponent "*all classes* in Catalonia combined their grievances."[50] This new sentiment was behind the creation of a new coalition on the eve of the Second Republic.

In the April 1931 elections, Maciá's and Companys's coalition of left-wing parties, the Esquerra Republicana de Catalunya, resoundingly defeated Cambó's Lliga. The mainstay of the new wave of nationalism was the middle stratum broadly defined, made up of salaried and professional people (but not of employers), that "was growing in size and developing an awareness of [its] role and position." Pi-Sunyer also emphasizes the educational foundations of this stratum, which was "a culturally conscious middle sector which read a good deal and attended all manner of meetings and performances— characteristics which reached right down into the class of artisans and small shopkeepers."[51] A lower layer of non-manual-laboring group also aspired to resemble the middle stratum and adopt its values. Another group of Esquerra supporters came from the *rabassaires*, the small tenant farmers, whose side it took against larger landowners.[52]

The Esquerra, for the first time, also commanded the vote of a portion of the workers in Catalonia, though many of them were Castilian and anarchist, hence internationalist in outlook. The CNT concluded that some of its demands, such as the legalization of its syndicates, were more likely to be attained under a republican regime. The preponderance of syndicalist influence in Catalonia seemed to guarantee that the legal framework of an autonomous Catalan region would safeguard present and future social gains against more hostile Castilian central governments.[53] Setting aside its traditional abstention in elections, the CNT threw its support behind the Esquerra and assured the latter's victory.[54]

The defense of constitutional liberty, that is, of the shell of democracy, served on two occasions as the foundation of regional alliances in Catalonia. The formation of Solidaridad Catalana around the conservative bourgeois Lliga was a response to an ominous weakening of the legal bases of civil jurisdiction over the military.[55] CNT's support of Esquerra was due to the desire to win amnesty for its prisoners and attain the legalization of its syndicates. The solidity of the Popular Front in Catalonia during the Second Republic was the strongest result of the same sentiments and calculations.[56]

Borrowing Antonio Gramsci's terms, we may argue that the protection of Catalan national interests led to the creation of a "political bloc," in this case an interclass alliance under the hegemony of the nationalist leadership.[57] The nationalist hegemony was not unshakable. For example, on the eve of the second national elections in 1933 the Esquerra split over the relationship with a radicalized CNT, and the appearance of the more moderate Acció Catalana enabled the Lliga to elect the majority of the Catalan representatives to the Cortes.[58] But a hegemonic social bloc is not just the papering over of differences but a genuine, even if temporary, meeting of minds and interests. Its recurrence justifies the description of the nationalist alliance not just as a marriage of convenience but as a hegemonic bloc. Not all nationalist movements attain hegemony, many become mass parties that contend with other mass parties representing other factional interests, such as Socialist or Social Democratic parties, or supernational interests, such as Christian Democratic parties.

Another illustration of the commanding character of Catalan regional interest was the regional focus of the workers' organization in Catalonia. All-Spanish, that is, unitary, parties failed to muster support in Catalonia. The PSOE was organized as an all-Spanish party and in spite of its Herculean attempts found little room for expansion in Catalonia. Its trade union, the UGT was founded in Barcelona but, having failed to galvanize support among the Catalan workers, had to be transferred to Madrid in 1899.[59] The same was true of the Spanish Communist Party after its foundation in 1920. In response to the rejection of unitary parties in Catalonia, Catalan socialists and communists created their own breakaway, regionally based parties: the tiny Unió Socialista de Catalunya (USC, Socialist Union of Catalonia) and the Bloque Obrero y Campesino (BOC, Workers' and Peasant's Bloc), which expressed nationalistic sympathies in the 1920s.[60] The strength of the anarcho-syndicalists, especially after the establishment of the CNT in 1911, always rested in Barcelona, and in essence they were a Catalan organization.

In short, "pre-Civil War Catalan parties, though divided along class lines, were, in most cases, locally based entities and not part of nationwide political organization."[61] Conversely, as we shall see in the next chapter, the workers of the Vizcayan factories and mines were successfully organized by the all-Spanish PSOE; Basque nationalism did not assume the mantle of hegemony.

Two factors combined to make Catalan nationalism *hegemonic*. The first was the uneven character of development in Spain, which set the modern regional interests in opposition to the conservative interests represented by Madrid governments. In the complex tug-of-war between centralizing and regionalist tendencies the primary lines of division separated not social strata organized throughout Spain, but Catalan from Spanish organizations. The geographical, rather then social, matrix in which classes splintered signalled the hegemony of Catalan nationalism, which was able to detach the various Catalan social strata and their political groupings from their Spanish moorings. Second, the combination of national and social oppression in the policies of monarchical and dictatorial, conservative agriculturalist and centralizing liberal regimes, in Madrid[62] brought together willy-nilly the opposing classes of the region in a political alliance that shared the goal of protecting the limited freedoms that allowed each to struggle for its own visions and interests. In sum, the common interests of overdeveloped Catalonia in modernization and reform, as well as in democracy, proved stronger than Spanish social divisions; regional interests dominated and ordered class interests.

The same hegemonic tendency appeared with renewed strength in the context of Catalan opposition to Franco. Franco's regime, as ever committed to centralization like its Absolutist and liberal predecessors, but driven by its own brand of fanatical dedication, undertook a campaign of "forced assimilation" in Catalonia (and the Basque country, as we shall see in Chapter 4). Catalan scholars and intellectuals describe its aims in Catalonia as nothing but "cultural genocide."[63] The authoritarian government "embarked on a deliberate policy of imposing the Castilian language and banning or ostracizing the local language, outlawing all its uses in the administration, education, mass media, translations...as well as making impossible any association that directly or indirectly would foster the national sentiment."[64] The repression of Catalan (and Euskera) was unparalleled: their use for worship was proscribed, books written in them were burned, inscriptions were removed from tombstones, street and shop signs were prohibited. Initially even casual conversation in the streets invited police attention.[65] This massive cultural oppression began to be relaxed only in the late 1960s and early 1970s.

During Spanish transition to democracy in the aftermath of Franco's death, the nationalist hegemony reemerged much strengthened. Franco, after all, was the worst adversary of both socialists and regional nationalists! Because "Franco's repressive use of Spanish unitary nationalism made it easy to identify the worst of Francoism with Spanish nationalism" it was possible to organize against it in defense of the regional interest.[66] The repression of the authoritarian regime brought together the classes of Catalonia and produced an alliance even stronger than the Esquerra that emerged after Primo de Rivera's dictatorship. Anti-Franco sentiment was strong in Catalonia and Catalanism was equated during the Franco years with the anti-fascist struggle for democracy and, as such, commended the sympathy of many Spaniards both outside and inside Catalonia. Throughout the

Franco years, regionally organized underground Catalan Socialist and Communist parties remained in being,[67] and the Spanish Socialist and Communist parties accepted political decentralization as "an integral part of the process of democratization and were the most ardent supporters of autonomy and of the recognition of the multilingual and multinational character of Spanish society."[68]

After Franco's death in 1975, his regime's highly centralized and forcefully assimilationist tendency was rejected and replaced with a new willingness to recognize the legitimacy of demands for regional autonomy. The rapid reemergence of the historical Catalan and Basque nationalist parties and the birth of additional ones in the mid-1970s demonstrated the connection between democracy and regional nationalism and the urgency of attending to the distinctive national identities in a democratic Spain. Article 2 of the 1978 Constitution bridges the old and new conceptions by proclaiming that "the Constitution is based on the indissoluble unity of the Spanish Nation, the common and indivisible fatherland—*Patria*—of all Spaniards, and recognizes and guarantees the right to self-government of the nationalities and regions of which it is composed and solidarity among them all."[69]

By drawing an obviously unsustainable distinction between the terms *nation* and *nationality* the Constitution fudges some of the central issues of regional heterogeneity. But by acknowledging the "the multi-national and multi-lingual character of Spanish society," the Constitution's practical corollary was the establishment of "the principle of decentralization of governmental authority along regional lines" and the institution of regional governments (known as the *Generalitat* in Catalonia) with a president, parliament, and ministries.[70]

This Spanish policy is similar to the approach undertaken under the League of Nations for the protection of minorities though goes much beyond it. The similarity is rooted in the official recognition, protection, and cultivation of the cultural diversity of Spain without seeing them as mortal threats to the Spanish national identity through seeking, at the same time, to contain the expressions of peripheral nationalism within Spanish nationalism. The Spanish constitution, however, sanctions not only cultural and linguistic autonomy of territorially concentrated permanent national minorities but also their political autonomy. This approach represents a willingness to forgo the homogenizing tendencies associated with modern nation-states, and this affinity makes it easier to accommodate in places where a policy favoring national minorities is in effect, as we shall see in the second part of this chapter, allowing regional cultural diversity, and adopting a multiculturalist policy vis-à-vis the immigrants to the domains of the minority nations.

Catalan nationalists are no longer the major source of opposition to the central Spanish authorities they used to be in the period from the mid-1830s to the end of the Civil War. The "reconciliation" in Spanish-Catalan relations is due, it seems, to both the democratic character of Spain and the partial closing of the gap of economic unevenness between Catalonia and the Madrid region. The Suárez government was very clear about the importance of finding a satisfactory solution to the nationalist demands of centrifugal regional forces.

As part of the democratization process, negotiations between the central government and Basque and Catalan representatives yielded two autonomy statutes. These statues transferred to the regional governments exclusive jurisdiction over education and culture as well as major areas of the economy such as agriculture, forestry, and land-use planning. In addition they retained administrative authority over economic development planning and internal commerce, as long as their policies remained in accord with Spanish governmental norms.[71] The Constitution was very popular in Catalonia, and following the call of most Catalan parties, with the exception of small extreme right and left parties, the Catalan statute was ratified overwhelmingly in the referendum. The participation rate in the referendum over the Basque statute, the Statute of Guernica, was much lower but 95 percent of the voters approved it.

The slow pace of the devolution of the central government's functions in both Euskadi and Catalonia created a great deal of antagonism and considerable use was made of the Constitutional Court in adjudicating conflicting interpretations of the statutes, but the process was completed. The *estado de las autonomías* had come to be accepted by all parties, and even the conservative Alianza Popular (today Partido Popular) reconciled itself ex post facto to regional devolution. The regional issue lost, if not its saliency, then at least its explosive potential in Catalonia and in the Basque country its volatility was blunted.

Economic changes have also diminished interregional diversity in Spain. Already in 1967, Madrid was fifth among Spanish provinces with the highest per capita disposable income and trailed Barcelona only marginally. Soon after, Madrid overtook Barcelona, and in 1985 the disposable per capita income in Madrid was about 10 percent higher than in Barcelona. (See Tables 2.1 and 2.2.) Barcelona and the other Catalan provinces were still among the most developed of Spain's provinces, but the smaller gap made the authorities in Madrid less suspicious of Catalan demands to foster development that, after all, they were undertaking on their own initiative since the late 1950s. Spanish development made Catalonia less distinct and, therefore, more connected to Spain.

The combination of support for regional autonomy and lessened antagonism toward Spain in Catalonia is revealed in an analysis of electoral results. A distinctive characteristic of Catalan elections is the high frequency of split-ticket voting in choosing the Cortes (the National Parliament) and the regional parliament. Whereas the main Catalan nationalist party, the Pacte Democràtic per Catalunya/Convergència i Unió (PDC/CiU) consistently won the regional elections (see Table 3.2) and was able to put together a coalition government that dominated the Generalitat (the institution of the regional government), the PSOE (Partido Socialista Obrero Español, Spanish Socialist Workers Party) and its Catalan wing, the PSC (Parti dels Socialistes de Catalunya) were repeatedly the winners of the national elections (see Table 3.1). Admittedly, the gap in the Cortes vote between the two decreased, the PSC-PSOE falling from 41.2 percent in 1986 to 34.7 percent in 1993 and the CiU in the same period fluctuating around 32 percent, due in part to a countrywide decline of support for the PSOE (see Table 3.3), but in the regional elections a decisive interval of at least 15 percent remained between them in the period from 1984 to 1992.

Overall, in national elections Catalan nationalist parties (i.e., the PDC/CiU and the ERC) were chosen by a low of 21.3 percent in 1977 to a high of 36.7 percent of the voters in 1993, while the state-wide parties (UCD, PSOE-PSC, AP, and PSUC) were always chosen by about two-thirds or more of the residents of Catalonia.

One of the reasons for the disparity between the socialist vote in national and regional elections is that some of the Spanish immigrants to Catalonia vote for the PSOE and abstain in the regional elections, whereas many of the native Catalans vote for nationalist parties in both elections. In fact, the 1980 elections to the Catalan Parliament the Andalusian Socialist Party's leader Rojas Marcos condemned the Catalan Statute of Autonomy on the grounds that it is "an aggression against immigrants," and won two seats on the strength of Catalonia's immigrant population's votes.[72] But this tactic, which in nationalist circles invoked the memory of *lerrouxismo*—the pre-First World War

TABLE 3.1

Results of National Elections in Catalonia, in Percentages

Parties	1977	1979	1982	1986	1989	1993
Esquerra	4.5	4.1	4.0	2.7	2.7	5.0
CiU	16.8	18.6	22.2	32.1	32.7	31.7
PSUC/IC	18.2	17.0	4.6	4.0	7.1	7.4
PSC-PSOE	28.4	29.2	45.2	41.2	35.5	34.7
UCD-CC	16.8	19.0	2.0	—	—	—
AP/PP	3.5	3.6	14.6	11.4	10.6	17.0
Others	11.8	8.5	7.4	8.6	11.4	4.1

Sources: Shabad 1986, Table 7, p. 38, published with author's permission; El País, Table: Evolución del voto en Cataluña (1977–1988), p. 102; El País, June 8, 1993.

List of acronyms and abbreviations:

AP/PP	Alianza Popular/Partido Popular
CDS	Centro Democrático y Social
Esquerra	Esquerra Republicana de Catalunya
PCE	Partido Comunista de España/Izquierda Unida
PDC/CiU	Pacte Democràtic per Catalunya/Convergència i Unió
PSC-PSOE	Parti dels Socialistes de Catalunya-Partido Socialista Obrero Español
PSOE	Partido Socialista Obrero Español
PSUC/IC	Partit Socialista Unificat de Catalunya/Iniciativa per Catalunya
UCD-CC	Unión Centro Democrático-Centristes de Catalunya

(Hyphenated names refer to electoral blocs, slashed names usually refer to name changes between elections.)

TABLE 3.2

Results of Regional Elections in Catalonia, in Percentages

Parties	1980	1984	1988	1992
Esquerra	8.9	4.4	4.2	8.0
PDC/CiU	27.6	47.0	46.0	46.4
PSUC/IC	18.7	5.6	7.8	6.4
PSC-PSOE	22.4	30.3	30.0	27.3
UCD-CC	10.5	—	—	—
AP/PP	2.3	7.7	5.4	6.0
Others	9.6	5.0	6.6	5.9

Sources: Shabad 1986, Table 7, p. 38, published with author's permission; El País, Table: Evolución del voto en Cataluña (1977–1988), p. 102; El Pais, March 17, 1992.

TABLE 3.3

Results of National Elections in Spain, in Percentages

Parties	1977	1979	1982	1986	1989	1993
PSOE	28.9	30.5	48.4	44.1	39.5	36.7
PCE/IU	9.2	10.8	4.1	4.6	9.1	9.6
UCD	34.0	35.1	6.3	—	—	—
CDS	—	—	2.9	9.2	7.9	1.7
AP/PP	8.0	6.1	26.6	26.0	25.8	34.8
PDC/CiU	2.8	2.7	3.7	5.0	5.0	5.0
Other Catalan nationalist parties	0.8	0.7	0.7	0.6	0.4	0.8
PNV	1.7	1.7	1.8	1.5	1.2	1.2
Other Basque nationalist parties	0.3	1.5	1.3	1.6	2.2	1.5
Others		12.7	5.2	8.5	8.9	8.7

Sources: Gunther, Sani, and Shabad 1988, Table 57, p. 402, published by permission of the University of California Press and the authors; Blondel and Eseverri 1983, Table 1, p. 77; Molins and Vallés 1990, Table 1, p. 249 Reprinted by permission of the publishers, Butterworth-Heinemann Ltd.; and El País, June 7, 1993. (There are small differences in the percentages reported between the authors because they derive their data from different Spanish government sources.)

split between native and immigrants Catalan classes that played into the hands of (and maybe was even encouraged by) the Madrid authorities, was short lived.

Whereas anti-Catalanist approaches had only limited appeal, the acceptance of Catalan nationalism's hegemony led to electoral success. The PSOE as well as the Spanish Communist Party, "conducted much of their campaign in Catalan," thus indicating the existence of "considerable reserves of support for the regional cause."[73] In the parliamentary elections of 1977, "the socialists won a clear victory in Catalonia, as they had done nowhere else in Spain, because they were able to present socialism and Catalanism as complementary ideologies in a way that convinced the electorate."[74]

Pinilla de las Heras concluded that PSOE-PSC won because it was in the process of becoming a catch-all party, a concept we usually identify with the nonideological American parties. But he also recognized the unique Catalan character of this socialist "coalition," between the PSC, the party of the intellectuals with an effective rank and file (I would prefer to call it the educated Catalan middle class), and the PSOE, a mass party that represents the majority of the immigrant working class. In Pinilla de las Heras's view this coalition was "a sum, rather than a synthesis, of the electorate's tendencies and orientations."[75] While this evaluation seems appropriate, any implication that the coalition was unstable, as four more electoral campaigns demonstrate, was not borne out. The acceptance of the leadership of Catalan middle class intellectuals by socialist voters, many of whom hail from other parts of Spain, remained a central fact of Catalan politics. It seems that the majority of the residents of Catalonia feel at home both in Spain and in Catalonia.

The hegemony of nationalist goals, and the consensus over their meaning, is manifested even more clearly in regional politics. In the regional parliament "Catalan nationalists were able to rally behind one authoritative spokesman,"[76] a single major party—the PDC/CiU. In contrast, the nationalist movement in the Basque region (as we shall see in detail in Chapter 4), was split between three or four parties, so much so that an observer described the results of the 1986 regional elections as having yielded a "political map in which the competing parties resemble pieces of a jigsaw puzzle that refuse to interlock."[77]

The reason for the difference is that Catalans are by and large satisfied with regional autonomy, while in the Basque region there is a split between parties satisfied with autonomy in Spain and those demanding independence from Spain. In Euskadi, "moderate nationalists, associated with the *Partido Nacionalista Vasco* - the PNV, constantly...counter the risk of being outflanked by intransigent advocates of complete independence,"[78] and the wing of Catalan nationalism that aspires for independence from Spain is tiny. The Catalan independence party, the revived but radicalized Esquerra Republicana de Catalunya, doubled its strength, growing from 4.2 to 8 percent of the electorate between 1988 and 1992, but a long-range view shows that it has not yet regained the highest level of its support in 1980.

In general, Catalan elections reveal a less polarized electorate than Basque elections. Furthermore, Catalan voters are more willing to make complex decisions when practical considerations demand it. Many split their vote between the national and regional parliaments, and even though this indicates a cleavage between voters of Spanish origin and those of Catalan origin, many of the same voters are willing to support broader multiclass and multiethnic electoral alliances for the regional parliament.

Although current trends indicate that most Catalans found the satisfaction of their nationalist desires within Spain the gradual homogenization of the economic space of the European Union, which potentially weakens the political boundaries of the European states, creates a new disjuncture between the forces of economic and cultural homogenization in Spain and provides an incentive for over-developed regions, like Catalonia, to pursue their advantage through strengthening their direct ties with the EU. Spain's, and within it Catalonia's, integration into the European Union redraws political and economic borders and potentially reopens the question of the latter's membership in the former.

Immigrant Integration and Language Normalization

Immigration to Catalonia was the direct product of industrialization, which required an ever-growing labor force. The first trickle, it is estimated, commenced in 1845, and evolved into a torrent between 1888 and 1897. Immigration continued ever since, with the exception of the 1900–1910 and 1936–39 periods, when its volume was negligible.[79] The Franco regime's July 1959 Stabilization Plan, which signalled the end of autarky and a major shift toward renewed development through tourism and industrialization, catalyzed immigration into Catalonia into a new rapid phase. The number of immigrants in the two and half decades from 1950 to 1975 reached a staggering 1,387,731—of which 720,808 arrived in 1961–1970 alone (see Table 2.5). The largest group of immigrants in this period, constituting 43.6 percent of the new arrivals, were natives of Andalusia. Because the population of Catalonia in the 1970s was about 3.25 million the impact of such massive immigration was very noticeable. Immigration from less developed parts of Spain to Catalonia still continues but at a much reduced pace.

As part of the transition to democracy in the wake of Franco's death in 1975, and especially during the campaign for the referendum on the Statute of Autonomy and the working out of the contours of the their regional party system, Catalans experienced, what I can characterize only as a collective identity crisis. With over 36 percent of the residents of Catalonia being born outside the region, the question, Who is a Catalan? forced itself onto the public agenda. Demography alone, however, could not account for the centrality and extensiveness of the public preoccupation with the question, let alone with the answers given to it; no such identity question ever emerged in the context of the public debates made possible by *glasnost* or independence from the USSR in the Baltic republics—not even in Latvia, where the native and immigrant populations roughly match one another.

For the Catalan people, "the Catalan language [is] the living center of Catalanism,"[80] the key to their collective identity. In Conversi's words, for Catalans "language always appears as an indispensable and all-pervading factor" of their unity as the great texts of Catalan nationalism, from Almirall to Prat de la Riba, testify.[81] What is the place of language among the possible criteria—ethnic background, place of birth, descent, religion, or civic affiliation—for pinpointing identity?

The historical record shows that language is a flexible criteria: its uses ranged from the pseudo-scientific Nazi attempt to transform language families into immutable racial categories, through an identification of ethnicity with native language, to assimilation of foreigners who acquire the local language. But Catalans seem to have taken this flexibility one step further.

Although most would consider the local language inseparable from Catalan national identity, a civic criterion was given pride of place in the definition of Catalan identity. Most parties during the 1977 campaign adopted the slogan coined by the moderate nationalist leader, Jordi Pujol, "All those who live and work in Catalonia are Catalan." Another popular slogan to emerge was, "Now more than ever, one single people."[82] Such inclusionary civic definitions, though obviously and willfully ignoring important divisions between the native born and immigrants (as we shall see later in this chapter), are significant in that they not only leave open the possibility of individual absorption, and maybe even assimilation, but encourage this process for large numbers. The civic delineation of Catalanness empowers immigrants to make demands on native Catalans and Catalan institutions and, in some areas, such as politics, encourages the formation of nonethnic political parties that place some, even if limited, power in the hands of immigrant representatives. This definition of Catalan identity is an example of an *assimilationist* approach by applying a civic criterion of membership to immigrants, in "violation" of the customary definition of a Catalan as one who is proficient in Catalan. For this approach to work, the push-and-pull of immigration to Catalonia has to lead to a certain measure of social mobility.

To again anticipate, under much different conditions, the process of democratization in Latvia and Estonia, even under the exigencies of a relatively free electoral system, brought about much more rigid and at times exclusionary programs and legislation in both the linguistic and electoral spheres against the Russian and other Slavic immigrants. Certainly no Baltic leader shares the equivalent of Jordi Pujol's vision of the "Catalan mission"—glorious and full of responsibility at once—of welcoming the masses of the immigrants and creating a new Catalan community that includes the immigrants.[83] However exaggerated, self-congratulatory, and politically motivated Pujol's language is it helped him be elected president of Catalonia in 1980 and stay in that position since then; in the Baltic republics such pronouncements most likely would have disqualified him as a leader. A comparative framework easily shows up a remarkably tolerant attitude toward immigrants in Catalonia and the willingness to integrate them.

Integration, however, is just one possible consequence of ethnic contact; "reactive nationalism" is another. In the 1980 elections to the Catalan Parliament, the leader of the Andalusian Socialist Party condemned the Statute of Autonomy on the grounds that it is "an aggression against immigrants." This sentiment commanded sufficient sympathy in Catalonia's immigrant population to win his party two parliamentary seats.[84] Many Spanish born professionals in Catalonia also look unfavorably upon the prospects of absorption into Catalan culture. In 1981, in the midst of the debate over the meaning of the language clause of the Constitution and the Statute of Autonomy (which I shall discuss later), 2300 non-Catalan professionals issued a manifesto in which they interpreted these documents as mandating a fully official bilingualism and parity in education and public expenditure for Catalan and Castilian language activities that, they concluded, are discriminatory against them. They also complained that, by focusing on language policy issues, the Generalitat diverts attention from the "real" issues that confront the immigrants of Catalonia.[85] But their ambition to catalyze among the non-native-born working class an anti-Catalan nationalism has not yielded long-term results. Similarly, the Andalusian Socialist Party soon after lost its electoral support.

In the first section of this chapter I discussed the hegemonic attraction of Catalan nationalists—especially under the Esquerra during the Second Republic and after Franco—which enabled them to forge electoral and class coalitions under their own aegis. In this section I will analyze a related dimension of the hegemony of nationalism in Catalonia: the willingness of immigrants born in other regions of Spain to voluntary loosen or abandon parts of their native culture and be absorbed into the population of Catalan speakers. Both dimensions of hegemony are based on the confidence and experience of continuous economic and demographic expansion found in a region that is more developed than its neighbors. Although there are clear indications of Catalan readiness as well as ability to integrate at least some portion of the immigrants, the hegemony of Catalan nationalism does not mean a seamless unity and, therefore, I will examine the forces that keep Catalans and immigrants apart, especially in the areas of housing and employment, even against the countercurrents of absorption and integration.

Immigrants from other parts of Spain live in distinct residential concentrations in Barcelona and its industrial belt. In 1970, in all but one of the seven districts surrounding the city of Barcelona, immigrants made up at least one third of the population, and in one they were 53.8 percent of the residents. In a few of Barcelona's tenement suburbs immigrants outnumbered Catalans by a ratio of three to one.[86] These dormitory tenements are neither suburbs in the American sense nor the shantytowns of the Latin American experience, but low-income housing projects located on the margins of the city. The tenements consist of "row after row of grimy cement-block apartment structures," where "infrastructural services are minimal" and "the polluted atmosphere is unrelieved by greenery or the graceful architecture for which Barcelona is famous."[87] Few Catalans live in these worker tenements. Residential segregation is a prominent characteristic in the lives of immigrants to metropolitan Barcelona.

The residential segregation is nothing but an extension of the lopsided occupational distribution that characterizes Catalans and Spaniards from other parts of Spain. A depiction of the Catalan occupational structure in a study by Sàez reveals striking socio-economic differences between Catalans and immigrants (see Table 3.4). In the upper two occupational categories, which carry managerial responsibilities, Catalans outnumbered immigrants at a ratio of three to one, whereas in the bottom two categories of manual labor, the ratio was almost the reverse: five to one in semi- and unskilled labor and three to two in skilled labor. In clerical work, Catalans had a much smaller advantage.

Pinilla de las Heras's more detailed study, one of the rare empirical studies of social mobility in Catalonia (or, for that matter, in Spain), confirms and sharpens Sàez's picture (see Table 3.5). The

TABLE 3.4

Occupational Distribution of Native Born and Immigrants
in Catalan Industry in Percentages.

Occupation	Native Born	Immigrants
Directors and upper management	74	26
Middle management and technical personnel	75	25
Clerical personnel	56	44
Skilled labor	40	60
Semi- and unskilled labor	18	82

Source: Sáez 1980, Table 7, p. 32.

TABLE 3.5

Occupational Distribution of Native Born and Immigrants
in Catalan Industry in Percentages.

Occupation	Native Born	Immigrants
Directors and upper management	80	20
Professionals and technical management	73	27
Middle level technical experts with administrative tasks	69	31
Middle level technical experts with technical tasks	57	43
Administrators with management tasks	69	31
Administrators with mostly technical tasks	61	38
Clerical personnel and low level technicians	64	36
Clerical auxiliaries	42	58
Foremen	37	63
Skilled laborers	37	63
Semi-skilled laborers	22	78
Unskilled laborers	11	89

Source: Pinilla de las Heras, Table 25, p. 107. Reprinted by permission of
Centro de Investigaciones Sociologicas.

advantage of Catalans over non-native-born residents, in both the higher and middle level managerial positions of Catalan industry, is clearly demonstrated.

In the upper echelon of management, Pinilla de las Heras found the Catalan's edge to be only a trifle higher, in middle management a bit lower, than in Sàez's data. Breaking down the category of clerical employees into two levels demonstrates considerable polarization in this occupational grouping as well, more representation for Catalans in the higher and less in the lower status jobs. Finally, among foremen and skilled workers, Sàez's numbers are well-nigh duplicated, and the two lowest manual labor classifications again polarize his data: four out of five semiskilled, but nine out of ten non-native-born residents are unskilled workers. The subdivision of the occupational categories clearly demonstrates that the divergence between Catalans and immigrants from Andalusia, Old and New Castile, Leon, Galicia, and so forth is systematic at all levels of employment and continuous from level to level. Pinilla de las Heras and Sàez's studies show that Catalan industry is built on an ethnically stratified labor force in which Catalans occupy the management and higher and middle status jobs while immigrants are, by and large, concentrated in manual labor.

An examination of the dynamic pattern of intergenerational mobility reveals that over time ethnic stratification is less pronounced. Pinilla de las Heras isolated the 575 respondents of his sample who belong in the younger age group (23–27 years of age) found an indication of intergenerational upward mobility in employment (see Table 3.6).[88]

Pinilla de las Heras draws our attention to one process, shown in Table 3.6. While the native-born and immigrant groups remain far apart in the self-employed and manual-wage-earner categories over time, in the category of non-manual-wage employees, a process of equalization takes place between the native and non-native born. In Pinilla de las Heras's words, "there is a section of the non-native sub-population...that possesses its best resources, that benefits more than the native-born from its insertion into the occupational structure, in terms of social mobility. This might partially explain how the coexistence of two populations within such unequal occupational structure is achieved with minimal or no social tensions."[89] A small minority of the immigrants attained upward mobility, thus becoming either a model or buffer (Pinilla de las Heras does not say which) for other, less fortunate, immigrants and keeps the latter's hopes alive and its frustrations under rein. Limited intergenerational mobility, together

TABLE 3.6

Occupational Distribution of Native Born and Non-Native-Born Sons,
Age 23–27, According to Father's Occupational Position, in Percentages.

Fathers	Native-Born Sons			Immigrant Sons		
	Nonmanual		Manual	Nonmanual		Manual
	high	low		high	low	
Self-employed	42	29	13	34	27	31
Nonmanual						
wage-earner	42	33	15	44	30	10
Manual						
wage-earner	16	38	72	22	43	59
Total	100	100	100	100	100	100

Source: Pinilla de las Heras, Table 101. (N = 575) The category of self-
employed (*por cuenta propia*) includes, among the native born, small
entrepreneurs, and among the non-native born, usually small farmers and
providers of personal services. Reprinted by permission of Centro de
Investigaciones Sociologicas.

with structural mobility that upgrades whole occupational categories
and the higher standard of living enjoyed by immigrants to Catalonia
joined to lessen the likelihood of ethnic conflict in the Catalan labor
market. Because the labor of the immigrants contributes to the prosperity of Catalonia without threatening the Catalans' hold on the
better part of the economy, most Catalans obviously have little reason
to engage in the kinds of exclusionary practices that lead to ethnic
conflict.

An examination of enterprise sizes also reveals the significance
of the intersection of occupational distribution and ethnic distinction. Most small (and medium size) companies are likely to be owned
by Catalans and produce for the local market (frequently in the area
of services), hence they speak and are culturally more Catalan.[90] Large
firms, on the other hand, are frequently modern companies producing
for a national or international market and, sometimes, are branches
of multinational corporations. As such they are less likely to favor
hiring local management or employing its language. This general
observation is borne out in the case of Catalonia, but is overshadowed
by a much more powerful trend.

A comparison of enterprises demonstrates that Catalans are
better represented in higher status jobs as the size of the enterprise

decreases but, more significant, that they are preponderant in upper and middle management positions in enterprises of all sizes (see Table 3.7). Conversely, nonnatives supply a smaller percent of unskilled workers as the size of the enterprise increases, but provide the bulk of manual workers in enterprises of all sizes. (The one exception is their overrepresentation among skilled workers and foremen in small enterprises, though probably there skill distinctions are harder to make, hence less indicative of occupational hierarchy.) The advantage that large-scale corporations provide to nonnatives is minimal: their overrepresentation in unskilled labor decreases from 14.8 percent (calculated as total employment minus their share in the category) in small, to 13.1 in medium, to 12.6 in large enterprise. Simultaneously their underrepresentation decreases from -3.0 percent in small to -1.6 in large enterprises in upper management, from an underrepresentation of -7.1 percent in small-, to -4.1 in middle- and -2.7 in large-scale enterprises in middle management; and from -9.3 percent in small-, to -7.3 in middle-, to -6.3 in large-scale enterprises in clerical work. The absolute difference between Catalans and non-Catalans still remains overwhelming. Catalans, in sum, manage the majority of all enterprises, including multinational companies, in Catalonia. An engineer employed by a multinational corporation in Barcelona reported to one of the researchers that "his co-workers and clients were...predominantly Catalan...[and] that he was being pressured...to use Catalans in order to be successful in his work."91 Even multinational corporations are managed and staffed by Catalans (even when partially owned by foreigners) and, rather than serving as tools of Castilianization, are themselves nationalized in Catalonia.

In sum, Catalans control every sector and type of enterprise of their region and are the undisputed masters of the Catalan economy. Migration does not threaten the Catalan control of the regional economy and, more than likely, contributes to Catalans' social mobility and prosperity.

The majority of immigrants from the rest of Spain who live and work in Catalonia remain manual workers who, according to Pinilla de las Heras's data, have enjoyed little or no intergenerational mobility. The occupational distribution curve of Catalans in the 1970s was bell shaped, with a clear overrepresentation in the upper part and in the middle, the largest, part of the curve. Spanish immigrants in Catalonia have a different occupational distribution: they compose the largest part of the group at the occupational scale's lower end. Without underestimating the importance of intergenerational mobility found

TABLE 3.7

Distribution of the Male Labor Force According to Origin, Occupation, and Size of Enterprise in Barcelona and Surrounding Municipalities in 1970

Size of Enterprise	Small (-51)			Medium (100-499)			Large (500+)		
Origin:	Total	Native	Immigrant	Total	Native	Immigrant	Total	Native	Immigrant
Occupation:									
Directors and professional	3.9	7.6	0.9	2.8	4.7	0.9	2.8	5.9	1.2
Middle management and technical personnel	10.4	19.4	3.3	6.6	14.2	2.5	4.7	9.7	2.0
Clerical personnel	22.4	34.1	13.1	22.5	36.0	15.2	18.0	30.0	11.7
Skilled laborers and foremen	29.4	23.5	34.1	30.6	31.2	30.3	23.5	27.2	21.5
Semi- and unskilled laborers	33.8	15.3	48.6	38.0	13.8	51.1	51.0	27.1	63.6
Total	100	100	100	100	100	100	100	100	100

Source: Pinilla de las Heras, Table 43, p. 138. The enterprises include private sector, industry, commerce, services, and public transportation. (N = 17,156) Reprinted by permission of Centro de Investigaciones Sociologicas.

by Pinilla de las Heras, we need to beware of painting an oversimple, optimistic picture of ethnic stratification and ethnic relations in Catalonia. Pinilla de las Heras's data allowed him to draw only limited conclusions,[92] and of course, these inferences might be dated by now. A new study is needed to fill in the information for the 1980s and 1990s.

Social mobility, as we have seen in the theory of immigrant assimilation, is the major source of integration into and identification with any host society. An important question, therefore, is whether such mobility will continue and whether it will also effect the residential segregation of immigrants and hosts. In its absence, class confrontation can become ethnic conflict, and it is far from sure how the Catalan-born sons and daughters of first generation Spanish immigrants would respond to lack of signs of such mobility, especially if it is coupled with continued residential segregation and cultural alienation. Although Catalan society has gone a long way toward integrating its immigrants, this process is far from complete and there are some who worry about its potential reversal.

"Catalan society," Llobera warns, "will have to make provisions for a system of economic rewards and mobility that is seen to operate freely and equitably by the Spanish speaking working classes." The danger is that at times of a potential economic crises "this is not always easy to implement."[93]

What is the impact of Catalan control and management of the regional economy on the cultural identity of the Spanish immigrants employed in manual and subordinate positions?

Given the prominence of the Catalan language in the regional culture, the cultural assimilation of immigrants presupposes bilingualism: the learning of Catalan in addition to Castilian. It is generally agreed that pre-Second World War immigrants to Catalonia (like most immigrants to other Western European states and the United States, respectively) "integrated themselves into the fabric of Catalan life and assimilated to the Catalan language."[94] Because close to a quarter of the nonnative population of Barcelona in 1930 was made up of expatriates of Valencia, a Catalan-speaking province of Spain, the knowledge of the native language might have facilitated the absorption of this group of immigrants.[95]

A study of the relationship between immigrant and Catalan workers, undertaken before the First World War, found that in spite of feelings of national and technical superiority shown by Catalan workers vis-à-vis the immigrant workers, the latter absorbed the "general ideas" of the former and their children learned to speak Catalan as if it were their native tongue. Its author resolved that "Catalonia nationalizes the immigrants."[96] The data from this early study, and from subsequent ones surveyed in 1963 by Maluquer i Sostres, present a very consistent picture, and the aforementioned conclusion is repeated as these studies' refrain.

Maluquer i Sostres observed that immigrants have had to partake in two processes to become assimilated to Catalonia: as peasants arriving to the city and the factory they had to adapt to industrial labor, and in addition, they had to undergo social and cultural assimilation. In a study he conducted in a textile factory in Teressa, some 30 miles outside Barcelona and, therefore, not a part of its industrial belt, he found both: "the general attitude of the majority of the immigrants...was, overall, extremely favorable to assimilation, especially regarding the desire to speak Catalan well." Immigrants less than 8 years of age and those who have been in Catalonia over 30 years have completely assimilated, and among other immigrants he detected patterns of partial assimilation.[97] Overall, he expected that the class differences between the Catalan middle class and the non-native-born workers will gradually fade, with the attainment by the latter of both social mobility and cultural integration through intermarriage.

It is particularly telling that Maluquer i Sostres's conclusions regarding the willingness of immigrants from the other Spanish provinces to learn Catalan are from the Franco period when Catalan was officially suppressed and the legal and state institutions in Catalonia used Spanish exclusively in conducting their affairs. Not even the prestige imparted by the authority of the Spanish state to its language, and the reduction of Catalan to a private language, made immigrants demand priority for their spoken language. The opposite was true, Spanish immigrants were willing to become bilingual and even to effectively cast off their language, the language of the state, in favor of the regional language, in spite of its lack of official sanction. The time-honored European state-building practices of enforcing linguistic homogeneity through state institutions, such as the bureaucracy and the military, did not "work" in Catalonia. Woolard's study of bilingualism in Catalonia explains the reasons for this apparent anomaly.

In 1980, Woolard found that in a matched-guise test in which listeners were asked to evaluate the personal qualities of tape recorded speakers who used Catalan and Castilian alternately (thus holding text, context, and speaker constant), the use of Catalan enhanced the prestige of the speaker.[98] Her explanation is that language prestige in

Catalonia is established not in the political but rather in the economic sphere: not formal settings or schools but personal relations formed in the workplace and the neighborhoods influence the relative status of languages. In the latter, Woolard concluded, "it is the greater economic power of Catalans that is the basis for the assignment of linguistic prestige."[99] This economic edge is the result of Spain's uneven pattern of economic development, which gives Catalonia an edge over most other Spanish regions. Catalonia, then, meets both of the conditions set by Inglehart and Woodward for the ability of a language to exercise strong centrifugal influence in a multilingual situation: Catalan is spoken in a country (or in this case region) in which the level development is high and it is not used to exclude nonspeakers.[100] Each of these conditions encourages linguistic assimilation and their coincidence makes it a likely outcome.

One expression of the Catalan language's high prestige is the allegiance to it of the Catalan social and economic elites. Catalan elites that were the main beneficiaries of Catalonia's status as an overdeveloped region in Spain retained, with the exception of a small minority at the top, their loyalty to Catalan through thick and thin and in this fashion contributed to the solidarity of Catalan society. By sticking by its tongue the Catalan bourgeoisie followed the well-worn path that since the 1830s emphasized the distinct "personality" of its region, its culture, and employment patterns. Whereas for Spaniards employment in the civil service and the military were important channels of upward mobility, Catalans had their own path of economic mobility and remained underrepresented in the institutions of the Spanish state.[101] Given Catalonia's position of relative overdevelopment vis-à-vis Spain, knowledge of Spanish was not a necessary tool for development; as Pi-Sunyer indicates, neither the Catalan language nor culture was "an impediment to change and modernization."[102]

The "language war" between Catalan and Castilian reflected an underlying reality of social stratification in which economic and linguistic prestige reinforced one another. Catalan's high status, expressed in its continued use by Catalan elites, prevented its reduction to a low-prestige dialect with the loss of its public status under Franco. This is the reason that Catalan is flourishing relative to most European minority languages that have also been besieged by the central state's language, such as Breton and Occitan in France or even ones such as Romansh in Switzerland and Welsh in the United Kingdom, which have been officially recognized as minority languages.[103] Catalans succeeded in maintaining their language and subsequently in expanding its users. "The higher status of Catalan helps explain why Catalonia is almost unique among European minority languages in maintaining and even recruiting speakers."[104]

The high prestige associated with Catalan for immigrants to the Barcelona industrial zone is due to its potential as a tool of integration and social mobility.[105] Sociologists have long since pointed to modifications and adjustments that take place in a person's cultural choices with corresponding changes in his or her social status; in Catalonia linguistic conduct also tends to change under such conditions. Either in anticipatory socialization or to ensure a higher spot on the social ladder, Spaniards from other regions are favorably disposed to learn and speak Catalan.

Because most immigrants to Catalonia also had less education and a lesser "Castilian" national consciousness than those immigrating to the Basque provinces,[106] they and their children are less likely to feel a loss due to assimilation. Language choice by children from mixed marriages, where one parent is Catalan and the other is from another Spanish region, clearly indicates the pull of Catalan. Eighty percent of such children, according to O'Donnell's study in one somewhat atypical town, tend to chose Catalan as their dominant home tongue.[107] Studies of children from mixed marriages in Barcelona also demonstrate very high rates of linguistic assimilation to and much smaller linguistic defection from Catalan.[108] A study of 10- to 12-year-old sons from mixed marriages reported by Strubell i Trueta found that 64 percent identified themselves as Catalans in comparison to 23 percent who viewed themselves as Spaniards (13 percent did not identify themselves), a percentage lower than among sons of Catalan parents but higher than that of sons of immigrant parents.[109] Since, the percentage of such mixed marriages is increasing, from 25.4 percent in 1950 to 34.6 percent in 1973,[110] they tend to serve as an accepted path of assimilation.

Sometimes it is pointed out that Catalan, like Spanish, is a Romance language, that the grammatical structures of the two languages are fairly similar and their vocabularies also bear resemblance and, therefore, that it is "easy" for Spanish speakers to learn Catalan.[111] This is very likely the case, but I would like to warn against linguistic reductionism: language also includes components such as intonation and accent that are harder (and after a certain age almost impossible) to come by and may easily be used to exclude nonnative speakers. Language acquisition, therefore, is not just a linguistic act but also a social process, and the two may operate independent of each other. In fact, nonnative speakers cannot assume that Catalan speakers will automatically reward their efforts, because social barriers are sometimes more difficult to overcome than the linguistic ones. The overwhelming majority of Catalans speak Castilian fluently and are willing to speak it with nonnative speakers, frequently as Woolard reports, preferring to speak it out of politeness but, occasionally, as a mechanism of exclusionary boundary maintenance.[112] Catalan is a distinct language and treated as such by Catalans, and its acquisition is a complex linguistic and social process. In general, the linguistic proximity of Catalan to Castilian is relevant only because it rewards an already existing willingness on the part of the immigrants to learn it and a fairly generalized openness of the native speakers to welcome new speakers.

Given this willingness on the part of many of the immigrants to learn Catalan, Catalan language planning policy can afford to be broadminded and tolerant. The 1978 Spanish Constitution and the 1979 Statute of Catalan Autonomy of the Spanish Cortes contained potentially contradictory aims. Although they declared Castilian as the official language of Spain they simultaneously recognized Catalan as Catalonia's "proper" language (and the other "languages of Spain" in their respective autonomous communities), without clarifying the difference between the two. I do not wish to enter into the ensuing constitutional debate but rather examine the outlines of Catalan language planning, the foundations of which were laid down in April 1983 by the Catalan parliament.

The aim of the policy of language "normalization," as clarified by Woolard, is to make Catalan the preeminent, that is, the normal language of communication, in the territory of Catalonia, with Castilian as a second language that serves to unite Catalans with other Spaniards.[113] In the interim this means parity between Catalan and Castilian and ultimately the primacy of Catalan.[114] Although ostensibly the attempt is to privilege Catalan, and by so doing privilege Catalan speakers—the common aim of language status planners in other places—Woolard is quick to point out that "in no sense is the enhancement of the status of the Catalan language conceived as a deliberate means of enhancing the social status of speakers of Catalan." The reason is simple: "the status of native Catalans is already elevated in comparison to the mass of Castilian speakers in the community,"[115] and they have no need to "reverse" historical and socio-economic tendencies through the use of political and legislative power to regain control of their society and lives. An examination of the means for implementing language "normalization" lends supports Woolard's assessment.

The time frame for making all residents of Catalonia primary speakers of Catalan is a generation (understood as 20 years).[116] Such generous time horizon obviously accepts the limitations posed by the concentration of masses of Castilian speakers in Catalonia who are either likely to learn Catalan partially or not at all and seems willing to give up on segments of the current nonnative populations in favor of imparting Catalan to the younger generation. The generosity of this framework as will become obvious when we will compare it with the severely restrictive time frames of the Baltic language laws. Furthermore, Catalan language normalization is to be achieved not through exclusionary practices or confrontational tactics against those who have not become Catalan speakers at the end of the era but through persuasion.

The language law, in fact, establishes not exclusiveness but parity for Catalan in government administration, education, and the media, and when it creates special institutions to foster Catalan, "these are compensatory rather than preferential measures."[117] It sets up Catalan language classes for civil servants and requires that candidates to new positions and applicants to universities pass a test in Catalan to prove that they are bilingual. Primary and secondary school teachers are required to know both languages, but a Spanish constitutional court struck down the requirement to test new teachers before they are hired, and, presently, they are tested after they having been hired and, if found deficient, are required to study Catalan and be retested later. No jobs are known to have been lost for lack of knowledge of Catalan.

Catalan language planners are free to display such unusual tolerance because, to use again an overused idiom, time seems to be on their side: there is willingness on the part of the majority of immigrants to learn Catalan as long as it remains a key to social mobility. The results of the tolerant and long-term character of the Catalan "nationalities policy" may be seen in two time series studies. A comparison of the findings of Carlota Solé's attitudinal surveys in 1978 and 1983 demonstrate that differences between the views of native Catalans and Catalan residents born in other parts of Spain have diminished in regard to the institutions and symbols of Catalonia.[118] Kathryn Woolard's studies that compare language use between 1980 and 1987 found that "there may now be rewards of increased solidarity feelings from Catalans for non-native Spaniards who use Catalan as a second language, and fewer sanctions against such use from Castilian speakers."[119] Solé and Woolard's conclusion testify to the integrative results of the first years of Catalan autonomy and Catalan language planning and, therefore, to the hegemonic influence of Catalan nationalism and culture on immigrants into the region.

Similar indications are found in studies of Catalan language use, though they are less clear cut because of differences in data collection methods. In a large-scale survey administered throughout Spain in 1979, Gunther, Sani, and Shabad found that 78 percent of the sample in Catalonia reported that they spoke Catalan; among them were 97 percent of the natives to the region and 38 percent of those born in other parts of Spain.[120] A large survey of the Barcelona metropolitan area from 1986 that used more restrictive categories found that close to 90 percent of Catalan natives and 27.3 percent of immigrants from other Spanish provinces (excluding Valencia and the Balearic islands) speak Catalan, to yield an average of 61.7 percent Catalan speakers. In addition, almost all native Catalans and close to 40 percent of the immigrants report understanding the language. More significant than speaking and understanding in a bureaucratic and industrial environment, however, is the ability to write in a given language—here the gap between those born in Catalonia and in the rest of Spain is huge: 45.9 percent of the former and only 5.3 percent of the later report that they write Catalan. On the average only 26.7 percent of Barcelona's residents write its language.[121] But among 10–19 years old, who have been exposed to Catalan language education at school, household heads report that 96 percent understand, 75 percent can speak, 78 percent can read, and 60 percent can write Catalan.[122] This is a clear indication of the impact of language normalization through schools and the mass media.

Yet, the nationalization or assimilation of post-Second World War Spanish immigrants in Catalonia is far from being a simple or unproblematic process and seems to have been much less thorough than the integration of the prewar wave. The obstacles to the spread of Catalan among all immigrants are the heavy concentration of the nonnative population in Barcelona's tenement neighborhoods and surrounding townships. Where immigrants make up the majority of the population they encounter Catalan speakers with less frequency and have fewer opportunities to learn and use it. Although the integration of immigrants into the host society has gone the furthest of the regions under study in Catalonia, even there questions marks hang over the future of the process.

In spite of all the changes that have taken place as part of Spain's democratization, the establishment of the Generalitat, the free functioning of Catalan parties and associations, and the energetic policy of language normalization that slowly spreads the use of Catalan, some observers wonder whether these changes might not be too little and might not have come too late.[123] Indeed, it is very likely that using low-key methods Catalans will not make Catalan into the normal tongue of Catalonia within their time frame, if ever. The "vocation" or "mission" of Catalonia, however, might not be, as wished by Pujol, the foundation of a new Catalan community that absorbs in its totality the masses of immigrants,[124] but the acceptance of Catalonia's unavoidable diversity and the safeguarding of the continued peaceful coexistence of its Catalan and Spanish members. For the effectiveness of a multicultural approach, whose virtue seems to be in part in its ambiguity, it is necessary that the occupational gap and the residential segregation of the immigrants and their descendants from the Catalan speakers will continue to be diminished and not become rigidified and, subsequently, ethnicized.

The assimilationist approach might yield partial results that have to be rounded out, if the openness toward immigrants is to prevail, with multiculturalist practices. This the Catalan government began to recognize. Since the restoration of democracy and Catalan self-government, the Generalitat and local authorities have supported the *cases regionales* that have for long served as the social centers of immigrants, especially from Andalusia, to Catalonia. They also helped financially and accepted the legitimacy of the main forms of Andalusian cultural expression that began flourishing in the past half century. Among these are two big fairs, Feria de Abril de Bellvitge and Feria de Abril de Pubilla Cases, and the Semana Andaluza festival as well as religious parades and dancing schools (*sevillanas*).[125] Not only the older generation of immigrants but also their children participate in these events in large numbers. These festivities are not just replications of similar celebrations in Andalusia, but have evolved in Catalonia and seem to represent a Catalan version of Andalusian culture. They represent the broadening of Catalan culture and the acceptance of an unavoidable diversity that resulted from the immigration of masses of Spaniards to Catalonia.

In the late nineteenth and twentieth centuries, the strength of states in their historical confrontation with multiethnic empires was found in the former's uniqueness, which was accentuated through processes of political, economic, and cultural homogenization. However, modern societies, as Emile Durkheim suggested, are dominated by an organic division labor of specialists dependent on each other, and therefore, their fortitude and vitality are found as much in their diversity, openness, and absorptive capacity of people as well as ideas. The increased opening of Spain, and Catalonia within it, to the rest of Europe as part of the European Union's internal integration will only increase regional diversity. Because, in comparison with other culturally mixed areas, as Giner points out, Catalonia is "one of the least 'racist' societies in the world,"[126] it is well prepared to take advantage of its varied population and cultures.

4

FROM RACISM TO "PRIMORDIAL SOCIALISM" IN THE BASQUE COUNTRY

Nationalism Under Combined Development

Of all the relatively developed regions under study, Nairn's and Gourevitch's theories appear most wrongheaded as already noted by Diez Medrano, in explaining Basque nationalism.[1] Instead of promoting modernization, the PNV (the major political vehicle of Basque nationalism) was conceived as an instrument for forestalling, or at least slowing down, the industrialization of the region. Although such forms of "defensive nationalism" are widespread, they are an exception in developed regions.

On top of this anomaly another one arises. Until the 1960s, in Carr's words, Catalan nationalism "hung like a milestone" around the necks of Spanish government whereas Basque nationalism remained "a local irritant rather than a national problem."[2] But during the second wave of the Catalan and Basque nationalisms that emerged in the waning years of the Franco dictatorship, the two movements "traded places": Catalan nationalism proved "more ready of solution than the Basque question." Indeed, the terrorist methods of ETA have "represented the largest single obstacle to a peaceful transition" to democracy and made Basque nationalism a "formidable challenge to the Spanish state."[3] In the new democratic era, ETA supplied the major reason for Prime Minister Suárez's downfall and the excuse for the February 1981 coup attempt.[4]

The rebirth of Basque nationalism as the most intractable nationalist movement of Spain and its terrorist extremism that continues to this very day (long after other urban guerrilla groups in Germany and Italy disappeared) are even more atypical of well-developed regions. Although this anomaly makes the task of comprehending Basque nationalism a particularly arduous, and in several respects a frustrating, task, the movement's broadest contours seem fairly clear: Basque nationalism at its various stages was opposed not only to administrative centralization but also to capitalism itself.

The powerful current of anticapitalist sentiment was begotten by unevenness in development, though not between the Basque provinces and Spain but, rather, between modern and traditional regions within the Basque country. This type of internal, or intraregional, uneven economic development was called by Trotsky *combined development*.[5] The Basque economy, furthermore, evolved in the context of a dualistic type of political relationship to the Spanish state that predated the region's industrialization. This doubly combined and, obviously, contradictory, character of development and centralization accounts, I believe, in large measure for the cast of the extremist wing of the contemporary Basque nationalist movement and its attempts to make up for past weaknesses by present excesses.

The four Basque provinces that make up the Spanish Basque country (there are three French Basque provinces as well) "never formed a single political entity,"[6] with the exception of a few years during the eleventh century, when the leaders of Alava, Vizcaya, and Guipúzcoa accepted the personal rule of the king of the fourth Basque province, Navarra, who reconquered large areas of Spain from its Muslim rulers and made Navarra into the staging area for the Reconquista. The three provinces were in fact "associated in one form or another with Castile already by the year 1200." Vizcaya was closely allied with Castile and its troops invaded Alava under instructions of the Castilian king. Guipúzcoa's relationship was even closer to Castile since its leaders consented to become a province of the Castilian dynasty.

In spite of their distinct and powerful ties with the Castilian monarchy "all the Basque territories...retained autonomous political systems and constitutional frameworks until [well into] the nineteenth century."[7] The major reason for the ability of the Basque provinces to retain their autonomy for centuries was their strategic location near the French border. France and Spain are separated by the 260 miles of the Pyrenees Mountains, but along the Basque coastline and in mountain corridors located in Basque territory there existed a number of invasion routes. Consequently, "a successful northeast border policy was a vital element in the survival of the Spanish state."[8]

The strategic location of the Basque provinces lead to the bifurcation of their internal structure. Already in the twelfth century, Castilian (as well as Navarrese) kings established in the Basque provinces strategically located urban centers—walled villas—for

Spanish, French, and Latin speakers, while the Euskera speaking Basque *baserriak* (farmsteads) continued to dominate the countryside. The *villas* received individual royal charters that granted them economic and political privileges to encourage their rapid growth, but kept them under the direct jurisdiction of the crown. The rural hinterland remained under the jurisdiction of provincial Juntas Generales (General Assemblies) and the municipal councils that ensured a measure of popular participation.

The urban centers were well positioned to take advantage of their location in the crossroads between the grain growing and sheep raising Castilian *meseta* and the English and Flemish markets and became flourishing commercial centers, but the countryside, with the exception of Alava, suffered from chronic overpopulation, steep terrain, and infertile lands.[9] The austere conditions of the Basque countryside offered a stark contrast to Bilbao and the other thriving Hispanicized townships. "From very early times," Heiberg concludes, "the Basque country has been populated by two culturally differentiated, but inextricably linked, types of people operating in different economic, political and social contexts."[10]

Additional aspects of the Spanish monarchy's solicitousness to gain Basque loyalty at low cost involved granting them separate sets of legal privileges, known as the *fueros*. The *fueros* laid down in minutia the economic and political life and domestic law of each of the Basque provinces. In addition they exempted Basques from paying tariffs and limited their taxation rates to encourage the growth of their population. Finally, in return for a grant of the noble status of *hidalgo* to all natives of Vizcaya in 1526 and Guipúzcoa in 1610 the residents of these provinces pledged to defend the region without compensation. The grant of collective nobility gave Basques direct access to public offices in the Spanish administration and military. Further, the monarchy could not impose but had to request taxes and conscripts.[11]

Basques enjoyed the best of both worlds: the *fueros* ensured their autonomy and privileges, and collective *hidalguía* provided them with a unique path of social mobility and, consequently, tied them strongly to the Spanish state. The sentiment expressed in the famous sixteenth century tract of Zaldibia, the compiler of Basque customary law, was that "a perfect compatibility existed between being Basque and being Spanish." He wrote that the dedication of Basques to both faith and defense made them "the best Spaniards of all."[12] These sentiments and bonds remained strong, and until the

MAP 4.1

The Basque Country

nineteenth century "relations between the Castilian monarchy and the Basque foral authorities tended to collaboration rather than confrontation."[13] "The unity of Basque and Castilian interests was such," Payne points out, "that there were never any Basque revolts against the Spanish crown under the old regime."[14]

The relations between the Basque elites and the Spanish state remained cordial, however, internal changes restructured Basque society but always within the framework provided by the foral privileges. Gradually a small-holding peasantry emerged and the lower classes in general improved their standing, but in the seventeenth century the social relations in the countryside were transformed, as a new elite of rural notables—the *jauntxo*—was consolidated. Although many of them lived in small *villas*, the economic basis of the notables was rural: a significant portion of their income was derived from small, technologically backward, uncapitalized, landholdings that they rented to landless laborers or tenant farmers. The notables supplemented the income they derived from the land through the ownership of small iron foundries and mills.

Because the *jauntxo* (*jaun* is a Euskera term of respect, equivalent to the Spanish *don*) was not a legally sanctioned corporate entity but a small self-made and not particularly wealthy stratum, acclaimed through custom, its members sought to anchor their ascendance in extraeconomic protection. An important prop of their status were the municipal councils and provincial Juntas Generales, from which they were able to exclude the majority of the peasantry through property qualifications and literacy requirements. Though the *jauntxoak* were responsible for the loss of land of about half of the small-holding peasantry and for the effective disenfranchisement of most of them, the notables used the foral system to evolve a paternalistic relationship with the geographically and socially isolated peasantry under the protective umbrella of the Church. This political and economic dominance enabled the notables to gain control of the *fuero* apparatus, which became their status symbol, and through which they enforced their privileges.[15]

The foral regime provided four important defenses of the rural notables' status and power. First, the Basque provinces enjoyed the benefits of being a duty-free zone. The integration of the Basque country into the national Spanish market, by moving the custom posts from the Ebro River to the coast, would increase the price of imported food products into the Basque country and transfer the locally collected custom dues to the Spanish government. Second, the foral system placed iron ore and lumber under municipal ownership and in this fashion ensured the effective control of the major resources of the Basque provinces by the rural notables. The privatization of these resources and the abolition of the Vizcayan Junta Generale's prohibition of iron export would transfer the control of these resources out of the notables' hands and permit the penetration of intensive capitalist practices into the Basque country. Capitalist transformation would also adversely affect the artisan classes, which could not stand up to competition by large-scale enterprises and, therefore, viewed their own and the rural notables' interests as coinciding. Third, the *fueros* shielded the population from state-imposed military conscription and state-levied taxes. Instead, the Crown had to ask for soldiers and taxes, which were assessed and collected by the local authorities. Finally, by allocating one vote to each township, regardless of its size, the *fueros* privileged the political power of the countryside over the city. The extension of Spanish centralization into the Basque provinces would replace the Juntas Generales, to which property and literacy qualifications restricted suffrage, with democratically elected Diputaciones Provinciales and, thus, undermine the political power of the *jauntxoak*.[16] The abolition of the foral regime could mean an end to the privilege and, therefore, to the whole way of life, of the notables of Basque society. At the same time, as long as the foral regime was intact, the economy of the Basque provinces remained undeveloped and gave little indication of the region's potential as an engine of industrial development in Spain.

The centralizing tendency of the Spanish state was renewed in response to the "demonstration effect" of Napoleon's conquest of parts of Spain. Most of nineteenth century Spanish history is marked by the drive of the Spanish liberal elite to impose the post-Revolutionary French model of administration on all regions of the Spanish monarchy.[17] Whereas during the nineteenth century Catalans fought a losing battle to regain their autonomy, the Basques provinces, the possessors of the last regional *fueros*, struggled to preserve them.

The centralizing drive and pro-capitalist economic reforms of Spanish liberalism, such as the deentailment of commons, municipal, and Church-owned land, or the imposition of mining laws that extended exploitation rights, threatened the traditions and traditional way of life of Basque notables, artisans, peasantry, and the Catholic Church. The response in Basque rural areas was a massive show of support in the two Carlists Wars (1833–1840, 1872–1877) for the antiliberal side. Ironically, the failure of Spanish Absolutism to subjugate the Basque provinces allowed the monarchy to pose as the protector of their fueros and religiosity and draw its major support from the Basque countryside. The Carlist Wars were fought by diverse coalitions whose support and motivations varied greatly from region to region. At the danger of oversimplification we may say that the civil war between the supporters of Don Carlos and Isabel II, customarily made out to be an old-fashioned war of succession, combined, in fact, a political struggle between an incomplete Absolutist and a partially evolved constitutional or liberal regime, a social battle between rural and urban Spain, and a cultural confrontation between Catholicism and anticlerical liberalism. This struggle united Basque "rural notables, peasantry, and clergy under the slogan of "God and *Fueros!*"[18]

The demise of the Carlist challenge to Spanish liberalism carried devastating consequences for the rural notables and the traditional way of life of the peasantry and doomed the *fueros*. The political power of the *jauntxo* was broken and the economic resources of the Basque provinces were opened for capitalist exploitation and export-oriented production. The step-by-step elimination of the foral system and its final abolition in 1876 was a major victory for the Basque urban elite. Only a single regional privilege, the local levying of taxes, was retained. Basque *fueros* were replaced by *concierto económicos*, which permitted the Basque authorities to assess their own taxes and pay part of it into the national treasury, with the result that "Basques paid little more than half of the proportionate tax burden on other Spaniards." Even after 1876 the Basques "enjoyed greater privilege than any other part of the peninsula."[19] The *conciertos económicos* of the provinces of Vizcaya and Guipúzcoa were abolished only by Franco, and even he left the agreement with Navarra intact.

The relocation of the custom houses from the Ebro River to the coast after the military defeats increased the pace of economic activity, especially the mining of iron ore. The low extraction costs, due to the proximity of the mines to the port of Bilbao and the near-surface location of low-phosphorous ore that was especially well suited for steel production, made for rapid expansion in production. Extraction rose from 30,000 tons in 1875, the year before the abolition of the *fueros*, to 2.68 million tons by 1880, and double that by the end of the century.[20] By then Spain became the producer of one fifth of the world's annual iron ore output and exported most of it to England.[21] Although about half the profits were siphoned off by English export and transportation companies, a propitious legacy of the *fueros* was the retention of the mines under Basque ownership. The profits of mineral extraction provided Basque entrepreneurs with the resources for the rapid development of related industries: railways, steel and metallurgy, electricity, chemicals, shipbuilding, and the first decades of this century saw them expand into banking and insurance. Most of this Basque industry was concentrated in the two coastal provinces of Guipúzcoa and Vizcaya, especially in the latter's capital, Bilbao. Basque industrialization evolved on a larger scale and under a more concentrated ownership structure than Catalan industry. Basque industry also developed at a spectacular rate to become, next to Catalonia, the second nucleus of the Spanish industry and make the Basque country the fastest growing region of Spain.

"Basque development," Diez Medrano points out in his authoritative comparative work, "took place without a previous agrarian revolution and without the development of a powerful textile

industry like in Catalonia; it was mostly induced by foreign demand
for its rich iron resources."[22] A legacy of the foral system that cast a
long shadow over Basque industry and society was the absence of a
commercialized agriculture and, hence, an unbalanced, or in terms
used here a "combined," pattern of development. Basque mining,
heavy industry, and banking were concentrated in the hands of an
urban oligarchy of about five to ten families linked by marriage. The
Ybarra family, for example, were the largest stockholders of both
Altos Hornos de Vizcaya, the largest iron and steel company, and the
largest bank in the Basque provinces, the Banco de Bilbao. In 1908,
about a generation after the abolition of the *fueros*, one third of
Spain's investment capital was Basque and "the Basque capitalists
became the most important single financial interest in Spain."[23]

Side by side with the tiny, powerful, and tightly knit oligarchy
of monopoly capitalists there remained the resentful stratum of rural
notables and traditional artisans of small means. Because of the high
capitalization costs of steel, related industries, even those members of
the rural *jauntxo* who owned small mines or iron foundries, could
not join the new elite and fell behind.

The historical division of city and country in the Basque country
now took on a new significance. A particular feature of the Basque
oligarchy, which distinguishes it sharply from the Catalan industrial
bourgeoisie but is a direct continuation of erstwhile Basque urban
traditions, was its Hispanicization and integration into Spain. In
Medhurst's telling words: "Basque entrepreneurs were linked to
nation-wide financial or banking concerns which dominated the
entire Spanish financial system. They therefore had a much closer
relationship with the Spanish state and little or no stake in the
regional cause."[24] Although Catalan light industry depended on and
was held back by the restricted purchasing power of Spain's large
rural population, Vizcayan and Guipúzcoan producers of ships, steel,
and related products were the recipients of important military con-
tracts from the Spanish government and derived a significant part of
their prosperity from their links with the Spanish political and military establishment.[25] After the First World War, Basque banks, like
their counterparts in Germany, also assumed the pivotal role in
capital accumulation in Spain.[26] The Basque oligarchy, in short,
assumed the national role that the Catalan industrialists aspired for
and failed to attain.[27] "The point at issue," according to Heiberg, "is
not that this upper sector of Basque society was *loyal* to the Spanish
government and establishment; but that *they were an integral part of*

it."[28] Both the financial and intellectual segments of the Basque elite spoke Castilian and was Castilianized; they were more Spanish than Basque.[29]

The same economic processes that begot the Basque industrial oligarchy also generated a modern working class. A process of land concentration sent an unwilling wave of Basque peasants to the industrial cities. But by far the largest portion of this proletariat, and the majority of the industrial workers in Bilbao, was formed by immigrants from other agricultural regions of Spain in search of higher wages.[30] The immigrant workers were concentrated in the large mines and steelworks, while Basque workers dominated the smaller factories.[31] According to Linz, the immigrants to Basque provinces had more education and more "Castilian" national consciousness than immigrants to Catalonia and, therefore, were less likely to be assimilated into Basque society and culture.[32] The laborers from the other Spanish provinces, organized under the auspices of the Spanish Socialist Party (PSOE) and its trade union (UGT), further strengthened the ties of the Basque provinces with the Spanish state. The socialism and anticlericalism of the Castilian workers were seen as further weakening Basque solidarity.[33]

The long shadow cast by the powerful Basque oligarchy and the Castilian working class over the rural notables and artisans of the Basque provinces provided the fertile ground for the emergence of Basque nationalism. Basque nationalism had a complicated birth: it emerged out of Carlism but already in opposition to it. The defeat of Carlism sealed the hopes for the revival of Basque regional autonomy under the auspices of the ancien régime. Basque Carlism was still a premodern movement attached to medieval institutions and, thereore, was articulated in terms of provincial particularism with no "concept of a single Basque people or nation."[34]

When Basque nationalism appeared in 1893 in the writings and political activity of Sabino Arana Giori, it involved, in Medhurst's view, two major departures from Carlism. First, Arana viewed the Carlist program for the restoration of political and financial autonomy to each of the Basque provinces separately as insufficient. Initially he also evolved a provincial nationalism only, a program of Vizcayan nationalism, but with the spread of industrialization to Guipúzcoa and Alava, he evolved an all-Basque nationalism that set as its goal the unification of the seven Basque provinces (the four Spanish and the three French ones) into a confederation that would break away from Spain and France and become an independent country. Second,

Arana shared the strong religious dedication that singled out Carlism but, as part of his separatist design, supplemented it with claims of Basque racial superiority over Spaniards.[35]

Arana was born into a *jauntxo* family: his father was a deputy of the Junta General of Vizcaya and owner of rural property and a preindustrial shipbuilding firm.[36] Arana was a student in Barcelona, but his nationalist views evolved only after his return to Bilbao; and under the impact of the Basque context their character differed significantly from Catalan nationalism. Catalan nationalist sentiments, as we have seen, were championed by the bourgeois class that industrialized Catalonia, and they were accompanied by a powerful wave of linguistic and cultural revival. Catalan industrialists wanted to speed up modernization throughout Spain and, by recreating Spain in the image of Catalonia, sought to dominate both.

Basque nationalism also emerged in response to a rapid process of industrialization, but the leaders and cadres of Basque nationalism, like Arana himself, originated in the *jauntxo* and artisan stratum and were supported by the lower clergy and some segments of the peasantry.[37] Rather than seeking to hurry industrial development, these strata felt threatened by the new wave and sought to hold it up. For them, industrialization, the ascent of the industrial oligarchy, and the influx of an industrial labor force were so many threats to the very way of life by which they defined themselves and on which their status and power rode.[38]

Basque nationalism was formulated by Arana on the pages of his journal, the *Bizkitarra*, and in his many pamphlets.[39] It became a political movement with the foundation of a political party, the Partido Nacionalista Vasco or PNV (Basque Nationalist Party), in 1894. The ideology of the new movement drew on the Basque cultural revival the followed on the heels of the foral system's demise and on certain themes of the Carlist worldview. The *renacimiento euskerista* evolved a romanticized notion of Basque history and culture that revolved around the epic struggle of the Basque provinces to defend their liberties and tradition against foreign invaders and the moral and egalitarian character of traditional Basque society.[40] Carlism inspired Basque nationalism with its vision of the Church's predominance over the state.

Initially Arana's nationalism was constructed around an emphasis on the historical legacy and attendant rights of Basques. But there was no precedent for the political unification of the Basque provinces, and therefore, history, even in its mythical form, could not carry the movement far enough toward its desired goal.[41] Euskera, the Basque language, provided the movement with even less succor than the doctrine of historical rights could; Euskera was, and remained, the Achilles heel of Basque national revival. Urban centers in the Basque provinces, as I already noted, were traditionally Hispanicized, and Euskera was the preserve of the peasantry. In the eighteenth century over half of the population spoke Euskera, but the spread of literacy through primary schools in which the language of instruction was exclusively Spanish decimated the number of Euskera speakers in the nineteenth century.[42] Abandoned by urban elites in the past and unused by the Basque industrial oligarchy or in large Basque-owned enterprises, Euskera could not serve as a tool of social mobility for immigrant workers. As an essentially oral language, used exclusively only in church service,[43] Euskera commanded low status.

A comparison with Catalan culture was equally sobering. The Catalan language experienced a cultural revival and modernization during the Romantic era while the Basque language was rejected as a literary instrument by the greatest Basque writers, such as Miguel de Unamuno and, remaining unmodernized, was in steady retreat before Castilian. Nor did Basque culture produce a literature comparable to the Catalan one, and its cultural achievements remained on the level of folklore and ballads.[44] Overall, Carr comments, "while Catalan nationalism could attract the best in Catalan life, Basque nationalism appeared an archaic concern, 'savage' and primitive."[45]

Arana, with his customary flair, dismissed historical rights, language, and culture as the primary markers of Basque nationalism and argued for another basis for Basque identity. He wrote:

> the extinction of our language matters little; so does forgetting our history; so does the loss of our own saintly institutions and the imposition of foreign liberal ones; so does the political enslavement of our homeland; none of this matters at all, absolutely at all, considered by itself, if compared with the rubbing of our people with the Spanish people, which immediately and necessarily causes in our race ignorance and loss of reason, weakness and corruption of the heart, that is an absolute deviation from the goal of all human society.[46]

The "core value" of Basque nationalism in Arana's vision was racial purity. Arana vehemently condemned those Vizcayans who had inter-married with "Spaniards," who, in his words, had "confounded themselves with the most vile and despicable race in Europe."[47] Using the extreme language of xenophobia and racism, Arana gave expression to the hostility of the Basque notables to the influx of Spanish immigrants. "Arana's overriding concern" in Sullivan's opinion "was his belief that the Basque race was in danger of extinction because of an invasion of foreigners whom he considered to be racially degenerate, immoral, non-Catholic and socialist. Basque independence would…make it possible to deny admittance to the Basque country to Spaniards, prohibit intermarriage between them and Basques, restore traditional morality and shut out liberal and socialist influences."[48]

Arana's racism, a product of late nineteenth century thinking, had little of the "scientific" pretensions that racism evolved in the twentieth century but was based on a mixture of religious and secular themes from Basque history. The Basques were not only a race by virtue of their common origin and shared blood, argued Arana, they were also endowed by supreme religious gifts that increased their prospects of salvation. In addition, pointed out Greenwood, Basque notions of being a group apart evolved from the early medieval category of "collective nobility" that was granted to the residents of the provinces by the Spanish Crown and passed down through their supposedly democratic traditions.[49] Finally, it was also argued, this time using distinctly racial categories, that because the Basque country was not conquered by Muslims (some of it actually was ruled by Muslims) or had Jewish inhabitants its residents alone in Spain remained pure of blood. Arana's justification of Basque uniqueness and superiority was strongly denounced already at the end of the nineteenth century by, for example, Unamuno, who ridiculed Basque nationalism's reliance on an "absurd racial virginity."[50]

Ultimately, the weakness of Basque historical precedent and linguistic competence must have played an important role in Arana's choice of race to define Basque identity.[51] The use of race, however, erected an unsurpassable barrier between Basques and Spaniards; its *corporate conception of Basque nationhood* repudiated, in effect, any possibility of naturalizing immigrants from other Spanish provinces. Though the test of "racial purity" was indirect—race was traced through individual's and his or her parents' surnames—it was used for excluding non-Basques from early Basque nationalist organizations and trade unions.

This *defensive* character—a profound ambivalence toward modernity—marked Basque nationalism from its inception. Arana's catchall nationalist slogan, Jaungoikua eta Lagi-Zara (God and Old Laws), known by the anagram *JEL*, well testifies to this revulsion from modernity. The support of the clergy that used the vernacular in its services and, therefore, was identified with the autochthonous culture, and through it with the prospective nation,[52] was another crucial basis of Basque nationalism. Most of its leaders were anticapitalist as well as antisocialist, though they viewed the socialism, atheism, and internationalism of the immigrant workers as the most dangerous threat to Basque society as they knew it and immigration itself as an invasion that threatened the Basque Country with "denationalization."[53]

Heiberg went as far as arguing that Basque nationalism was a response of the Basque middle classes to "the rising tide of Spanish socialism" and that it can be seen as a movement "geared to the containment of socialism."[54] Although socialism was seen as one of the enemies of Basque nationalism, it was not the only one: modernity as such was the grand adversary.[55] Unable to employ the discourses of modernity, the response of Basque nationalists was cultural and ethnocentric, and it aimed at building an impenetrable wall between Basques and Castilians. Basque separatism, in this respect, resembles nationalist movements of underdeveloped regions that are exploited economically and have only their cultural distinctness to mobilize to fight the larger forces of homogenization, both political and economic, that intrude on them from the outside. The threat posed by all things modern, which came from Spain, not just to the power and privilege of the *jauntxoak* but to the whole way of life by which they portrayed themselves explains in large part the extreme and shrill language used in their defense.

Although Basque nationalists initially did not attract much attention and Arana himself was more of a propagandist than a political organizer, the Spanish government did not take separatist programs lightly. Arana's journal was banned, and he was jailed in 1895 and again in 1902, shortly before his death. The PNV's electoral support increased only slightly under the Restoration regime; and as long as it could not displace the alliance between provincial Basque particularism and Carlism that was supported by the peasantry, it was bound to remained a marginal force. Basque nationalists attempted to set up their own trade union, the Solidaridad de Obreros Vascos (SOV, later renamed STV-ELA) to divide Basque-surnamed workers from the immigrants organized in the socialist UGT, but registered only limited support, mostly among white-collar employees.[56] The basis of the

PNV remained restricted to its urban base in Vizcaya, and it met electoral success only in municipal elections and the elections to the Provincial Council of Vizcaya.

For a short interlude, in 1917 and 1918, the PNV gained control of the Vizcayan Diputacion Provincial and sent seven deputies to the Cortes. The auspicious constellation, in Harrison's view, was due to the tactical support of significant elements of the oligarchy, which fell out with the Madrid government over its attempts to tax war profits (a policy equally opposed by the Catalan Lliga Regionalista), for the PNV. This alliance of convenience dissolved as soon as the tax proposal was defeated, and the massive strike waves on the heels of the First World War already sent Basque industrialists to solicit government support. In 1919 and 1920, the dynastic parties presented a common front that defeated most PNV's candidates.[57]

Diez Medrano has shown that the basis of the coalition that supported the PNV was narrower than Harrison presented it but also had a long-term impact. The anticapitalist PNV actually had a small pro-capitalist wing, led by Ramón de la Sota, a rich and somewhat eccentric member of the oligarchy, who probably joined and bankrolled the nationalist movement (without ever becoming a member of the PNV) out of status considerations. This wing resembled in some ways the nationalism of the Catalan Lliga Regionalista without, however, evolving an equally coherent political program.

The importance of the capitalist members of the PNV was due to their systematically moderating impact on Basque nationalism, especially in convincing the mainstream members to give up the dream of national independence in favor or regional autonomy.[58] Between 1921 and Primo de Rivera's dictatorship in 1923, the PNV split between Sota's moderate wing and a coalition of the ideologically purist old guard and a younger generation that retained the party's name. In spite of the Sota wing's considerable measure of influence within the PNV, the oligarchy of the *fuerzas vivas* remained opposed to the local nationalist movement, because of their "fear that Basque autonomy would disrupt the economic integration of Spain" from which they benefited.[59]

The era of mass-based Basque nationalism arrived only after the fall of the Primo de Rivera dictatorship. The PNV's two wings united again under the old Arana program to continue their tug of war within the party. The reason for the PNV's renewed growth again demonstrates the difference between Catalan and Basque nationalism. The creation of the Esquerra resulted from the opening of the

Catalan petty bourgeoisie to the left, toward the anarcho-syndicalist workers, whereas the PNV was embraced by the Carlists and monarchist conservatives as a bulwark against the rising influence of Spanish socialism and syndicalism.[60] While Catalan nationalism incorporated social reform, a religious, moralistic, nostalgic Basque nationalism projected its influence to its right. In 1931, the PNV-Carlist coalition sent fourteen representatives to the Cortes. In 1933 and later in 1936, for the first time it outpolled the monarchists parties and attained an electoral majority in Vizcaya and Guipúzcoa.[61]

The difference in the two nationalist movements' social program also led to vastly different trajectories for the approval of their respective statutes of autonomy. The Catalans received their statute in 1932, the Basque statute of autonomy was approved only in October 1936, three months after Franco's uprising in Morocco. The reason for the delay was the desire of Basque nationalists to encapsulate in the autonomy as much as possible of their conservative platform both in content and in the form of its ratification and the continual distrust of the Republican governments, especially in their left-wing phase, toward the religious predilections of Basque nationalism. The PNV's demands that were unacceptable to the Republican governments was the right for direct relations between Euskadi and the Vatican and the limitation of the political and civil rights of Castilian immigrants through a restrictive naturalization process. At each stage of failed negotiations with Madrid the more conservative elements of Basque nationalism dropped out, leaving the stage vacant for more moderate elements until finally Prieto, a leader of PSOE in Bilbao, became actively involved in the preparation of the draft of the statute that was finally adopted.[62]

Although Catalans were united during the process that took them from the San Sebastian pact, which plotted the overthrow of the monarchy, until the attainment of regional autonomy, Basques were polarized both politically and regionally. After Franco's coup in 1936, the Basque provinces split. Alava, and especially Navarra, became strongholds of Franco's forces. Industrialized Vizcaya and Guipúzcoa, though socially and politically equally conservative, were the centers of Basque nationalism and, consequently, threw in their lot with the leftist and atheist Republic that finally granted them autonomy and not with conservative Franco, even though he was supported by the Church, because of his vision of one indivisible Spain. The crumbling away of the conservative elements left at the helm of the PNV only the most dedicated nationalist, who, forced by the radical circumstances of the Second Republic, forged a "strange alliance...which was to be consummated in the common defense of the Republic in the Civil War."[63] In this way the Republic left its imprint on Basque nationalism, which emerged much changed when a younger generation revived it in the latter years of the Franco regime.

The defeat of the Second Republic's forces also "brought the complete defeat of all the Spanish regional nationalist movements."[64] With the Republic's demise, the provincial governments of Catalonia and Euskadi went into exile. During the Franco dictatorship, Basque nationalists were driven into exile and underground. For a short period after the Second World War, the PNV renewed its activities mostly by organizing strikes but the 1953 U.S.-Spanish defense agreements undercut the hopes it entertained about the possibility of Franco's ouster and Spain's democratization. During the 1960s, when the grip of regime began loosening somewhat, socialists emerged as the major organizing force in the region. But, already in the 1950s there was a slow rebirth of Basque nationalism among the new generation. The young nationalists initially only formed discussion groups but, by the end of the decade, these coalesced into the underground organization Euskadi ta Askatasuna (Freedom for the Basque Country) that came to be known as ETA. ETA was yet another breakaway body from the moderate, and by now ineffectual, PNV.[65]

By the early 1960s ETA embarked on a terrorist campaign against representatives of the Spanish state, mostly police officers, and industrialists. This path was inspired by Third World urban guerrilla movements, especially the Algerian and the Vietnamese ones that, according to ETA ideology, struggled against similar colonial and capitalist opponents.[66] Whereas the PNV's anticapitalism was inspired by a backward looking glance to a precapitalist social order, the ETA justified its brand of anticapitalism by a revolutionary socialist ideology that looked beyond the capitalist organization of the economy and society. Of all the types and movements of nationalism examined in this study, the second wave of Basque nationalism is the most difficult to account for; it is at once the most complex and most paradoxical. I will turn now to an examination of the social sources of ETA's nationalism as a way of illuminating these contradictions.

It is much harder to pinpoint ETA's social background than it was to explain the PNV's roots. Whereas the PNV was born during the Bourbon Restoration and with the exception of the 1937–1975 period was able to act openly as a political party, ETA was the product of Franco's dictatorship, hence an illegal underground body. Nor has it emerged from its illegal existence to this day. As a conspiratorial body, ETA's membership always remained in the dozens and the hundreds; and it was possible to gather systematic information about only those ETA members who were captured.

There is agreement among observers and participants on the importance of ETA's intellectual strata, which rose from the lower middle classes, though there is a dispute whether this petty bourgeoisie was salaried or self-employed. One leader of ETA argued that the petty bourgeoisie that generated ETA makes its living from "small scale production based on a small industrial shop or family craft, or the small property based on small-scale trade, administered by a family. In both cases, with a few salaried workers."[67] Ortzi is convinced that, in addition to this artisan stratum, low-level clerical and technical cadres were also radicalized by the erosion of their type of employment by large industrial monopolies during the years of rapid industrial growth.[68] A more serious bone of contention between observers of ETA concerns the participation of industrial workers in the movement. Whereas some argue that relatively few workers are in the movement, the most careful assessment seems to have been made by Garmendia, who notices a transition among the recruits from the petty bourgeois intellectual founders to young Euskera speakers (eskaldunes) from rural regions of relatively recent industrialization, who suffered the ignominies of forced proletarianization. These new industrial workers, he argues, experienced directly the crisis of the values of traditional Basque society and were radicalized by it.[69]

The roots of ETA in the lower middle class and the increased recruitment of new members from the industrial work force help explain the puzzle of ETA's continuous existence in spite of Spain's democratization since the movement's emergence. In contrast, other Western European guerrilla movements—the Bader-Meinhof group in Germany and the Red Brigades in Italy—disappeared over a decade ago. Because middle-class-based terrorist groups, argues Waldmann, evolve out of ideological splits and suffer from the tension between their members' radicalism and relatively affluent social background, their organizations and activities remain discontinuous. Terror organizations that mobilize lower-class elements (usually after the initiation of the movement by middle-class intellectuals), in contrast, once they reach a certain level of intensity, are less likely to die out.[70]

Explaining the activity of a relatively small group, especially one that is highly charged ideologically, on the basis of its social origins is potentially full of pitfalls and needs to be rounded out by other types of evidence. Robert Clark has enlarged the purview of the sociological analysis of ETA's membership by examining three of its interconnected geographical dimensions. ETA is best known for blowing up Carrero Blanco, Spain's prime minister and Franco's purported successor, on the streets of Madrid but most of its urban terror acts were committed in the Basque provinces. Clark plotted these acts on a map and found that a large percentage of ETA attacks were concentrated in a distinct geographical region of the Basque country: the Goierri in Guipúzcoa province. Furthermore, he found that ETA "tends to recruit its members predominantly in the regions in which its attacks are concentrated."[71] Finally, the Basque parties that emerged out of ETA (Herri Batasuna and Euskadiko Eskerra, to be discussed later in this section) also draw most of their support from the same region.[72] He concluded that the Goierri region is the heartland of the ETA and, consequently, argues that ETA's roots are to be found in this region's character.

The Goierri region is cleaved by low mountain chains and, consequently, dominated by numerous villages and midsize towns, even the largest of which, Mondragón, has only 25,000 inhabitants. The layout and character of this region helped "Basque language and ethnicity survive and flourish" in it. In general, the Basque-speaking population is concentrated in small towns of fewer than 2,000 residents.[73] At the same time, in late 1950's—that is, relatively late in comparison with the rest of Guipúzcoa province—the Goierri underwent rapid industrial development. Whereas the PNV was situated in the Basque cities, especially in Bilbao, in the Goierri industry is located in the very midst of traditional smalltown, in many places agricultural, concentrations. The penetration of industry has not altered considerably the ethnic homogeneity of the region: very few non-Basque neighborhoods have sprung up in this region. In Clark's words: "the confluence of all these forces has produced an unusual blend of traditional and modern in the lives of its residents," and the ETA is the product of this blend.[74]

ETA, like its predecessor PNV, is a product of offended tradition, although it is defending not privilege and status hallowed by tradition, but a traditional way of life and culture.

Medhurst is helpful in making the connection more explicit. Rapid economic change under the aegis of a dictatorial regime, introduced considerable polarization between the new and old, the city and the countryside, the smalltown elites and the large industrial and financial institutions, and provoked a general process of radicalization of which the emergence of ETA was just one symptom. Illegal strike movements were undertaken by mostly immigrant workers under communist and socialist auspices, but also a reassertion of Basque culture connected with the lower Basque clergy's ecclesiastic dissent was the manifestation of a broader movement that affected the entire Spanish Church. The Marxism of ETA is seen, in this view, as a response to the twin problems of political repression and economic upheaval, while the strong bonds between the economic elite and the dictatorship, combined with massive repression undertaken by the latter, gave credence to the notion of the Basque country being a colonized area in need of liberation.[75]

Medhurst points out that "such rapid and dramatic changes drew attention to and aggravated precisely those dilemmas or tensions which, at the outset, had underlain the emergence of Basque nationalism."[76] In the terms used here, the discontent channeled by ETA is the product of the region's dualistic development, which spread into the previously less affected countryside. The often indiscriminate repression of the Guardia Civil, when provoked by ETA, "served to raise levels of popular consciousness and to reinforce a distinctive local political identity."[77] The deep politicization of the Basque population by the cycle of ETA terrorism and state repression accounts in large part for the continuation of ETA activity in the democratic era. At the same time, the support enjoyed by ETA has shrunk considerably since Spain's democratization: today, the various fractions of ETA combined represent a minority view in the Basque country.

In light of the continued unbalanced development of the Basque country we can make better sense of the complexity of contemporary Basque politics and the changing electoral fortunes of the Spanish and Basque parties in national and regional elections since the return to democracy in 1975. Basque nationalists have historically rallied around a single party—Arana's PNV—which, by and large, was able to contain its two contending wings and prevent serious splintering. The early opponents of Arana's orthodoxy were Soto's moderate wing, which possessed its own party between 1923–1930, and the tiny Jagi Jagi group, a socially conscious Christian Democratic but pro-independence party, which broke away during the statute of autonomy negotiations of the 1930s.[78] Today's PNV is still the champion of regional autonomy for the Basque provinces.

During the democratization process and since, the PNV prevailed as the largest Basque nationalist party, and its main opponent

remained the Socialist Party, which for the first time also evolved a
Basque spinoff—the Partido Socialista de Euskadi (PSE). The PNV
won the largest number of votes in every election between 1977 and
1990, in both national (see Table 4.1) and regional (see Table 4.2)
elections, overtaking the Socialist Party by a few percentage points in
national and by about 10–20 percent in the regional elections (with
the exception of 1986, when the PNV split).[79] The PNV continually
represents the wish of the largest bloc of voters in Euskadi.

The PNV, however, is no longer the sole representative of Basque
nationalism. It shares the support given to Basque nationalism with a
growing nationalist left wing (which, by comparison, is tiny in
Catalonia). The *abertzale* (socialist-nationalist) parties demand independence for Euskadi and are the political arms of ETA fractions.

TABLE 4.1

Results of National Elections in the Basque Provinces,
in Percentages of Valid Votes

Parties	1977	1979	1982	1986	1989	1993
PNV	28	27	31	25.7	22.8	23.9
EA	—	—	—	—	11.2	9.8
HB	—	15	14	16.4	16.9	14.5
EE	6	9	8	16.8	8.8	—
PSOE-PSE	25	19	29	24.3	21.1	24.3
PCE/IU	5	5	2	1.1	2.9	6.2
UCD	12	16	—	—	—	—
AP/PP	7	3	11	11.0	9.4	14.6
Other	17	6	5	4.7	6.9	7.6

Source: Shabad 1986, Table 4, p. 35, published with author's permission;
computed from *Anuario El País, 1989*, Resultados provinciales de las
Elecciones Legislativas de 1989 and from *El País* (June 8, 1993).

List of acronyms and abbreviations:

EA	Eusko Alkartasuna
EE	Euskadi Ezkerra
HB	Herri Batasuna
PNV	Partido Nacionalista Vasco
PP	Partido Popular
PCE/IU	Partido Comunista de Euskadi/Izquierda Unida
PSOE-PSE	Partido Socialista Obrero Español—Partido Socialista de Euskadi

TABLE 4.2

Results of Regional Elections in Basque Provinces,
in Percentages of Valid Votes

Parties	1980	1984	1986	1990
PNV	38	42	23.7	30.0
EA			15.8	12.0
HB	16	15	17.5	19.4
EE	10	8	10.9	8.2
PSOE-PSE	14	23	22.0	21.0
PCE/IU	4	1	—	—
UCD	8	—	—	—
AP\PP	5	10	4.9	8.7
Other	5	1	5.2	0.7

Source: Shabad 1986, Table 4, p. 35, published with author's permission; *El País* (October 29, 1990), p. 18.

ETA itself underwent repeated splits. The schism of 1974, on the eve of Franco's death, was the most important one in ETA's history. The ETAm (i.e., ETA *militar*) insisted on continuing the unrelenting campaign of urban terrorism that was undertaken during the last decade of Franco's rule; and the ETApm (i.e., ETA *político-militar*) decided to change its tactic, in view of the anticipated changes in Spain's political life, by limiting terrorism to selective actions and by seeking to involve itself in mass politics.[80]

ETApm created the Euskadiko Eskerra (EE, Basque Country Left) Party, which, together with the PNV, called on its supporters to vote in favor of regional autonomy in the constitutional referendum of December 1978 (though viewed it as an intermediary step toward self-determination), and its delegates have played active parliamentary roles on the local and national levels.[81]

Though ETAm also created a political wing—Herri Batasuna (HB, People United), a coalition of radical separatists and Marxist-Leninists—this party advocated abstention in the autonomy statute referendum. Since 1979, HB has participated in elections but boycotted the Parliaments in Vitoria (capital of Alava) or Madrid and refused to accept governmental posts in either, though it participates in municipal governments.[82] HB is what political scientists describe as an *antisystem party*, a party operating on the margins of the national political system with the aim of gaining support to create an alternative system, in this case, an independent state. Of the two *abertzale* parties, Herri Batasuna, the more radical nationalist party, is the larger one, and together with EE it attains about the quarter of the votes in elections for the regional parliament. Basque nationalism, in short, is fragmented between moderate and radical wings that disagree over the goal of the nationalist movement, autonomy or independence, as well as over social goals, a market economy or some form of socialism or communism.

Although the significant programmatic divide of the Basque nationalism runs between the PNV and the *abertzale* parties, on the eve of the 1986 regional elections the PNV itself was split by a disagreement over the proper degree of tying together the three Basque provinces.[83] The new Eusko Alkartasuna (EA, Basque Solidarity) subsequently justified its separate course by accusing the PNV of being too accommodating to the Spanish government. Ironically, this split opened the way for the Socialist Party to win the regional elections for the first time (the PSOE-PSE received one more representative in the regional parliament than PNV though the latter received more votes).

The Basque electorate is divided not only between different political programs and between the native born and the immigrants, it is also fragmented geographically. In the regional elections that took place in 1986, different parties commanded the largest blocs of voters in each of the three provinces. In Guipúzcoa, the winner was EA; in Alava, the PSOE-PSE; and in Vizcaya, the largest of the provinces, the PNV. In 1990, HB succeeded EA in Guipúzcoa, and in Alava the PNV replaced the PSOE-PSE as the winner of the largest bloc of votes.[84]

Basque nationalism suffers from serious internal divisions, but the parties that make up the nationalist camp (PNV, EE, HB, and EA) regularly obtained the majority of the votes for the Cortes (with the exception of 1977, when HB boycotted the elections) and increased their share from a low of 51 percent in 1979 to a high of 59.7 percent in 1989. In 1993, however, this trend was reversed when the votes cast for the nationalist camp fell to 48.2 percent. In part this was the result of the disappearance of EE and the transfer of many of its votes to the Communist Party but, in part, also the result of the growth of the electoral support for Spanish parties: the communists (PCE/IU), the socialists (PSOE-PSE), and the conservatives (PP). It is too early to tell whether the 1993 national elections herald a new trend. In the regional parliament the nationalist camp consistently receives around two thirds of the votes cast (see Tables 4.1 and 4.2). In the Basque country, in short, the nationalist camp, at least till 1993 and maybe beyond, was expected not only to run the regional government but also represent the region's interest vis-à-vis the rest of Spain. The majority of the residents in the Basque provinces think of themselves as Basques first and Spaniards second. They are considerably less willing than their Catalan counterparts to distinguish between their regional and national interest, in fact frequently viewing the former as encompassing the latter.

At the same time, the heavy fragmentation of the ideological, political, cultural, and intraregional aspirations that reflect the internal instability of Euskadi witnessed some unexpected repercussion in Spanish-Basque relations: a greater willingness to be integrated into the larger Spanish political order. The best example of this trend is the cooperation of the PNV and the PSOE that commenced in 1985. In consequence of the split between two leaders of the PNV (which led in 1986 to the creation of the competing EA), the PNV's new leader and the Vitoria government's new *Lendakari* (Premier), José Antonio Ardanza, reached an ad hoc agreement with the PSOE-PSE. The Socialist Party agreed to support the legislative initiatives of the PNV, while the PNV promised "to honor the Constitution, the Statute of Autonomy, other related laws, and the decisions of the [Constitutional] Court."[85] The PNV also promised to oppose ETA's separatist violence in a more vigorous form. This pact "signalled a turning point in the dynamic of constant confrontation between the PNV and Basque socialists and between the Basque and central governments."[86] The greater willingness of the PNV to uphold the Spanish constitution also expedited the devolution of central government functions to the regional government. In short, the fratricide between the two wings of moderate Basque nationalism, the PNV and the EA, placed the socialists in position of "arbiter in regional political life."[87] In 1987, the cooperation between the PNV and the Socialist Party led to the formation of a coalition government that included both. As part of taking these steps the PNV has expressed its opposition to ETA's terrorist activities in forceful terms.

The support that ETA enjoyed during the Franco years and the period of transition has been considerably reduced since then. Only around 10 percent of the respondents in opinion polls taken in Euskadi express support for ETA. The defense of the traditional way of life, which Clark identified with the Goierri region, seems to carry less weight. In January 1988, all six major Basque regional parties—including the Basque Socialist Party but with the exception of Herri Batasuna—signed an antiterrorism pact that was designed to isolate

ETA terrorists. Until the signing of the pact, the PNV and the smaller *abertzale* parties used to condemn ETA's terrorist tactics but not its separatist aims. The January 1988 pact attempted simultaneously to take the wind out of ETA's sails by demanding increased Basque autonomy without, however, breaking away from Spain.[88] Although ETA has not abandoned its terrorist campaign, the rapture with most Basque nationalist parties and its dwindling public support is likely to corrode its basis of legitimacy and eventually erode its activities.

Basque nationalism has had a checkered career and was not able to establish itself as the hegemonic force in Euskadi on the basis of its nationalist program alone. Only its participation in the struggle for the democratic renewal of Spain made that possible, but the preponderance of radical terrorism in the Basque struggle, which continued even after the restoration od democracy to Spain, has not allowed the consolidation of Basque nationalist hegemony among Spanish immigrants. The new wave of Basque nationalism, however, was also wedded to socialism and within the program of Basque socialist nationalism there was room for reaching out to immigrants who, as in other developed regions, responded positively to such opening.

The Transformations and Contradictions of Contemporary Basque Nationalism and Immigration

What ideological shifts took place between the founding of the PNV by Sabino Arana and the appearance of ETA and the second wave of Basque nationalism? The history of the PNV, and of Basque nationalism in general, is the gradual waning of its initial convictions and aims and attempts by splinter groups to restore its doctrinaire purity. Two major areas of internal debate may be singled out: the dilemma of independence versus autonomy, and the dilemma of anti-immigrant belligerence versus the immigrants' integration into Basque society and culture.

Basque nationalists adhered to the overall aim of Basque independence from Spain during periods of political repression, but when the likelihood of attaining regional autonomy—usually during the democratic phases of Spanish political life—increased, their more moderate autonomist wing asserted itself within the movement. Already Arana himself, while serving a five months jail term, acknowledged the unfeasibility of the secessionist course and acquiesced in the less ambitious goal of autonomy within Spain. After his death in 1903 his supporters resurrected the platform of independence.[89]

In practice, however, Letamendia argued that "the two tendencies [always] coexisted in the PNV, but the legalist and autonomist orientation dominated the party."[90] Indeed in 1908, the PNV's platform omitted the call for secession and even changed its name to the more traditional sounding Comunión Nacionalista Vasca. The more radical wing, led by Luis Arana, the founder's brother, revived the old doctrinaire PNV in 1921. Under Primo de Rivera's dictatorship both parties were forced underground only to unite in 1930. The reborn PNV again labored under Arana's program of independence, but the PNV's willingness to collaborate with the Carlists during the Second Republic was yet another indication of its retreat from aspirations for independence to satisfaction with regional autonomy.

The PNV-Carlist alliance on its part folded in 1932, mostly along geographical lines: Navarra sided with the more religious Carlists who only wanted to restore their *fueros*, whereas Vizcaya, Guipúzcoa, and Alava, which sought a central administration for all Basque provinces, remained in the PNV's camp.[91] After the receipt of the statute of autonomy for the Basque region in 1936, the PNV remained a steadfast supporter of the Second Spanish Republic.

The split between the proponents of regional autonomy and the supporters of complete independence reappeared during the era of transition to democracy after Franco's death. For "the ETA hardliners, the enemy was never Franco, but rather Madrid, and those Basques who participate in the current political process are simply collaborators."[92] Consequently, even when ETA entered into negotiations with the Spanish government with an aim of bringing terrorism to an end, it keep insisting, in addition to amnesty for its prisoners and the withdrawal of the Civil Guard from the Basque country, on the "recognition of the national sovereignty of Euskadi and the right of the Basque people to self-determination."[93] And yet the strength of the pro-independence organizations and parties related to various ETA factions "reinforces and brings to the surface the inherent ambiguity of the PNV's objectives regarding the status of the Basque country within the Spanish state."94 In short, even though the PNV does not actively campaign for independence and, in fact, seems content with the general outlines of the current regional autonomy, its leaders find it hard, in view of the party's past position, to actively oppose the demand for Basque independence. Clarity was never the strength of Basque nationalism.

The other area in which the PNV's position showed considerable strain was its view of the preferred relationship with the Spanish immigrants in the Basque country. At the end of the nineteenth century, the PNV called for the expulsion of non-Basques by an independent Euskadi[95] with the exception of temporary residents who had essential business in the region. Furthermore, it opposed the naturalization of individuals not originally of Basque parentage.[96] There was a yawning gap between Catalan and Basque nationalism in regard to immigration. Arana was well aware of this difference and expressed it in the following fashion:

> Catalan politics...consist in *attracting to it* other Spaniards, whereas the Vizcayan program is to *reject from itself* all Spaniards as foreigners. In Catalonia every element coming from the rest of Spain is Catalanized, and it pleases them that urban elements from Aragón and Castile speak Catalan in Barcelona....The Catalans want all Spaniards living in their region to speak Catalan; for us it would be ruin if the *maketos* resident in out territory spoke Euskera. Why? Because purity of race is, like language, one of the bases of the Vizcaya banner.[97]

The fear of "denationalization" through immigration was more acute in the Basque than in the Catalan provinces, though both had about the same percentage of immigrants, because the Basque country already included a large percentage individuals who ethnically were Basque while culturally Spanish. But, in 1908, simultaneously with its disregard of the secessionist stand, the PNV also began moderating its rigid racial stand toward immigrants, for example, it reduced the number of Basque-named grandparents required to be admitted to membership in the party and its trade union from four to one.[98] A draft autonomy statute prepared at the onset of the Second Republic by the PNV and the Carlists included a clause that still would have required ten years of residence from nonnatives before becoming eligible for citizenship. Although this requirement would have severely limited the civil and political rights of immigrants it also signalled the acceptance, for the first time, of the possibility of their naturalization.[99]

Dramatic change in the position taken by Basque nationalists toward Spanish immigrants came only with the appearance of ETA.[100] The new movement was born, like the PNV itself, in a period of rapid in-migration and debated the proper relationship between the host society and the immigrants repeatedly, not to say incessantly, without ever reaching a coherent and agreed upon resolution. The horns of the dilemma were the conflicting interpretations of ETA's goals in class versus ethnic terms pitting the "socialist nationalists" against the "nationalist socialists."[101]

The socialist nationalist, or revolutionary socialist, position, articulated in ETA's main journal, *Zutik*, was that in an industrial society, such as existed in the Basque provinces, the working class holds the key to the future. Only an all-Spanish revolution was seen as capable of overthrowing Franco, and later capitalism, and liberating the Basques. The logic of class struggle demanded that Basques join forces with other Spanish parties and recognize that the majority of the workers in Euskadi itself were Spanish. This revolutionary perspective led to the conclusion that unity with the Basque bourgeoisie had to be abandoned and Basque chauvinism toward the immigrants needed to be uprooted.[102]

The nationalist, or traditional, socialists led by Txillardegi and Krutwig repudiated any alliance with Spanish forces, including immigrants, and preferred to conduct class struggle through a Third World-type guerrilla strategy that did not require the active involvement of large masses.[103] The nationalist wing, however, also rejected Arana's racism and, therefore, was opposed to anti-immigrant chauvinism. Consequently its leaders preferred to base Basque identity not on race but on language. At the same time, this faction still viewed Spanish immigrants who spoke Spanish and supported Spanish political parties as "behaving in an imperialist way."[104] Both factions, in short, used different arguments from the socialist arsenal to reject the purist position of Arana, but one wing was willing to go a longer distance than the other toward the immigrants. The shared aim of all ETA factions was to connect national liberation with social revolution through the creation of an independent socialist state for Basques.[105]

In 1967, ETA sustained the first of its many ideologically based organizational splits between its wing that emphasized the primacy of nationalism and the wing that stressed the primacy of socialism. The nationalist faction that remained in control of ETA subsequently saw the rebirth of the same struggle within itself. For a while the division within the nationalist wing was patched up by adopting a formula that combined the Marxist and nationalist elements. The compromise solution, pointing to aspirations of hegemonic influence over immigrants, redefined the social entity expected to carry out the Basque revolution as the "Basque working people," that is, "those who earned their living in the Basque country and supported Basque aspirations," but it did not work for long because of its vagueness.[106]

The major question, Are immigrants welcomed by the movement or not? was left unanswered, and consequently, it gave rise to subsequent schisms. Sullivan is right in concluding that "ETA was never to resolve the question of what attitude to take to the immigrants." On the one hand, rejection of the immigrants as objectively imperialist colonizers would have eliminated one of the most politically conscious groups opposed to the Francoist dictatorship. On the other hand, their "complete acceptance would have cut [ETA] off from the grass roots [Basque] nationalist feeling"[107] and exposed it to the charge of collaborationism.

The type of nationalist perspective adopted toward the Spanish immigrants, hegemonic or corporate, also determined to a large extent the options available to ETA's factions in other areas. The nationally leaning organizations that contemplated a semihegemonic-semicorporate approach—partial opening toward the immigrants, based not on ethnic but socialist criteria of exclusion and inclusion, revived the old aim of independence and insisted on the exclusive use of Euskera as the language of the Basque provinces. The socialist wing of ETA, which followed a hegemonic plan for accepting the immigrant workers as full partners and liked to call itself *popular nationalist*, "substituted the demand for autonomy for independence, and bilingualism for a Basque-speaking Euskadi."[108] Ironically, neither wing of ETA acquired "an extensive working class base"[109] but the political parties associated with the two wings of ETA, especially the HB, were able to mobilize electoral support among immigrants.

In summary, the changes adopted by ETA's nationalist wing departed from the PNV's original views in two contrary directions: ETA's positions combined a radical insistence on secession from Spain with an incongruous, if only partial, accomodationist attitude toward Spanish immigrants. ETA's smaller socialist wing showed readiness to integrate the immigrants into Basque society in return for their assistance for a partial Basque rejection of its association with Spain. What are the relations between the native-born Basques and Spanish immigrants? The presence of a large number of immigrants means, as Shabad puts it, that "the center-periphery cleavage which divides the Basque country (and Catalonia) from the rest of Spain is replicated, but in reverse, within each."[110] Basque nationalist parties garner the majority of their votes from native-born Basques, whereas the Spanish parties (called by the nationalists *sucursalistas*, or branch offices) receive the largest part of their votes from immigrants. Shabad found in her survey that in the 1979 national elections, three quarters of the *peneuvistas* and EE supporters, 62 percent of HB voters, but only 44 of the UCD and 20 percent of the PSOE voters, were native born. The results in 1982 were similar.[111] Another feature of the native-born–immigrant split indicates that immigrants felt the local parliament to be less relevant to their concerns than the national Cortes, consequently the abstention rate among the immigrants was higher by 8–9 percentage points in the 1979 national and 1980 regional elections than among the native-born voters.[112]

Voting patterns point to a schism between immigrants and hosts in Euskadi. Most other indicators, however, lead to a much different conclusion. Among these indicators the most important ones are connected with the struggle for democracy, occupational stratification, language acquisition, and national identification.

In the waning years of the dictatorship, Basque nationalism and specifically ETA, presented the most daring challenge to Franco and as such attracted "a novel degree of sympathy for the local cause which even extended to workers of non-Basque origin."[113] The common platform of the anti-Franco opposition was the demand for democracy. For socialists, democracy was the precondition for the legalization of their political and economic organizations that, under Franco's regime, were a major target of oppression. For nationalists, democratic institutions promised to undermine the particularly pernicious forms of centralization and Castilianization practiced by the Francoist regime. At times of confrontation with the dictatorship, whether caused by the workers' short-term economic demands or the massive and frequently indiscriminate governmental repressive practices (which included mass arrests and systematic torture) in response to ETA's terrorist acts, this coalition was mobilized.

The best known example of such protest, which also spread outside the Basque provinces, was the Burgos crisis in December 1970, when, in a carefully choreographed show trial seeking to destroy the ETA once and for all, a military court condemned to death six ETA members. Mass mobilization of the major oppositional bodies—illegal parties and trade unions, intellectuals and professionals, and the regional (both Basque and Catalan) Churches—forced the commutation of the sentences, and helped consolidate the democratic opposition.[114] In the early 1970s, just as in 1907 and again in 1931, the defense of political freedom served as the platform for the formation of Solidaridad Catalana and the Esquerra Republicana de Catalunya under, respectively, the aegis of the Catalan regional parties and leaders. But in the Basque country (as in the Baltics during the *perestroika* years), this coalition never congealed into a permanent organization. Basque nationalism had not acquired permanent hegemonic influence over nonnationalist classes and parties in the region.

Although the struggle for democracy served as a magnet for diverse interests, Spanish workers in the Basque provinces did not assimilate into Basque society and culture. But Spanish immigrant workers in the Basque country had no incentive to be absorbed. In terms of income, in 1973 immigrants trailed Basques both of whose parents were also born in the Basque country by less than 5 percent and trailed even less those Basques who only had one parent born there.[115]

I will examine the occupational stratification of the labor force in the Basque provinces by ethnic origin through its comparison with Catalonia. Because the percentage of immigrants in the two regions is roughly one third, the most important demographic factor is kept constant in this comparison. The data from Catalonia and the Basque provinces are from the same period, but Pinilla de las Heras's survey is more precise (see Table 3.5) than the Basque data, and hence, the comparisons across categories are harder to make. We need, therefore, to use Sàez's data (see Table 3.4) which has fewer subcategories, (and supplement it, when possible, with the Pinilla de las Heras survey) as our basis of comparison between the employment pattern of Spanish immigrants in Catalonia and the Basque provinces (the Basque data includes Navarra in addition to the other three provinces of the Basque country).

Such comparison demonstrates that social strata are less polarized in the Basque country than in Catalonia. The percentage of nonnatives employed in management positions (see Table 4.3) is roughly equal between the regions: 26 percent in the Sàez study and 20–27 percent in the appropriate categories of the Pinilla de las Heras survey as compared with 27 percent in the four Basque provinces. The divergence between middle-level employees is relatively small, 29 percent in the Basque provinces versus 25 percent according to Sàez, though the Pinilla de las Heras survey shows that in Catalonia the more technically defined jobs of the same category employ more immigrants than the managerial jobs (38–43 percent versus 31 percent). At the same time, we need to keep in mind that the middle-level categories are not defined in the same way in the two surveys: in addition to middle-level technicians they also include middle management in Catalonia and in the Basque provinces also include middle-level employees. The fact that the categories used for Catalonia are skewed upward might be responsible for the smaller representation of immigrants in this category in Catalonia.

TABLE 4.3

Occupational Distribution According to Place of Birth in the
Basque Country (including Navarra).

Occupational Category	Native-Born Basque	Immigrant
Management, executives, professionals, and high-level technical workers	73	27
Middle-level technicians and employees	71	29
Skilled workers and clerks	72	28
Semi-skilled workers	62	38
Unskilled workers	53	47

Source: Miguel 1974, p. 265.

Clear differences appear between Catalonia and the four Basque provinces at the lower end of the occupational pyramid, and they seem to favor immigrant workers employed in the Basque country. We find that 44–60 percent of the combined categories of skilled workers and clerical personnel are drawn from immigrants in Catalonia in comparison with 28 percent in the Basque provinces. In the combined semi- and unskilled workers, 82 percent of the employees are immigrants (78–89 percent in Pinilla de las Heras's data) in contrast to 38–47 percent in the Basque provinces, to yield the largest occupational gap between Spanish and the native born between the two provinces. In short, as we move down the occupational ladder Catalans outnumber immigrants in the higher status jobs and immigrants outnumber Catalans is the lower status jobs: as skilled laborers and, more dramatically, in semi- and unskilled work; in the Basque provinces, however, the majority of the workers at all levels are native born.

In high- and middle-status occupations, such as manager, middle-level executive and technical employee, professional, and clerical personnel, the employment patterns of immigrants were roughly the same in Catalonia and the four Basque provinces in the early 1970s. Immigrants outnumbered the native-born Catalans among unskilled workers by 64 percent in Sàez and a whopping 77 percent in Pinilla de las Heras's survey but are themselves outnumbered by the native born in the Basque country by 6 percent. The concentration of immigrants at the bottom end of the occupational hierarchy that we encountered in Catalonia is not repeated in the economy of the Basque region. Basques are both managers and unskilled workers, Catalans are more heavily concentrated as we move up the occupational status ladder. On the basis of Nuñez and Amando de Miguel's data we may conclude that association between employment and ethnicity in the Basque country is weaker than in Catalonia.

Nuñez's argument that under such employment conditions antagonism between immigrant and native born Basque employees must be due only to psychological causes such as mistrust and cultural friction probably plays down political disagreements but there is no reason to assume that it would be greater than in Catalonia.[116] Some of the antagonistic sentiments are also because immigrants in the Basque country, like those in Barcelona, are concentrated in the urban ring around the industrial metropolis, especially in Bilbao, where housing and factories are mixed together. A chronic shortage of housing forces many of the immigrants to reside in rundown housing and in shantytowns with inadequate sanitary conditions.[117] Although there are many indications of the integration of immigrants into Basque society, even here it remained limited. It is too soon, therefore, to proclaim in the Basque country the triumph of the integration theory of immigrant-host relations over its neo-Marxist counterpart that expects hosts and immigrants to remain divided.

A variety of reasons diminishes the potential incentive, so clearly present in Catalonia, to learn the regional language. A very large proportion of the immigrants to the Basque country hailed from Castile and León, which, as Linz explains, were "areas of relatively high levels of education, independent property-owning peasantry, and strong Spanish identification" and, therefore, would probably exhibit less willingness to lose part of their cultural background in the process of assimilation than the poorer Andalusian immigrants of Catalonia.[118] The main reason behind the desire to become bilingual that we encountered in Barcelona and its environs—to improve one's chances of social mobility—is not present in the Basque country. Much of economic life, as well as politics and culture, in the Basque provinces are conducted in Spanish and therefore knowledge of Euskera would be of marginal advantage in securing professional advancement and social mobility for immigrants. In fact, the extent of Hispanicization in the region is such that the majority of the Basques themselves have only limited knowledge of Euskera. "Ability or inability to speak Basque does not help or hinder career opportunities. Even many political leaders of Basque nationalist parties," reports Coverdale, "cannot speak Basque."[119]

Historical studies and surveys estimate that the number of Euskera speakers between 1856 and 1868 was between 400,000 and

660,000. In 1930, the number of those speaking Euskera was 500,000, and in 1970 it was 455,000. The number of Euskera speakers has not changed much over a century but during the same period the overall population of the provinces has more than tripled. A hundred years ago slightly over half of the Basque provinces' population were *euskaldunes* (speakers of Euskera), and in 1970 they made up less than 20 percent; consequently, Euskera speakers have steadily lost ground.[120] Furthermore, most *euskaldunes* live in the rural districts and small villages with a population of 5,000 to 20,000; while in the industrial towns and cities knowledge of Euskera is sparse.[121] The only provincial capital in which knowledge of Euskera reaches the average of the Basque country is San Sebastián; in Bilbao and Vitoria less than 1 percent of the population use it.[122] Clark concludes that "as people move from small town to large industrial city, they have a tendency to abandon the language of their origins in favor of the more modern and utilitarian language of their new surroundings."[123] This linguistic shift is even more marked among the children of second-generation urban dwellers.

Spanish immigrants have little reason to learn Euskera, a language unlike any other they know, when neither occupational mobility nor cultural integration demands it. Furthermore, immigrants seem to be concentrated in large and multinational corporations in which Spanish is the dominant language (in contrast, in Barcelona even many large enterprises are managed in Catalan), while smaller companies, among them the cooperatives of Guipúzcoa, recruit Euskera speakers.[124] Beltza reports that in the 1960s even in smaller towns, such as Mondragón, Hernani, and Elgóibar, no more than three percent of immigrants and their children learned to speak Euskera to any degree, and around 95 percent remained ignorant of it, while in large cities the numbers of immigrant *euskaldunes* was even lower.[125] Linz's more recent data reveals only a moderate increase. By 1985, 5 percent of the immigrants claimed to speak Euskera and 13 percent to understand it.[126]

The Basque nationalist movement, in view of its shifting emphasis from a racial to a linguistic definition of the Basque identity, refuses to accept that the bells had tolled for Euskera and seeks to increase the percent of Euskera speakers in the population of the Basque provinces. As part of the nationalist activities in the 1950s, *ikastolas*, small Euskera language schools, began operating in clandestine settings in churches and private houses. Enrollment started rising only in the 1970s: whereas in 1971–1972, 18,500 children studied in 67 *ikastolas*, in 1979–1980, 54,000 were enrolled in 234 *ikastolas*. But even this growth increased the number of children studying in Euskera language schools to only 10 percent of school-age children.[127]

The 1981 census of the government of the Autonomous Community of Euskadi also indicated only a slight increase in the percentage of individuals who reported speaking Euskera. The census found that 21.4 percent of the population speaks Euskera, but also relates that an additional 14.5 percent of the residents of the Basque provinces speak it nearly or imperfectly (*cuasi-euskaldunes*). Of the fluent Euskera speakers 9.5 percent and of the imperfect speakers 7.7 percent, that is, altogether 17.2 percent, claim literacy in Euskera. It seems to me that even these numbers are inflated. By breaking down the census into too many loose categories, as the government of Euskadi did, respondents were disposed to overestimate their command of the language and the overall results tend to be inflated. For example, it is hard to know how much real knowledge one is to attribute to the 4.1 percent of imperfect speakers who also claim to possess partial literacy in Euskera, let alone to the 2.7 of imperfect speakers whose level of literacy is "passive."[128] Literacy, especially in our literary era, is by far a more important indicator of language use than speech, and with a literacy rate of 17.2 percent among the population of the three Basque provinces—a percentage that itself is probably inflated—there is little reason to expect the recovery of Euskera.

The distribution of the *euskaldunes* among the major economic sectors is another indicator of its marginal place as a public language. Euskera speakers over 16 years make up the majority (60.1 percent) in only one major economic sector, agriculture; in industry they compose 22.3; in services, 19.8; and in construction, 15.8 percent of the employees.[129] Euskera has remained the preserve of the traditional part of society and is only a marginal language in the city and among the manual and middle-class employees. In most Eastern European societies in which peasant languages, some used only orally, were modernized and transformed in the nineteenth century into the language of urban life, industrialization has only begun. In a society with highly advanced industry, as in Vizcaya and Guipúzcoa, the likelihood of transforming the language of the countryside into an urban and high status, "urbane" language is slim.

Basque language planning also had only limited impact on the expansion of Euskera. The Franco regime conceded the teaching of regional languages in primary schools and legalized the *ikastolas* in

1968. Another significant step was taken in 1979 when the Spanish Ministry of Education "accepted responsibility for programs of instruction in Euskera at all levels of education in the Basque provinces from preschool through to university." This plan, however, made Euskera obligatory only for students in regions where "Euskera was still a functioning language"; in other parts of the Basque provinces, parents have to initiate such programs, which, however, remain based on voluntary attendance.[130] As part of the autonomy statute of Guernica, Spanish and Euskera were made coofficial languages and the regional government of Euskadi was authorized "to regulate its use and to undertake policies designed to support and strengthen the language."[131] The results of this facet of regional devolution in democratic Spain have been mixed. The creation of a television channel that broadcasts in Euskera has been made possible as part of this policy. At the same time, there is continued friction over the funding of local education. Attempts to use this provision to the exclusion of Spanish, for example by making knowledge of Euskera a precondition for public employment, have been struck down by the Spanish Constitutional Court. The court holds the position that learning and speaking regional languages "is a right...[and] not an obligation."[132]

The desire to resort to coercive practices, in fact, is probably an indication of the limited success of voluntary *euskaldunzación*. In Laitin's view the difficulty that besets attempts at language revival is that a critical mass of speakers is needed to make it worthwhile for new people to learn it. It is hard to reach that "tipping point," and therefore, he believes that "the brutal politics of regional separatism can best be understood in terms of assuring that a sufficient number of people alter their language of normal, everyday, use so that the culture of the region would be altered."[133] But Woolard's surprising finding in Catalonia, namely, that relative language prestige is established not in the formal settings or schools controlled by the state but rather by interpersonal relations formed in the workplace and the neighborhoods in which "greater economic power" matters,[134] indicates that coercive measures are not likely to succeed where voluntary ones fail. The difficulty of using Euskera as an effective marker of ethnic Basque identity makes the lingering corporate tendencies of Basque nationalism difficult to sustain and its more recent hegemonic aspirations and civic criteria of membership easier to justify.

Although the study of electoral preferences indicated that immigrants and Basques have different voting patterns in three other areas we found greater communality between them. First, during the years of struggle for democracy, Spanish immigrants in the Basque country like Spaniards from the rest of the country expressed their sympathy with the Basque struggle, which they accepted as part of the war against a common enemy. In the second and third spheres, the process of integration works in a negative fashion by reducing potential gaps between the groups. The relatively limited occupational differentiation between hosts and immigrants eliminates a potential source of conflict between the two groups. The third sphere, spoken and written language, the relatively sparse knowledge of Euskera in the Basque country also removes a potential barrier; though knowledge of Euskera is highly prized in nationalist circles it cannot be used to exclude those ignorant of it from social mobility. There is no, or little, segmentation on the basis of occupation or language use between immigrants and hosts in the Basque country. As a result of the difficulty in imposing clear divisions between the groups, symbolic identification has taken on a larger significance.

On their part, immigrants to the Basque country have shown remarkable willingness to identify with their hosts. In lack of data on intermarriage and the irrelevance of language acquisition, the most pertinent indicator of identity change is subjective national identification. In a study undertaken in the early 1980s, a comparison of immigrants according to their descent clearly demonstrates that the more family members of an individual born in Euskadi the higher is his or her measure of Basque identification on a scale that seeks to distinguish the Spanish and Basque components of national identity.

As we would expect, among second-generation Basques there is higher self-identification as Basque or more Basque than Spanish, and the reverse is true for immigrants. But, remarkably, almost half of those who consider themselves to possess two national identities of equal weight, Basque and Spanish, are immigrants, almost a quarter of those who feel more Basque than Spanish are also immigrants, and among those who identify exclusively as Basque about 10 percent are immigrants (see Table 4.4). And breaking down the category of immigrants reveals that 45.6 percent of those identifying themselves as Spanish or more Spanish than Basque but 35 percent feel equally Basque and Spanish, 8.3 percent as more Basque than Spanish, and another 11.1 percent as Basque only. Obviously one can question the depth of this identification but the willingness to be expansive rather than restrictive in one's choice of national identity seems to indicate that instead of conceiving of themselves as a Castilian national minority, many of the immigrants view themselves as existing within a

TABLE 4.4

National Identity by Descent in the Basque Country

Self-Identity of Immigrant Respondent	Both Parents Born in Euskadi	One Parent Born in Euskadi	Born in Euskadi of Immigrant Parents	Immigrant
Spanish (and more Spanish than Basque)	10.1	2.5	7.0	80.4
As Basque as Spanish	29.7	10.9	13.2	46.2
More Basque than Spanish	50.8	15.6	9.8	23.8
Basque	71.8	10.1	8.0	10.1
Number	(438)	(92)	(92)	(351)

Source: Linz 1985, Table 10.11, p. 240.

multicultural framework, Spanish and Basque at once. They chose to partake in two cultures and two worlds in various degrees, without feeling the need to let go of one to affirm the other.

The complexity of the relationship between immigrants and the native born has obvious implications for Basque identity. A promising approach for disentangling this morass is Juan Linz's imaginative use of survey research in a fashion particularly well fit "to unpack" the multi-layered character of national identity. Linz, inspired by the Catalan identity debate, seeks answers to the fundamental question, Who is a Basque? This question indicates the problematic character of Basque identity itself in a society in which immigrants make up at least one third of the population, even more if one counts the descendants of the earlier wave of immigrants. Linz examines the relationship between four scales of identification with the Basque nation—some objective and others subjective—that span a continuum from primordial to civic criteria.135 Crosstabulation of the national *self-identification* of the respondent with his or her criteria for identifying *others* as Basque produces the most fruitful and revealing results.

The first two scales measure in different ways how people in the three Basque provinces report their *own* national identity. The answers to the first question produce the following scale from two primordial criteria—to be born to Basque parent(s), and to speak Euskera—via an intermediary category (to be born in the Basque country) to a civic criterion (which was copied from Catalonia: to live and work in the Basque country). The second scale ranks the respondents' *self-identification* in one of five categories: Spanish, more Spanish than Basque, as Basque as Spanish, more Basque than Spanish, and Basque. In cross-tabulating the results of the two questions, Linz concluded that "there can be little doubt that a purely Basque identity is found most often among those whom the primordial criteria would identify as Basque."[136] It would appear that the emphasis found in ethnographic and anthropological work on the distinctive culture of the Basques and the theoretical approach that roots the emergence of peripheral nationalism in the reassertion of primordial identification in the face of the threats of modernity are borne out by the strong correlation of these two types of identities.

The third scale lists the criteria (each asked and tabulated independently, hence the combined answer may exceed 100 percent) necessary to accept others as Basques, and its results radically change our intermediate conclusions—the significance of the primordial dimension diminishes and the civic criterion of identity gains in relative importance (see Table 4.5). In a comparable study conducted in Catalonia, 56.5 percent of the respondents reported that they viewed living and working in Catalonia as necessary for someone to be considered Catalan but 69.2 percent of the respondents in the Basque provinces did so. Furthermore, although 82.4 percent of the respondents in Catalonia view Catalan descent (lumping together the criteria of Catalan parent(s) and being born in the region) as a necessary condition of local identity, only 60.7 percent did so in the Basque provinces.[137]

Finally, among those who define themselves as Basques only, and thereby reject any Spanish identity, there is a much higher percentage than in the already high regional average of choosing the condition of living and working in the Basque country as necessary for being a Basque (79.8 percent versus 69.2 percent). In the same group, descent was seen as a necessary condition by 41.2 percent, and speaking Euskera by only 28.3 percent.[138] There is, in conclusion, a clear contrast, if not contradiction, between national self-identification and the identification of others as Basque: the former tends to be more primordial, the latter civic.

An examination of the fourth scale of Basque national identity, political party preference, helps us understand the reasons for this surprising divergence in the responses. Linz reports a clear correlation between national self-identification and party preference. The voters of the PNV tend to come from among those identifying themselves as "more Basque than Spanish," whereas among the voters of the

TABLE 4.5

National Identity of Those Who View "Living and Working in the Basque Country" a Necessary Condition to Consider Oneself Basque.

Self-Identity of Respondent	Sample Total	To Live and Work in Basque Country	
		Yes	No
Spanish	25.0	18.7	39.2
More Spanish than Basque	2.9	3.0	2.8
As Basque as Spanish	23.7	23.3	24.6
More Basque than Spanish	10.7	11.6	8.8
Basque	37.3	43.5	24.6
Number	(782)	(541)	(241)
Total	100.0	69.2	30.8

Source: Linz 1985, Table 10.2, p. 213.

abertzale parties (socialist-nationalist)—the *Herri Batasuna* and the *Euskadiko Eskerra*—there is a higher percentage of those who identify themselves as Basques only.[139] If we cross-tabulate party preference with necessary criteria for identifying others as Basques, we find that 47.2 percent of the supporters of EE, 41.4 percent of the followers of HB, and only 30 percent of PNV supporters chose "to live and work" in the Basque country as the criterion of Basqueness. Conversely, 24.3 percent of PNV partisans chose only primordial criteria of identity of Basqueness versus 17.2 percent of HB voters and 8.3 percent of EE voters.[140]

The gap between the primordial and the civic criteria in defining oneself versus defining others as Basque is obviously correlated with political worldviews. The likely reasons for the choice of civic definition of others' Basqueness by those individuals who, using primordial criteria, appear to be "pure" Basques are their socialist and communist ideologies. This view of Basque civic identity is described by Linz as a form of "utopia." In his words, "it is a utopia in the sense that it proclaims the ideal of a community that could ignore the complex realities derived from almost a century of immigration, the linguistic losses of Euskera over an even longer period of time, and the differing strength of primordial ties within the Basque community itself."[141] But to me it seems that the real utopia was Sabino Arana's vision; the new basis of multicultural identity actually fits the reality of the mixed cultural character of the Basque provinces more than the primordial ever did. Basque nationalists would remain utopian if they insisted on a continued primordial definition, but the "new" civic Basque identity is the result of an attempt to compensate for those losses that make a political struggle based on descent and language ineffective in the Basque case. The attraction of socialism for Basque nationalists who, using ethnic criteria of distinction, would qualify as "pure" Basques demonstrates a willingness to subsume under the principles of socialist solidarity the divisive ethnic principle and produce what I will call a *primordialist socialism*. This combination is based on a contradiction but its intent is hegemonic: the integration of the diverse inhabitants of the Basque provinces with its native-born population.

The change in the definition of Basqueness, as Linz observes, corresponds to a generational shift: the older generation, heir to Sabino Arana's racial definition, still employs primordial criteria of identity, but the younger generation is shifting from the primordial to the civic definition of national identity.[142] The generation of younger nationalists expresses its views in the socialist vocabulary that makes it possible to play down the importance of ethnic differences by emphasizing class solidarity. Both class and civic identity can accommodate cultural diversity.

The old, corporate, approach of Basque nationalism toward Spanish immigrants has giving way to a new one made up of a two elements. First, the primordial markers of Basque identity, whether based on putative racial purity or descent, has been abandoned by many younger Basque nationalists in favor of a civic criterion like its Catalan counterpart, which makes inclusion of immigrants possible though not certain. The second element of the new civic Basque identity is negative: the weakening of Basque culture, due to the long association of urban and upper class Basques with Spain, allows the filling of the Basque identity with a less demanding, less homogenous content. Under these conditions, immigrants to the Basque country can identify with their host society by adopting its symbols and without letting go of their Spanish culture. This is a multicultural context with a difference, the culture of the immigrants is more than likely to persist because the majority of the native born view it as their own.

Basque nationalism frogleaped its Catalan counterpart in its intensity after the 1950s and 1960s even though the respective movements have not changed: the overwhelming majority of Catalan nationalists were always were willing to be satisfied with regional autonomy, whereas Basque nationalists vacillated between home rule and independence. Catalan nationalists have not moderated and Basque nationalist have not radicalized their respective aspirations, though the emergence of ETA clearly signaled a greater determination to struggle for the goal of independence. What can explain this puzzle?

I believe that the changing relative weight of the Catalan and Basque nationalist movements is to be sought in the transformation of Spain itself. Catalan nationalism was an expression of the relative development of Catalonia, an organ that was too large and demanding on a body that could not support it. Starting with the stabilization plan of 1959, however, Spain has entered a sustained period of economic modernization that diminished the gap among different regions of Spain and specifically between Madrid and Barcelona. The traditional concerns of modern Catalonia were not strange to a more modern Spain. Spain has caught up with Catalonia, though after much delay, a significant detour, and great suffering to all of its regions. Catalan demands, therefore, could be met by the post-Franco regime without significant risk to the unity of Spain.

Although the modernization of Spain facilitated its rapprochement with Catalonia, modernization was bound to exacerbate Basque nationalism rooted in the traditional sector of the Basque country. Most of ETA's membership, scope of its activity, and its electoral support are from small townships of the traditional Basque countryside, which were adversely affected by the rapid industrialization that started with Franco's stabilization plan. The dualistic pattern of the Basque country's economy explains the character of both the first and second waves of Basque nationalism. Neither the PNV nor ETA represented the dominant economic and social forces of the Basque provinces, hence both were opposed to the rupture introduced by capitalist industrialization.

Considering the basic change in ideology—from traditional, even reactionary, to revolutionary socialist—there is a surprising continuity between the two generations of Basque nationalism. The vagueness and internal dissension that characterized the PNV, reappear in much sharper, indeed frantic, fashion in the ETA. Ultimately, neither was able to overcome the fundamental vagueness of its aims, one would surmise, due to the immensity of the task: the defense of tradition that was slipping away with tools of the modern world that are undermining that very tradition. The violent ways of ETA are a desperate method of compensation for its weakness. But, whereas the religious basis of the PNV's program and its racial criteria of ethnicity were distinctly antimodern, the socialist path of "national liberation" is opposed to capitalism but not to modernization. Immersion in socialism has modernized Basque nationalism in some respects at least. One of the dimensions of its modernity is the, at least partial, adoption of a civic criterion of Basque national identity. In the new identity there is room for both the native born and the immigrant.

5

Baltic Awakening and the Lure of Exclusivity

Unintended Independence

The eastern Baltic littoral, the present-day territories of Estonia, Latvia, and Lithuania, was one of the last pagan backwaters of medieval Europe. The Crusaders, after suffering defeat in Palestine, turned their attention to Europe and made the Baltic region the target of a savage northern Crusade. The westernmost of the Baltic tribes, the Prussians, were the first to be subjugated and assimilated into the German-speaking peoples, bequeathing only their name to their conquerors. The Estonian, Latvian, Kurish, Livonian, Lettgalian, and related tribes were conquered, christianized, and reduced to serfdom by the military-monastic orders of the Livonian Brothers of the Sword and the Teutonic Knights in the Crusades of the thirteenth century.[1] Consequently, the Baltic region remained divided into a confederation of ecclesiastical estates governed by princes of the Holy Roman Empire until the middle of the sixteenth the century.

After the Reformation the Teutonic Order lost its power and significance, and its lands were lost first to the Polish-Lithuanian and Swedish states and subsequently to the Russian empire. One consequence of repeated conquest was that the present territories of Latvia and Estonia were not unified as political entities until 1917. Instead they were known as Estland (northern Estonia), Livonia (the southern part of Estonia and eastern Latvia, also known as Livland), and Kurland (also Courland and Kurzeme, the southwestern littoral of Latvia on the Baltic Sea), and their political boundaries frequently shifted. But throughout these centuries, the *Ritterschaften*—the corporations of the landowning German nobility—and the German merchants and guilds of the Hanseatic League's towns retained a considerable measure of autonomy and remained the regional political elite.

Although Latvia and Estonia were conquered while Lithuania retained a measure of independence as part of the Polish-Lithuanian

Commonwealth, the native peasantries of all three lands remained enserfed and dominated by culturally alien nobilities throughout most of their history. The limited concern of the ruling nobilities with the lower classes' culture was satisfied by the imposition of their religious preferences and, thus, permitted the preservation of the peasantry's own traditions, folk arts, and the Estonians' Finno-Ugric language and the Latvians' Baltic Indo-European language into the modern era.

The victory of Peter the Great in the Great Northern War, confirmed in the Treaty of Nystad in 1721, brought the Swedish-dominated Baltic territories under Russia, and the partitions of Poland at the end of the eighteenth century delivered most of Lithuania (with the exception of Lithuania Minor, which accrued to Prussia) to Russian rule. For

MAP 5.1

Estonia and Latvia

the first time most of the northern Baltic littoral was dominated by one great power. Thus started the almost continuous close association of the Baltic region with Russia, spanning two and half centuries.

The incorporation of the Baltic lands into the Romanov empire led to few changes in their internal structure since the tzars esteemed highly the administrative and military skills of the German land-owning nobility and agreed not to interfere with its corporate privileges and political and cultural autonomy in Estland and Livonia.[2] In a series of capitulations and treaties, first granted by Peter the Great and subsequently reaffirmed by his successors, the "rights and privileges of the Baltic *Ritterschaften* and burghers received...confirmation in general terms without reservations." The *Ritterschaften* exercised their feudal privileges through the provincial Landtag (Diet) and its Executive Council and through local governments organized in the countryside coterminously with the parishes and in the cities through councils and guilds.[3] The nobles, as Michael Haltzel, the historian of the Baltic Germans, documents, "received confirmation of nearly unrestricted freedom over the land," self-government, an autonomous judicial system, and the use of German in the provincial bureaucracy. The continued preeminence of Lutheranism was guaranteed by the recognition of the Augsburg Confession and the Evangelical Lutheran Landeskirche.[4]

As part of their privileges, the Baltic German elites continued to exercise harsh control over the Latvian and Estonian peasantry. In the words of a contemporary German observer, Livland was "the heaven of nobility, the paradise of the clergy, the gold mine of foreigners, and the hell of the peasants"; Treitschke described Estland similarly as "the classical land of peasant oppression."[5] Serfdom was intensified in the eighteenth century to expand the production of grain for Western European consumption. But when the limits of increased output through extensive cultivation methods were met and led only to growing social unrest, the old system found itself in a crisis.[6]

The "essential point of departure" for the disjunction of the development of Latvia and Estonia and the rest of the Romanov empire was the emancipation of the serfs in Estland in 1816, in Courland in 1817, and in Livonia in 1819, some two generations before the emancipation of the serfs in the rest of the empire.[7] By freeing serfs from the manors, the localism inherent in feudalism was undermined. Initially the results of freedom remained limited because emancipation was not accompanied by land reform or even freedom of travel. But by the end of the 1840s Baltic peasants were permitted to buy land and the passport law of 1863 legalized their freedom of mobility. The abolition of compulsory guild membership for urban craftsmen encouraged a movement to the cities, and a process of occupational differentiation commenced.[8] The favorable location of the Baltic lands, on the much traveled coastline between Germany and Russia, encouraged the construction of "a significant railroad network and large industrial concerns." The railroads, however, were financed by Russian, Baltic German, and foreign German investors;[9] and in general, the "leading positions in all branches of the economy" remained in the hands of the Baltic German aristocracy and townspeople, which now evolved an entrepreneurial bourgeois stratum.[10]

Although economic modernization set the Baltics, with the exception of the Latgalian part of Latvia, apart from the rest of the Romanov empire, Latvians and Estonians did not yet have "the consciousness of belonging to a lasting political entity." The Baltic masses were not, in the terminology of late nineteenth century political theory, a "historical nation," because they did not have native nobilities in possession of political rights and privileges that could be claimed by the putative nation-people as its birthright.[11]

The domination of the German nobility, urban guilds, and the Lutheran Church ensured the high status of German language and culture in Livland, Kurland, and Estland. The major channel of mobility—formal middle-level and higher education—could also be attained only in German-language institutions. Because the peasant languages lacked prestige, educated Latvian- or Estonian-speaking individuals in the process of upward mobility "inevitably shifted to the language of culture and rapidly became Germanized."[12] It is significant that the term *saks*, used by the peasantry in Estonia to refer to Germans was extended in the nineteenth century to include an individual of any nationality who "had more than an elementary education, spoke some German, and did not live by manual labor."[13] The process of *Volkstumwechsel* was many shaded: it included the adoption of German names among literate peasants, and many urban artisans and laborers, even when intermarrying among themselves, spoke German at home.[14]

The distinctiveness of the Baltic peoples began to be recognized only after the emancipation of the Latvian- and Estonian-speaking serfs. Ironically, the first to express interest in the native culture of the peasantry and gather its folktales and folkways were Baltic German pastors and writers. Native authors and folklorists appeared only in the 1840s.[15] Plakans still views the designation of the inhabitants of the Latvian lands as *Latvian* for the first half of the nineteenth century premature because the localized experiences of the rural people did not allow for the formation of an all-encompassing solidarity. As late as 1860 most Latvians and Estonians viewed themselves as the *Landesvolk*, the "people of the country," and even in the 1860s and 1870s "peasanthood...was seen as a hindrance to the development of the modern Latvian nation."[16] Only subsequently, and gradually, had the word *people* assumed a national connotation in the Baltics: in Latvian by incorporating the new meaning into the old term *tauta* and in Estonian by differentiating between the *rahvas* (people) and the *rahvus* (nation) or between *eesti rahvas* (Estonian people) and *maarahvas* (people of the country).[17]

The continued economic and political supremacy of the alien nobility was a main cause of the growth of national awareness among the native Baltic strata. The inhabitants of the Baltic region already began enjoying the benefits of modernization but their ability to take full advantage of it remained severely constrained by the traditional structure and privileges of the German elites. Initially, in the absence of a vigorous native bourgeois stratum, the nationalist movement had a very heterogeneous social character. The dominant occupation of Estonian patriotic agitators was primary rural school instruction, because teachers were "almost the highest social group which had not accepted the language of the ruling nation."[18]

Most patriots in the 1860–1880s had rural origins, small-craft producers and the petty bourgeoisie also participated in nationalist activities in growing numbers.19 The rural supporters of nationalism hailed from the most fertile agricultural regions (Viljandi and Viljandimaa in Estonia, the environs of Riga in Latvia, which also evolved rural manufactures or food processing and, finally, were linked with international—and in Estonia, internal—agricultural trade).[20] In Latvia, and especially in the capital, Riga, the most important town in the Baltic region, the expansion of educational institutions and government administration and later industrial development gradually created employment opportunities for a broader native intellectual stratum. Between 1862 and 1865, individuals from such backgrounds formed the Young Latvia movement, which, restricted at home by the German elite, published the first nationalist journal in St. Petersburg.[21] The first large-scale nationalist body, the Riga Latvian Association, was formed by members of the evolving bourgeoisie and professional stratum in Riga, in 1868. In general, the most modern elements in both Latvia and Estonia, whether rural or urban, provided the leadership for the peasants involved in the movement in Latvia and to a somewhat smaller extent in Estonia as well.[22]

In contrast to the Catalan and Basque nationalist movements, Baltic nationalists could not rally around the protection of ancient privileges but fought to undermine them. The control of the Baltic autonomous institutions was in the hands of culturally alien aristocracies. Baltic nationalists could not act on their own but had to wait for the challenge of the tzarist central authority to the corporate principles of the Baltic German barons. The beginnings of a broader-based Latvian and Estonian nationalism around 1880 were due to changing political relations between the tzarist authorities and the *Ritterschaften* and the attendant cultural conflicts. But, although deliverance from the hands of the foreign elites by the Russian empire was a bright promise, it also implied a threat of new controls by yet another alien elite. A *three-way struggle* of emerging nationalities restricted the options of the Baltic nationalities and constrained the development of their national awareness.

The Russification of the western borderlands was carried out as part of the modernization of the empire and encompassed administrative and cultural reforms that sought to increase at once the political and cultural homogeneity of the empire. A multifaceted policy of Russification that encroached on Polish and German rights and undermined the privileged position of the Livland, Estland, Courland, and Russian-annexed Poland (of which Lithuania was part) provinces within the Russian empire began to be implemented already in the reign of Catherine II. Catherine's own centralizing reforms, however, have been to a large extent premature.[23] Even subsequent tzars were at times reluctant to press their policy of bringing the Baltic regions under their direct rule because of the fear that without the continued control of the German nobility and the Lutheran Church the Baltic peasantry would become restless. Frequently, therefore intended changes were suspended or carried out half-heartedly.

The Estonian and Latvian populations were targeted by two separate and antithetical drives of cultural homogenization: a weaker and unplanned drive for Germanization and a powerful Russification backed up by the resources of the tzarist authorities. The nobility on its part, having a culture distinct from the peasantry's, could not mobilize the culture and language of its subjects as a barrier against the centralizing drive of tzarist absolutism but enjoyed the mostly spontaneous "Germanization" of socially mobile natives. When some Baltic German leaders in Estonia called for an organized Germanizing drive in the 1860s it turned out to be counterproductive and further spurred Estonian nationalism and Slavophile reaction.[24] A debate between a leading publicist of the Slavophile movement Yuri Samarin, who wrote a six-volume study of the Baltic region, and the *Ritterschaften*, defended by Carl Schirren, a professor of history at the German-language Dorpat University (today Tartu University), erupted publicly in the late 1860s. Samarin warned of the danger of the peasantry's Germanization and demanded that the imperial government stop its vacillation and countermand the perceived threat by making Russian the language of instruction in the Baltic schools and by extending the tzarist legal and administrative system into the region. Schirren's *Livländische Antwort* called for steadfastness in face of Samarin's call to arrogate the *Ritterschaft*'s ancestral inheritance.[25] The Baltic Germans, on their part, attempted "to bend slightly with the wind [of reform], but at the same time essentially [sought] to preserve old privileges."[26]

Caught between the Baltic German anvil and the Russian hammer the Estonian nationalists were split and had to settle on moderate aims. One group, led by Johannes Jannsen and Jakob Hurt, viewed continuous German hegemony as inevitable and, therefore, saw "the Estonian mission in the cultural rather than in the political realm." Another group, led by Johann Köler and Carl R. Jakobson, sought equal representation of Estonians and Germans in the, until now, German-run institutions and set its store in tzarist intervention. Among the activities of the nationalists were the creation of school systems (e.g., the Estonian Alexander School movement), publication of newspapers in the native tongues, organization of large-scale song festivals, and temperance organizations. These were secular cultural institutions and the Lutheran churches of Latvia and Estonia played no role in fanning the sparks of nationalism. The reason was the lack of Latvian and Estonian native-born religious elites, because "the Lutheran Church remained a German institution until the twentieth century, and it appears to have been perceived as an alien one by the local people, both in its structure and religious content."[27] The Baltic Lutheran churches became "native" only after national independence was achieved.[28]

When, finally, in the 1870s and the 1880s a small native bourgeois stratum began playing an important role together with the other strata in the Latvian and Estonian nationalist movements, its demands, expressed in petitions that originated in Latvian and Estonian towns, to the tzarist authorities in 1880–1881, were the consolidation of Latvian and Estonian speakers, who were divided into the administrative regions of Kurland, Livland, and Estland, into two districts (to be called Riga and Reval, Tallinn's German name). In addition, it was demanded that the provincial diets be replaced with zemstvos elected in a more equitable fashion and election to city council not be based on unequal voting rights. It was requested that lower level administrators be supplied by the native populations, clergymen chosen by the peasantry, and the native tongues used for instruction. Finally, the nationalists requested the improvement of the peasantry's economic conditions through the clarification of their rights vis-à-vis the German landowners.[29] In short, Baltic nationalist leaders demanded the geographical unification and freeing of the motley upwardly mobile Baltic strata from the political and economic domination of the German *Ritterschaft* and urban entrepreneurs.

This quest was partially successful when the tzar implemented demands in those areas in which the empowerment of the Baltic peoples simultaneously strengthened the central authority; for example, in increasing Russian subjects in the elementary schools or introducing municipal councils to the larger towns in which Latvians and Estonians were able to gain a majority.[30] The call for redrawing the administrative boundaries, which would have amounted to the recognition of the principle of national self-determination as an organizational framework within the empire, was ignored by the tzar.[31]

The unification of Germany further increased the desire of the Russian government to deepen its hold in the borderlands and its willingness to assail the *Ritterschaften*.[32] Already in 1832, the Lutheran Church lost its favored status and became a "tolerated church." In 1877, tax-paying Estonians, Latvians, and Russians were allowed to vote in the elections for municipal councils, and in 1889 the Russian judicial system was incorporated into the Baltic legal system.[33] The Russian language replaced German in police, justice, and municipal institutions in the mid-1880s. The study of Russian was made compulsory in all elementary public and private schools and later the language of instruction for all subjects except religion.[34] By the reigns of Alexander III and Nikolai II much of the *Ritterschaften's* privileges were in tatters. In short, in the process of centralizing the Romanov empire, the German cultural enclave in the Baltics was cracked open and the political privileges of the German nobility were eroded.

Baltic nationalism originated out of the early economic modernization that set the region apart from the empire and was fostered in the limited space created by the mutually hostile political and cultural conflicts between the German elites and the tzarist regime. But their involvement in a three-way struggle considerably moderated the Latvian and Estonian nationalist movements and weakened their influence. Both Latvian and Estonian nationalist movements sought increased representation within their provinces, maybe a federated empire, but always remained loyal to the tzarist regime. As a result of these compounded obstacles, Raun and Plakans concluded that Estonian nationalism remained "pre-eminently a cultural phenomenon throughout most of its existence" and observed that its "maximum political goal before 1917 was autonomy, not independence."[35] With minor variations, these observations apply to Latvia as well.

The weakness of the urban bourgeois stratum in the leadership of Latvian and Estonian nationalism did not permit it to secure a hegemony of local political life. The class differentiation of Latvian and Estonian societies began at a time when nationalism was still in the process of gaining ground. In both Latvia and Estonia, socialist movements emerged in the very early years of the twentieth century led by a radicalized intelligentsia and not particularly favorable toward the nationalist movements. The Baltic socialists either accepted the internationalist premises of the Russian Social Democratic Party, or were willing to be satisfied with autonomy within a free Russian state.[36]

During the 1905 and 1917 Revolutions, Latvia and Estonia, underwent their own socialist revolutions, aimed at curtailing the remaining German baronic privileges. In 1905, for example, "Latvia was the most revolutionary part of the empire in terms of the ratio of strikers to total number of workers."[37] Estonia, likewise, experienced a revolutionary upheaval, pitting moderate versus radical socialist. National assemblies in Estonia and Latvia demanded autonomy whether within a reformed empire or in a transformed empire.[38] A Lithuanian National Congress also sought regional autonomy. No demands for outright independence were voiced.

The same experience repeated itself and the same demands surfaced during the February and October 1917 Revolutions. On March 30, 1917, the provisional government united the provinces of Estland and northern Livland to create, for the first time, the political entity of Estonia. Estonia was granted regional autonomy under a provincial assembly, the Maapäev, and the right to set up separate Estonian military units. An autonomous Latvian province was also proclaimed.[39] The aim of the Estonian parties was that "Estonia should become part of democratic Russian federation," but toward the end of the year other options were examined. These options included "a non-Bolshevik Russian federation, a Scandinavian alliance, a Finnish-Estonian union, and an independent Estonia."[40]

The conquest of parts of Latvia by opposing Russian and German forces intensified the dissolution of the old regime. Latvian Bolshevik groups proclaimed a soviet in the part of Latvia occupied by the Russian forces, while a national assembly declared independence in November 1917. The conquest of the Russian-dominated area by the Germans and the latter's attempt to set up puppet regimes in the areas ceded by the Bolsheviks in the Brest-Litovsk treaty allowed the creation of a provisional Latvian government in November 1918.[41] A committee of the Estonian Maapäev in February 1918, on the eve of German occupation, declared Estonian independent to make a potentially Russian-German bilateral conflict into an international concern.[42]

Only after Germany's collapse could real independence be attempted.[43] As late as 1919, Latvian rifle regiments of the Red Army fought against Latvian nationalist forces and after their defeat preferred to go to exile in the USSR.44 The effective attainment of independence lead through additional military conflict with German and Russian forces, and in 1920 the three new republics signed peace treaties with the USSR that renounced any claim to their territories.

As this brief historical sketch suggests, the independence of the Baltic republics (and even the creation of Estonia) were not inevitable but, perhaps, a last resort. The aim of even the more radical wings of the nationalist movements was to limit the traditional authority of the German Baltic barons and urban elites with the help of the modernizing Russian authorities and attain regional autonomy within the empire. As long as they were dominated by the German Baltic baronial and urban elite indeed Baltic nationalists needed the Russian countervailing power to free themselves. Only much later, after the Bolshevik regime did the Baltic peoples the service of delivering them from the Germans elites (establishing themselves in their place), could Baltic nationalist think of ridding themselves of the Soviets as well.

Baltic independence then was not a deeply rooted demand of a nationalist movement of independence or its creation, but the result of the intense competition between Germany and Russia over the Baltics, "the simultaneous collapse of the Russian and German empires" during the First World War, and the relatively quick radicalization of the nationalist movement through the catastrophes of war and revolution. This processes moved them from the demand for "a free Baltic in a free Russia" in March 1917[45] to, by years end, a demand for independence.

This process, however, drew on the historical development of the Baltic peoples to form them into relatively compact and modern solidarity groups, which started in the middle of the nineteenth century. Their wars of independence and twenty years of independent statehood have strengthened these sentiments. Their nationalists did not, however, attain the sustained intellectual and moral leadership we associate with hegemony over the German elites or the socialist parties before independence.

Baltic independence, however, radically changed the power relations among the local ethnic groups. Both Germans and Russians lost their predominance, the former by losing control over local administration and the latter through the departure of the Russian state. The German elite furthered suffered from the loss of its estates to land reform.[46] Together with other non-Latvian and non-Estonian groups they were transformed into ethnic or national minorities.

In Estonia the minorities made up 12.4 percent of the population in 1922; of these 8.2 percent were Russian, 1.7 percent German, 0.7 percent Swedish, 0.4 percent Jewish, and another 1.4 percent of other smaller groups. Latvian minorities composed 73.4 percent of the population in 1925; again the largest minority was the Russian that made up 12.6 percent of Latvia's population, followed by 5.2 percent Jewish, 3.8 percent German, 2.8 percent Polish, 1.3 percent Lithuanian, and an additional 1 percent of smaller minorities.[47] Estonia and Latvia were just two of the many successor states to address the problem of national minorities in the context of their constitutional deliberations and negotiations to join the League of Nations. Of these countries Estonia adopted the most liberal of the minority policies and maintained it relatively intact until the Second World War. Latvia's minority policy was more traditional and came under siege in the 1930s. Its application was undermined by an aggressive corporatist nationalist policy.

Both the Latvian and Estonian constitutions guaranteed equal rights to all citizens regardless of nationality. The Latvian minorities were allowed to establish and administer schools in their languages and did so under the auspices of the Latvian Ministry of Culture. The director of the minority educational administration were given the status of civil servants, and the director of the German administration was appointed Secretary of State in the Ministry of Culture.

Baltic Germans also attained the recognition of an autonomous German language university, the Herder Institute.[48]

The Estonian approach evolved in two stages. In 1918, the minority rights of territorially concentrated minorities, the Swedes and most of the Russians, were recognized and ensured through the establishment of local autonomous self-governments. In the February 5, 1925, Law for Cultural Self-Government for National Minorities, the needs of dispersed minorities, Germans, Jews, and the rest of the Russians were addressed. Inspired by the nationalist theorists of Austrian socialism, Otto Bauer and Karl Renner, the territorial dimension of nationalism was deemphasized in favor of personal or nonterritorial autonomy as a consequence of which any group of more than 3,000 individuals was empowered to constitute itself as a public corporation and establish its cultural institutions.[49] Estonian Germans and Jews registered as national minorities and elected their cultural councils and set up their cultural self-governments in 1925 and 1926, respectively. These bodies ran cultural institutions as well as elementary and secondary schools in their language; the compulsory elementary schools were financed exclusively by the state and local governments, and the secondary schools were subsidized by them. The Cultural Council also had the right to promulgate decrees within its areas of competence, tax its members, and draw funds for its activities from the governments's cultural budget.[50] There were no such bodies in Latvia but the unofficial Baltic German national community's executive council fulfilled similar functions.[51]

Estonian cultural autonomy was based on the explicit and far-reaching willingness of the majority to support the education of all minorities in their own national languages and under the auspices of the minorities' own elected representatives. In this respect it was "an exemplary solution"[52] to the problems of minorities that took the requirements of the League of Nations for the protection of minorities to their logical conclusion. The goal of the League's policy was the preservation of the minority's distinctiveness and the creation of the conditions for its unhindered cultural reproduction, which would in any case happen if it were the majority in its own state.

But the Estonian minority law had an unusual aspect that instead of fixing the boundaries of the minorities kept them open and instead of tethering their culture allowed for its evolution.[53] Membership in the minority's cultural self-government was voluntary and every individual had to ask for his or her name to be entered in its Nationality Register. According to the Estonian policy "the Cultural

Self-Government was granted to the individual citizens of the Republic who had their particular interests, rather than to a national minority as a closed group."[54] This individualistic approach allowed for the integration and eventual assimilation of minority members who so wished into Estonian culture and society. In this fashion the Estonian constitution and Law of Cultural Self-Government departed from the corporate approach of the minority protection policies and by leaving the choice of nationality to the individuals concerned, without coercing them either to belong or not to belong to a minority, showed a willingness to accept them in a fashion that is typical to hegemonic forms of nationalism. There is no indication, however, of the central tenet of multiculturalism to require changes in the dominant culture so that it can meet the minority cultures part way.

The adoption of the law in February 1925 followed closely on the heels of a failed Communist coup "which impressed on Estonians generally the need to muster support among all sections of the community interested in the maintenance of the young republic."[55] The common defense of the republic and its democracy had served as the foundation for bringing together the host society and the immigrant groups in Catalonia and the Basque country during the Franco regime. But less than a decade later both in Estonia and Latvia the democratic regimes were replaced by the authoritarian presidential regimes of Päts and Ulmanis, respectively. In both cases, the aim of the leaders was to preempt fascist putsches and in both the rights of minorities were curtailed. In Latvia minority school autonomy was abolished and, under the slogan Latvia for the Latvians, the Ulmanis regime display much of the same aggressive nationalist tendencies propagated by the proscribed Thundercross Association and encouraged the displacement of minority members, especially Jews, from Latvian economic and professional life. In Estonia, by contrast, the scope of cultural self-administration and education were limited but not abolished.[56] Minority members also were prevented from being employed in Estonian educational institutions or rise above the rank of corporal in its armed forces.[57] In the absence of the democratic framework minorities were particularly vulnerable.

National Flourishing and Convergence

The Soviet Nationalities Policy

While Russia's two neighboring multiethnic empires, the Hapsburg and Ottoman empires, were dismantled as a consequence of the

First World War, the energizing potential of the Russian Revolution made it possible—and the desire to be protected from the use of the outlying nationalities' territories as staging grounds for counter revolution made it imperative—for the Bolsheviks to revive and restructure the disintegrating Romanov empire. The USSR nationalities policy was based on Lenin's formulation on the eve of the war and Stalin's reformulations and practices.[58] This policy reflected the difficulty of reconciling, in Carrère d'Encausse's words, "the same dilemma that bedeviled the empire: consciousness of a common destiny, on the one hand, and national aspirations, on the other."[59]

The nationalities policy as it came to be formulated under Lenin has consisted of two, carefully balanced but potentially contradictory, parts. This policy was predicated on the recognition of the existence of nationalities within the USSR and legitimized their distinctiveness. On the eve of the USSR's dissolution there were fifty-three territorial administrations based on designated ethnic homelands: fifteen union republics, twenty autonomous republics, eight autonomous oblasts, and ten autonomous okrugs.[60] When pondering Lenin and the Bolsheviks' willingness to accept the legitimacy of the national principle we should keep in mind the considerable influence of that principle on the eve of, during, and after the First World War. The Bolsheviks shared an appreciation of the strength of movements of national self-determination with President Woodrow Wilson and his Fourteen Point Plan.

The geographical spread of Marxist ideas from the relatively homogenous nation-states of Western and Central Europe to the multiethnic Hapsburg and Romanov empires of Eastern Europe demanded a Marxist analysis of the national question. Lenin recognized the oppressive character of Great Russian nationalism as well as the relevance of national aspirations to the dismantling the Romanov empire and, therefore, expressed his support for the flourishing (rastsvet) of all national groups.[61] The geographical layout of the Soviet Union—with Russia at its core and the non-Russian nationalities surrounding it in a gigantic arc, spreading from the Baltic, via Belorussia, the Ukraine, and the Caucasus to Central Asia, with each group concentrated in a relatively distinct territory—meant that national flourishing required a federal principle. The structure of the Soviet state was consequently "formally shaped along ethnic lines."[62] Graham Smith argues convincingly that "in Lenin's 'federal compromise,' which granted territorially-based administrative status and limited cultural autonomy to...[the] union republic nationalities the

Soviet state set itself on a specific trajectory of having to continue to accommodate national aspirations."[63]

The long-term aim of the Bolsheviks, however, was not to preserve national differences but to gradually eliminate them by creating the conditions under which distinct groups were to shed their distinct characteristics and undergo a two-step process of convergence. In the first stage the goal was the equalization of the standard of living among the different nationalities through a policy that favored the development of the less industrialized regions, thus leading to social homogeneity (sblizhenie).[64] At a second stage the rise of the new Soviet man and woman was envisaged through the merging or fusion of nationalities through the homogenization of their cultures (sliyanie).[65] Since the mid-1970s the latter goal was expected to be realized only in the distant future. The fragile balance between the flourishing and convergence of the nationalities of the USSR was articulated in Stalin's formula "national in form, socialist in content," which offered national autonomy in cultural affairs within the overall parameters of Soviet state interests.[66] The alleged synthesis actually comprised conflicting centrifugal and centripetal tendencies in the spheres of social, cultural, political, and economic life. The Soviet nationalities policy in essence reproduced the ethnic divisions of the Soviet Union while aiming at their elimination.[67]

The pursuit of such contrary aims was not the exclusive preserve of the USSR but there the state-building interests and Great Russian nationalism have frequently upset the fragile equilibrium intended in the original nationalities policy, and in the lack of countervailing institutions, there was no possibility of readjusting their balance. The flourishing (rastsvet) of the nationalities and their equalization, convergence, and homogenization (sblizhenie), as we shall see in this section, found their organized expressions in mutually hostile bodies and produced discrepant results.

This contradictory policy also made a decisive contribution to the rapidity with which the USSR collapsed. Past empires, including the Hapsburg and Ottoman empires, lingered for decades or centuries while they declined or even crumbled, the Soviet one was gone with astonishing swiftness. Whereas dynastic empires were recognized as hodge-podge conglomerations in which the different territories were attached to the emperor with radically different bonds, modern states promoted and relied on cultural homogeneity to ensure the solidarity of their citizenry. The USSR sought to employ the Marxist-Leninist ideology as the unifying, or homogenizing, principle of legitimation

(and the Communist Party as its organizational tool) for its heterogeneous population. But the high degree of solidarity and uniformity
required by the Soviet regime and ideology violated the diversity of
interests rooted in the heterogeneity of the "empire's" regions and
peoples. The fusion of the principles of empire and nation building
was proven not possible.

I will scrutinize separately their contradictory results in the
spheres of culture, politics, and the economy. In the sphere of *culture*,
the universalist ideology itself was frequently subverted by a Russian
nationalism that continued tzarist practices of "official nationalism"
and forced assimilation in a variety of ways. Russianization was aimed
at persuading or coercing the members of other nationalities to learn
Russian, and more demanding Russification drives sought to impose
not only the Russian language but also Russian cultural, political, and
economic interests.[68] Even so, it was only under Khrushchev that "for
the first time the Russian language was officially thrust into the role
of the primary language of all the Soviet peoples."[69] Although this
policy remained tentative for some time, starting in the late 1960s, all-
union conferences and school reforms aimed at expanding and im-
proving proficiency in Russian throughout the USSR. The 1984 school
reform went as far as requiring the teaching of Russian in first grade
and kindergarten.[70]

As a result, there has been a systematic expansion in the percentage of most members of the eponymous nationalities who
reported to speak Russian as a second language. For example, a comparison of the censuses of 1970 and 1979 reveals that the percentage
of Latvians who reported using Russian fluently as a second language
within their republic increased from 45.2 to 56.7. Although the
percentage of Russian-speaking Estonians was reported to have fallen
from 29 to 24.2 percent in the same period,[71] there seems to be an
agreement, however, that this decline is most likely due to their
unwillingness to admit to knowledge of Russian.[72] The influence of
such factors on statistical results does not inspire confidence in the
rest of the numbers, especially in light of the difficulty, which we
already encountered in Catalonia and Euskadi, of finding a reliable
measure of "bilingualism." Self-reported speaking fluency is at best a
vague indicator and at worst an open call for overrepresentation (and,
correspondingly, underrepresentation).

We might find some comfort in a study of bilingual Russians in
Moldavia that acknowledges the need to carefully subdivide speakers
with different levels of knowledge. The Moldavian study observed

that if one counts among bilingual speakers not just fluent speakers but also those who speak it "fairly well," "with some difficulty," and "with great difficulty" the size of the group would increase fivefold.[73] There is no telling, however, whether the same conservative definition was applied in the case of Baltic bilinguals. Ability to write in Russian would serve as a more rigorous test and a far better indicator of the ability to put the knowledge to use in an industrial society. The fact that with minor exceptions the spread of Russian among most the nationalities of all the union republics was reported to have "proceeded at a relatively uniform rate,"[74] with the exception of Estonians in 1979, might also indicate bureaucratic rather than sociological logic in operation.

But even given these doubts, in comparable terms Latvians were reported to have the second largest percentage of fluent Russian speakers, almost on par with Belorussians (57 percent bilinguals), and higher than the percentage of Russian speakers in the Ukraine (49.8 percent bilinguals). The 1989 census results for Latvia further increased the percent of Latvian Russian speakers to 65.7 percent and put Latvia ahead of even Belorussia, where bilingualism was put at 60.4 percent.[75] Undoubtedly, this extraordinary level of Russian knowledge was a reflection of the influence and high concentration of Russians in the republic. Estonians in 1970 and 1979 were somewhere in the middle of the pack.

Cultural assimilation, however, was just one aspect of the Soviet nationalities policy. In spite of these efforts the native languages of the union republics occupied a relatively secure place in the educational and cultural life of the various republics. Neither Russianization nor Russification seem to have undermined the native languages of the union republics. Children in elementary and secondary schools in the union republics were allowed a choice between native-language schools, Russian-language schools, or mixed-language schools. Russian children and children from other nationalities usually attend the Russian-anguage schools, whereas children of the eponymous nationalities attended the schools in which the native tongue was the language of instruction. In the mixed schools of the USSR, the majority of which had been located in Latvia, the joint activities of children were reported to be truly bilingual, in contrast to many other republics where they were held in Russian.[76]

Most significant, the percentage of the eponymous nationalities who regarded Estonian and Latvian as its native, or first, tongue has stayed around 99 percent. Correspondingly, only 1.0 percent of the

Estonians and 2.1 percent of the Latvians regarded Russian as their first language in 1979. Latvians and Estonians were not different in this respect from the other union republic nationalities; in fact, among only the Ukrainians and the Belorussians had the rate declined below 90 percent by 1979.[77]

The Baltic peoples have certainly done much better than the Basques in retaining their language and even better than the Catalans. Not only has the knowledge and use of the Baltic tongues remained relatively unaffected by the incorporation of the Baltic republics into the USSR, the linguistic character of the three Baltic languages also reveals only "a surprisingly low number of borrowings from Russian."[78] The reasons, in Kreindler's view, were that the Baltic languages already had achieved full "functional" or "sociological completeness" during the years of independence, when they served the needs of a modern state and society and, furthermore, were used as the language of instruction from elementary to higher education. This development means that Baltic language speakers did not need Russian as an intermediary language when borrowing international terms.[79]

In Misiunas and Taagepera's estimation from the early 1980s the "utterly limited political autonomy" of the Baltic republics sharply contrasted with their "very real cultural autonomy." They conclude that by making full use of these cultural opportunities the Baltic nations "extended appreciably their historical depth," as compared to the 1940s.[80] The ability of the Baltic languages to "clearly hold... their own against Russian,"[81] it seems, is the combined result of their relatively advanced economies and corresponding educational systems, as in Catalonia, and also of the relatively effective guarantee of cultural autonomy under the Soviet nationalities policy.

A further aspect of the federal organization of the USSR that allowed the retention and development of non-Russian cultures was the policy of "indigenization" (*korenizatsiya*). As part of this policy, the attainment of high status and corresponding social mobility, without assimilation into the Russian culture, was made available for a segment of the native-language-speaking population. The provision of education in the native language of the eponymous nationality, as well as the creation of research institutions and republican academies, "has resulted in the demand for a large native intelligentsia equipped to read and speak the native language."[82] It has been argued that for the populations of some of the less-developed republics the policy of indigenization amounted to large-scale "affirmative action" programs or even quota systems.[83] In the relatively overdeveloped Baltic republics such policies were unnecessary, even during the years of Stalinist terror "the schools continued to produce and train a native intelligentsia in the native language."[84]

Although the implications of the statistics of language retention, bilingualism, and native language education are relatively clear, for example, for the creation of a republican cultural elite stratum, we have a serious difficulty in evaluating the extent of the Baltic nationalities' measure of autonomy in the sphere of *politics*. Because the Soviet leadership frequently appointed party leaders from one nationality into the institutions of other nationalities, a favorite preoccupation of Sovietologists had been the study of the ethnic composition of the Communist Party and the political bodies of the union republics as an indicator of their "self-administration."

Hodnett evolved a four-level scale of "native occupancy score" in "all leading" positions within the union republics. He reported that the Baltic republics, together with the Ukraine and Uzbekistan, fall in the category of "largely self-administering" republics (with 75–89 percent native occupancy), just below the "self-administering" category (score of 90–100 percent) that includes Armenia, Georgia, and Azerbaijan, but above the "partly self-administering" republics (score 50–74 percent) that includes Tadzhikistan, Belorussia, Turkmenistan, and Kirgizia, and the "administered" category (0–49 percent) that includes Kazakhstan and Moldavia.[85] He found that membership in the Communist Party as a percentage of the republic's population in 1970 also puts Estonia and Latvia in the top group (third and fourth, respectively).[86]

It would seem that Baltic nationalities were well represented in the political institutions of their republics. These percentages, however, do not distinguish between the participation of the eponymous and immigrant populations in the republic's Communist Party; if it included only the share of the former, Latvia's and Estonia's place on the scale would probably be lower. Another important distinction ignored in these numbers is between Latvians and Estonians who were born in their republic and those who reimmigrated from the USSR when their respective republics were reannexed to the USSR and are better seen as representing not the local people vis-à-vis the central authorities but rather the unifying designs of the central authorities. In Latvia and Estonia the percentage of Russified Latvians and "Yestonians" (so-called because of their different inflection of Estonian) in position of power was relatively high for many years.[87]

A more serious problem, however, is that the very meaning of these statistics remains unclear. For example, even where the First Secretary of the republic's Communist Party was a member of the eponymous nationality, he frequently had a Second Secretary, usually from Russian stock, to watch over him. In general, the political institutions of the union republics were designed not to represent but to control the eponymous nationalities. This should come as no surprise because these institutions were always dominated by the Communist Party, which was the main mechanism of centralization in the USSR. The union republics that "ostensibly guarantee minorities the framework for national self-determination and expression" did so "only within the overall parameters of Soviet state interests,"[88] and therefore, their sociological features need to be evaluated within a broader political context. The study of mere statistical distributions overlooks questions of power and its locus.

What can then we say then with some measure of confidence in regard to the political representation of the Baltic nationalities? First, although very little real power seems to have resided on the level of the union republics, the latter's very existence provided institutional barriers to the process of Russification and Russianization. In contrast, institutions that had a centralized rather than federal framework, such as the military where the Russian language was used exclusively, were instruments of control and cultural homogenization.[89]

Second, the framework of the territorially based union republic served to protect, even if tenuously, the legitimate existence of its eponymous nationality and facilitate its national existence. Union republics were, therefore, privileged in contrast to the nonterritorial nationalities of the USSR, such as the Jews and Germans, many of whom, though among the most assimilated groups in the USSR, have chosen emigration as a means of ensuring their individual and collective rights. Yet other groups, such as the Crimean Tatars, who have less clearly defined territorial bases and institutional frameworks, are well aware of being thereby disadvantaged and try to attain a territorially anchored political framework to provide them the protection afforded other nationalities.[90]

Third, within the republic's own institutions a political elite—a cadre of professional experts and leaders with the experience to run the affairs of their republic—was always available. In contrast, in the military, another centralized institution, no such cadre was formed. Like in the other unifying institutions of the USSR, the military had a clear ethnic stratification: the officer corps dominated by Russians,

Ukrainians overrepresented among noncommissioned officers, and the Slavic groups overrepresented in the technically more modern and strategically important branches.[91]

These conclusions, however, reflect only the relatively static differences between centralized and federal institutions. Important changes in the relationship of the central and republican authorities also occurred over time, especially in the Brezhnev era. Paradoxically, the economic stagnation of the Brezhnev years was paid for, in part, by the higher indigenization of appointments to republic-level administrative and political positions. In return for security of status and more extensive regional autonomy, the regional political class underwrote stability, when necessary even through the vigorous repression of dissidence such as in Lithuania and the Ukraine during the 1980–1981 Polish crisis. This tradeoff enhanced the power of the local cadres—in fact, some observers went as far as arguing that this era saw the formation of republic-level "networks of feuds and mafias" by the elites—but not yet of their peoples.[92]

In both the cultural and political spheres, the Soviet nationalities policy led to the formation and continuous replenishment of elite strata for whom the effective framework of reference was their republic's territory.

An examination of Soviet *economic development* plans again demonstrates the self-contradictory character of the Soviet nationalities policy founded on the recognition and cultivation of national differences with the aim of encouraging their elimination. We can best follow the evolution, accomplishments, and shortcomings of this policy through an examination of the regional dimension of subsequent Five Year Plans.

The planners of industrial development in the Soviet Union inherited a western regional emphasis.[93] Although the third Five-Year Plan intended to move from "concentrated" to "complex development"—that is, to establish the most basic branches of industry, such as local fuel and electrical power production, and self-sufficiency in construction materials, consumer goods and foodstuffs, in each region[94]—only the loss of the more developed regions of western Russia (the "Old West") to the Nazi occupiers during the Second World War brought about the development of the hitherto backward eastern regions: the Urals, Western Siberia, parts of Central Asia (the so-called Near East). The fourth Five-Year Plan of 1945–1950 sought to build on this expanded, though only partially developed, heavy industrial base. "Of the projects announced in the plan, proportionately more seemed to concern the eastern areas of the RSFSR and the Central Asian Republics."[95] Still, one half of the planned all-union investment was used for the reconstruction of plants destroyed in the western areas previously occupied by the Nazis, and some new plants were also built there.

In fact, neither the regional nor the overall 1945–1950 targets were met.[96] The eastern regions declined relative to their position during the war, but western reconstruction also was only partially accomplished. The exceptions were found in the unoccupied areas of the RSFSR and in the Baltic and Caucasian republics where "output targets for 1950 were comfortably surpassed."[97] Specifically, "the output of the new areas [i.e., the Baltic States, right-bank Moldavia, and the westernmost oblasts of the Ukraine and Belorussia] that had been incorporated into the USSR [during the Second World War] expanded by more than five times over the plan period." In Dunmore's view, the reason for the western emphasis in general and for the construction of new plants in the Baltic states in particular is to be attributed to the nationalities policy; that is, the desire to placate the potential opposition in the newly annexed territories to the loss of their independence.[98] During the period 1950–1953, that is, in the first part of the fifth Five-Year Plan, the same areas, including the Baltic republics and Moldavia but also the past-occupied areas of the Ukraine and Belorussia, again experienced the greatest industrial growth; this time, however, even though they "received rather less than their planned share of USSR capital investment funds."[99]

Why were the aims of regional redistribution from "Old West" to "Near East" and for "complex development" of all regions not carried out, and why did some western regions, especially the Baltic republics, enjoy disproportionate development? Dunmore's overall explanation is that investment yielded high returns only where qualified workers and construction materials were available, as in the Baltic republics and in the areas of the Ukraine and Belorussia liberated from the Nazis, whereas their shortage in Central Asia and Kazakhstan reduced economic growth.[100]

When faced with the conflicting demands of maximizing output and redistributing the productive forces among the republics of the USSR, the ministries "generally chose to maximize the output of the branch to fulfil their own plans rather than of particular regions for which some other organization (a party organ or Gosplan department) was responsible."[101] In short, the structure of Soviet administrative machine, because of its centralized structure—"organized along functional and branch rather than regional lines"—had a "built-in bias" against effective regional planning. In consequence the union-level ministries "directed these towards the areas that yielded most rapid returns in a bid to maximize branch rather than regional output,"[102] even when the political or planning agencies had different, regionally focused, goals. The reasons for higher short-term yields in the Baltic republics and some of the other areas, as we have seen, was due to their industrial experience, infrastructure, closeness to major population centers, and lower transportation costs. Ironically, the centralization of the Soviet economy furthered Baltic economic development.

When the Soviet economy was growing apace, as studies undertaken in the 1970s—of Komsomol youth by Grossman and of modernization by Graham Smith in Latvia and Shryock in the three Baltic republics—indicate, Baltic national sentiment was invested in Soviet economic development not in separation from it. Pride in industrial development became an important element of Baltic national consciousness. Economic development based on the integration of Latvia into the Soviet economy was an important vehicle for the integration of Latvia and Latvians into the USSR.[103] Grossman expected that "the vast reserves of Latvian national pride and effort in its industrial sphere" would further conform themselves to this integration. Rapid industrial modernization that has differentiated Latvia from the other parts of the USSR, Smith and Shryock judged, enhanced Baltic national pride.[104] We should not with the help of hindsight disregard this period of at least partial accommodation between Baltic national aspirations and Soviet economic growth. In a survey of ethnic relations in the USSR in early 1980s, Zaslavsky added that though, "the Baltic republics have always been considered the stronghold of ethnic nationalism in the Soviet Union...in fact... the Baltic example demonstrates how the Soviet regime manages to neutralize the nationalist threat by means of the centrally planned economy, federalism, and the passport system."[105] Much of the waning of separatist sentiment that Zaslavsky noted was due to the unabating repression Balts experienced under Soviet rule, but some of it, as other observers also noted, resulted from the continuous development of the Baltic economies and in the case of Lithuania from the industrialization of its economy.

And yet, the benefits accruing to the Baltic economies within the USSR were limited by another aspect of economic centralization. Economic production in the USSR, in a simplified fashion, was directed and supervised within one of three frameworks: by all-union ministries located in Moscow, which exercised direct control over enterprises all over the USSR; by identically named union and republican ministries, which were expected to share the responsibility for decisions but in fact the former retained predominant authority; and by republican ministries. The former two were in charge of the industries whose products were used throughout the USSR, the third, of products and services with a local clientele.[106]

By bifurcating the republic's economy into competing all-union and republican sectors, this control pattern reproduced the division between the Soviet state-building interest and a multiplicity of national interests and, therefore, was a fertile ground for the reinforcement and reproduction of republic-level elite strata and of peripheral nationalism.

Economic Bifurcation

The two economic sectors may be differentiated at least according to seven criteria. Their considerable overlapping reinforces the pattern of sectoral separation.

Bifurcation of Control. The management of industrial production was divided between all-union and republican ministries. This partition with few exceptions remained lopsided, for example, in 1956, the Moscow ministries were responsible for 90 percent of Latvia's industrial production. The centralized control over the republic's economies was interrupted only during Khrushchev's Thaw, when industrial production and construction were reorganized under the *sovnarkhozy* (regional economic councils).[107] As part of the new system the Estonian sovnarkhoz assumed charge over 80 percent of its industrial output, while all-union ministries retained control of only 3 percent of Latvia's production.[108] With the abolition of the *sovnarkhozy*, joint union-republic (so-called state-union) ministries were allocated the lion's share of control but, in fact, the economy was covertly recentralized by transferring effective control back to the all-union level without abolishing the republican ministries.

By 1971, all-union ministries regained control of 34 percent of Latvia's industrial production, and union-republican ministries retained 56 percent of the industries, leaving only 10 percent in the charge of Latvian ministries.[109] In Estonia, 90 percent of the enterprises was under union and union-republic ministries, and only 10 percent was left in local hands.[110] One reason for the massive centralization of control over industrial production was the extraordinarily central role of military production in the Soviet economy. It was estimated that about 40 percent of Estonian industry was tied to the Soviet military-industrial complex, and in Latvia, where heavy industry is more advanced than in Estonia, the rate must be even higher.[111]

In 1989, the share of republic-controlled enterprises in the Baltic republics was as low as 6–9 percent, and in no republic did it achieve 10 percent.[112] This division created a local economic elite, a managerial cadre, but systematically frustrated its desire to assume direction of a substantial portion of the republic's economy.

Bifurcation of Industries. Most heavy industry, such as machinery or energy production, and all the major enterprises, such as the huge Lenin Engine State-Union (Dvigatel) Plant in Riga, were under the responsibility of the all-union and union-republic ministries, while light and food industries, services, and so forth were the charge of the republican ministries.[113] The belief of the Soviet planners in the benefits of scale led to the creation of large-scale enterprises throughout the USSR in which ethnic bifurcation was further magnified. The average labor force of these enterprises was in excess of 800 workers, and it was estimated that over one third of the products in the USSR's industrial output was manufactured by a single enterprise.[114] Consequently, all-union enterprises tended to be more labor intensive and larger in scale than the locally controlled firms and increased the number of Slavic immigrants and their concentration.

Ethnic Bifurcation. Data from the Soviet censuses already presented give clear indication of the ethnic composition of the populations of Estonia and Latvia in Chapter 2. To recapitulate (see Table 2.6), in 1989 the percentage of Estonians in Estonia was 61.5 and of Latvians in Latvia, 52 percent. This division is closely associated with the patterns of industrial bifurcation we observed.

A recent study reveals that in Central Asia and the Baltic republics the share of the eponymous nationality was lower in the industrial labor force than in the republics's population. The share of Estonians, who make up 61.5 percent of their republic's population, was 43 percent of the industrial workers; of the 52 percent Latvian population of the Latvian republic 38 percent were employed in industry.[115] But, although while the Central Asian republics are underdeveloped and their population is less educated, the opposite can be said of the Baltic region and its people. Obviously the under-representation of Balts in the industrial labor force indicates the over-representation of the Russian and other Slavic populations of the Baltic republics in the same employment category.

The labor force of the all-union enterprises in Estonia was estimated to be about 80 percent Russian speaking.[116] Because the
percentage of Latvians in the industrial labor force is even lower than
in Estonia, it is fair to assume that the concentration of Russians in
the all-union enterprise sector was even higher there. The overlap of
ethnic and industrial branch employment leads to the conclusion
that "there [was]...ethnic segmentation in the Estonian and Latvian
labor markets."[117]

Occupational Bifurcation. It is important to emphasize that the
Slavic immigrants to the Baltic republics range the full scope and
hierarchy of the occupational structure. Because the decision to
establish the all-union enterprises was made in Moscow and they
were overseen mostly by Russian managers, the latter usually found
it easier to recruit not only the cadres but their unskilled labor force
in central Russia.[118] The pattern was established already under Stalin,
after the Second World War: "the most influential segment of
Russians consisted of thousands of officials assigned to direct and
supervise social and economic changes at the republic, district and
commune levels. The numerically largest segment consisted of
unskilled industrial labor."[119]

According to a very thorough study of Soviet economic policy in
Latvia from 1945 to 1965, the share of "managers and industrial
specialists" especially economists and planning specialists, employees
of administrative agencies, engineers, and technicians, not only grew
from a small fraction of the Russian migration into "a relatively
larger portion of immigrants from the Soviet Union, but also provided
the absolute majority of managerial and professional increments to
Latvian industry."[120] Although it was customary to look down on
unskilled Russian labor, in fact different sources indicate that Russians
and Ukrainians in the Baltic republics had more schooling than
Latvians and Estonians.[121] Whereas the share of professionals kept
rising, the majority of the immigrants always was made up of unskilled
workers, and there is a consensus that throughout the Soviet period
immigrants included both skilled cadres and unskilled workers. Even
immigrants who acquired their specialization locally, tended to be
acquire the skills possessed by other immigrants.[122]

Like the Slavic immigrants, Latvians were also employed at all
levels of the occupational hierarchy. The 1989 census reveals that
"Latvians have a smaller representation within [the managerial
stratum] than in the total population but a somewhat higher share
than in the workforce as a whole."[123] Latvians were overrepresented

as chairmen and leading personnel of kolkhozes and sovkhozes (68 and 83.7 percent) and among their republic's and its Communist Party's apparatus (55.3 and 63.6 percent) and underrepresented in the management of enterprises and production units (35.6 and 47.3 percent). Russians, Ukrainians, and Belorussians made up 45.7 and 53.8 percent of the management of enterprises and production units, their share in party apparatus jobs (for Russian 27.3 and 31.6 percent) was somewhat less than in the republic's population, and they were significantly underrepresented in the management of the agriculture.[124] Though the census provides no information concerning the affiliation of the enterprises in which individuals were employed, it seems that the sectoral division cuts across the managerial elite as well.

Another recent, but more detailed, survey of occupational distribution in various branches of the Latvian economy by ethnic background further refines the picture. In 1987, Latvians were employed most heavily in culture and arts (74.6 percent), agriculture (69.5 percent), public education (58.8 percent), communications (56.7 percent), administration (55.1 percent), and credit and insurance (55.1 percent). They were underrepresented in industry (38.1 percent), light industry (33.6 percent), machine construction (31 percent), chemicals (30.1 percent), railroads (26.5 percent), and water transport (11.5 percent).[125] This distribution demonstrates that immigrants "control certain key sectors of the economy" in the Baltic economies.[126] Transportation, which was viewed as of strategic importance in the USSR, was dominated by Slavic immigrants, as were to a lesser extent most branches of industry. Agriculture, education, and services were the preserve of the eponymous nationality.

A less-nuanced comparative study of the occupational distribution of the eponymous and Russian population in four union capitals in the late 1970s–early 1980s similarly found that in Tallinn Russians were better represented in the manufacturing, construction, transport, and communications, but Estonians in the science, education, and culture categories.[127] The authors' hypothesis was that industrial branches that have had a long history in the region will continue attracting the members of the eponymous nationality, but they were surprised by the decline of the employment of Estonians in metal working even though this industry dated back to the turn of the century. "Even the preservation of most traditions in the sphere of urban labor may be explained first of all by social interests and by particularities of the contemporary social situation in the republic," they plaintively concluded without specifying what these might be.[128] It seems, however, that the metal working industry, local employment traditions notwithstanding, conformed to the sectoral bifurcation by replacing Estonians with Russian metal workers. Similar divisions were found in Latvian trade unions, where employees in public education had proportionally more Latvians than the trade union composed of metal workers.[129]

Spatial Bifurcation. The large industrial plants are usually located in urban centers, giving them access to a large nonnative population, whereas the native groups usually predominate in smaller towns and the countryside. By 1979, only the Estonians remained a majority (51.9 percent) in their capital , Tallinn (even the Lithuanians made up only 47.3 percent of Vilnius's residents), whereas the Latvians were 38.3 percent (and 36.5 in 1989) of Riga's inhabitants.[130] Secondary cities in Estonia, such as Tartu, retained native majorities and provided an additional cultural center to the capital cities. Latvia had no such city. Latvians were in the majority in the republic only in the countryside and were a minority in the seven largest cities of their republic. In the large cities of Estonia, such as Tallinn, Russians and Estonians live in separate neighborhoods, but in Riga the Russian and Slavic population is scattered in all neighborhoods and makes up the majority in each of its six boroughs.[131]

The development of certain industries with Russian management and labor power has in several cases created large Russian territorial enclaves. The clearest example is the oil-shale industry, which was under the direct control of the all-union Ministry of the Coal Industry, in northern Estonia's Kohtla-Järve region where Estonians make up only 23 percent of the population. Other cases of immigrants' territorial concentration is the industrial center Daugavpils, where Latvians made up no more than 13 percent of the inhabitants.[132]

Educational Bifurcation. Because the immigrants were employed and frequently recruited by the heavy industry ministries, they tended to congregate in the technological fields. Slavic immigrants and their children in the higher educational institutions of the Baltic republics also preferred to study those disciplines in which Slavic employees constituted the majority. Balts pursuing higher education and white-collar careers were more likely to choose the educational, cultural, and artistic fields, where the knowledge of the native language and the maintenance of an internal "market" had favored them over the immigrants. A local observer called this separation *an inner intellectual apartheid.*[133]

A study of students in institutions of higher learning by language groups in 1977–1978, found that Russian speakers were overrepresented in engineering; Latvians in agriculture, creative arts, and medicine; and Estonians in economics, agriculture, and the humanities.[134] The fairly lopsided distribution of the ethnic groups in Estonia and Latvia—Russians favoring engineering and the eponymous nationalities teacher training, creative arts, and humanities, and agriculture—is indicative of the general bifurcation of occupational patterns.[135]

Linguistic and Cultural Bifurcation. The economic separation of Latvians and Estonians and the mostly Russian and other Slavic immigrants found its expression in the cultural sphere as well. The linguistic segmentation of "branches and types of industry" also led to "a division of the manpower market." In consequence, "members of different nationalities are limited in their choice of jobs by the language in which the enterprise operates."[136] In the words of the *Isvestia* journalist L. Levitsky: "The population was divided along linguistic lines. The Estonians had their own kindergartens, schools, enterprises, and regions. The Russians had theirs."[137] The sectoral bifurcation of types of enterprise, industries, schooling, and residential areas increased the interaction of Russian and other Slavic immigrants to the Baltics republics with each other thus reinforcing their distinct cultural identity. As the members of the dominant ethnic group of the USSR, Russian immigrants also had the benefit of speaking a major language in which education, literature, and culture were abundantly (and, under the Soviet system, cheaply) available, not to mention that it was also the language of the central authorities. For the Balts, Russian economic control coupled with cultural separatism were experienced as Greater Russian chauvinism and colonial control.

Misiunas and Taagepera's trenchant formulation sums up this multilayered separation: "[this] was an industry based on Russian investment and Russian labor, managed by Russians according to goals set by Russians, importing a large part of the raw materials from Russia, and exporting most of its products. The whole show was called 'Baltic' industrial growth because the Soviets decided to run it on Baltic soil."[138] Three researchers at the USSR Academy of Sciences Institute of Ethnography similarly reported in October 1988 that in the union republics: "for a long time…industries were developed by creating enclaves of residents of a different ethnic background, usually Russian."[139] In fact the term *enclave* is too limiting as a description of the Russian presence in the Baltic republics because it implies the existence of a distinct but small alternative community side by side with a larger dominant society. In fact, the economies, and consequently societies, of the Baltic republics were bifurcated into two full-scale self-reproducing *sectors*. Within each sector one national group dominated, although they were not fully exclusivist. About a fifth of the employees in the Estonian all-union enterprises were Estonians, and simultaneously there were immigrants in the republic's economic sector.

The result of the self-contradictory character of the Soviet nationalities policy was the legitimation of the multinational character of the USSR without, however, allowing the free expression of these nations' aspirations. In the institutional sphere, cultural, political, and economic institutions were reserved for the people of the union republics: national academies, research institutions and universities, branches of the Communist Party and trade union, and a republican economic sector, respectively. The cultural institutions, however, were besieged by the demands of Russification, political bodies were under the thumb of the Moscow authorities, and the republic economic sector was but a poor cousin to the gargantuan all-union enterprises.

The amount of repression varied among the three spheres. In comparing them with each other, it seems that culture remained the less fettered or at least the most legitimate area for the expression of national distinction while the political institutions were bound most severely by virtue of being subordinated to the Communist Party of the USSR, the institution that served as the main girdle of centralization in the USSR, and the economic institutions were somewhere in between, producing for the local market but inserted into a broader economic framework in terms of input, economic philosophy, and so on. However, each of the three spheres possessed institutions that were distinct to the republic and served as a glasshouse for the creation and reproduction of native elites.

An alternative, but in my mind too narrowly based, interpretation of the significance of the sectoral division is presented in Graham Smith's thesis that it led to competition between Russian immigrants and the eponymous nationalities. In Smith's view: "The largest cities of the non-Russian union republics represent places where the Russian language has become an important determinant of social advancement and where as a consequence of centrally-initiated interrepublic programs such as 'cadre exchanges' and various 'planned migration schemes' natives have to compete with incoming Russians for jobs."[140] Smith's thesis tried to cover all the non-Russian union republics, but whatever its merits are for interpreting host-immigrant relations in the other republics of the former USSR, its validity for the Baltic republics is limited. Not just knowledge of Russian, possessed by many Balts, but the whole bifurcated structure encouraged animosity and social conflict between Russians and Balts. The ethnic dimension of the bifurcation, which we already examined, was generated not by competition but rather by the many-sided *exclusion* of Latvians and Estonians from the parallel institutional structure erected in their republics. This exclusionary framework was expressed in the many-layered segmentation of the Baltic societies.

Two, only partially overlapping, societies existed in Latvia and Estonia: each with its institutions, language, industrial specialization, educational preferences, and geographical concentration. The Baltic elites were confronted with the existence of an alternative society of Russian and other Slavic immigrants that possessed its own elites, concentrated mostly in the economic sphere. The Baltic elites were threatened by the massive presence of this immigrant elite that arrived in the context of and under the justification of a Soviet state-building project. Furthermore, the Latvian and Estonian elite stratum controlled only the weaker and smaller of the economic sectors while the powerful all-union sector of the economy, built, managed, and staffed by Russian and other Slavic immigrants, had the priority by virtue of its closer ties to the Soviet authorities, which further enhanced its threatening foreign character.

Finally, the coexistence of two societies with clear identities within one republic created a multidimensional pattern of ethnic or national conflict in which no area remained uncolored by this contestation. Part of this division led to competition but, despite Smith, over resources rather than over employment. Under the Soviet statutory wage determination heavy industry was favored over other branches of the economy by higher wages and additional bonus payments.[141] Because most of the all-union enterprises were in the area of heavy industry, they paid higher salaries to their employees, most of whom were Russian. In addition, employment in favored industrial branches provided preferential access to a whole area of fringe benefits and resources that were in chronically short supply in the USSR, first and foremost housing.[142] Russian-language newspaper want ads in the late 1960s sometimes promised housing with employment, thus revealing the priority of immigrants over native Balts, who frequently had to wait years for scare housing.[143] Construction workers had the shortest waiting period for housing, but the construction industry was made up overwhelmingly—in Estonia close to 80 percent, in Tallinn itself over 90 percent—of nonnatives, who had been recruited to build housing that they were the first to occupy.[144] In consequence of the preference of Russians in housing allocation, "most new residential areas of the larger cities [in Estonia] are now predominantly Russian sections."[145]

The ethnic conflict between Russian and Slavic immigrants and the members of the eponymous Baltic nationalities was unique in that it was fed by the combination of two mechanisms that sociologists usually view as contradictory: exclusion and competition.[146] Because of the sectoral division in the union republic's economies there was a measure of exclusion in the sphere of production that operated against the eponymous populations. At the same time, in the area of consumption there was competition over scare resources, which also led to discrimination against the Baltic peoples. The two mechanisms were linked; for example, the employment of Slavic immigrants in heavy industry also gave them better access to limited resources. Although lack of competition may lessen conflict, competitive advantages that are the result of exclusionary mechanisms will add fuel to the ethnic conflict.

The segmentation of the Latvian and Estonian societies between the native-born and the immigrant populations was different from the Catalan case but similar in many ways to the Basque one. In Catalonia, the control of the economy remained firmly in Catalan hands even under Franco. In the Basque region, two alternative societies were created, or rather the old bifurcation between Spanish-dominated urban and Basque rural and smalltown life was extended in a radical fashion as a result of industrialization. The type of segmentation that evolved in Catalonia is typical to the immigrant experience—confined by and large to the labor market, and within it to the lower rungs of the occupational hierarchy—and its central question is the extent to which immigrants may integrate into Catalan society inter alia through occupational mobility and language acquisition.

Neither the Basque nor the Baltic experience is typical: immigrants in the Basque country were low-skilled, low-status employees before the Civil War, and the industrial elite that employed them was native born but already within the Spanish cultural ambit. At the early period, therefore, two alternative societies, though the origins of their elites were different, coexisted and led to a particularly harsh form of nationalism aimed against Spain and the Spanish immigrants.

The lessening of these differences also raised the question of integration for immigrants. However, in Estonia and Latvia two alternative sectors, or societies, with immigrant laborers and immigrants elites, were created in the twentieth century. This atypical form of segmentation, vertical rather than horizontal, that posed a threat to the predominance of the native-born elites was translated within the context of Gorbachev's reform policies into a nationalist project for regaining control over Latvia and Estonia and making them independent once again.

The Popular Fronts and the Politics of Demography

The Movement Toward Independence

The incorporation of the three Baltic republics into the USSR changed the character of Baltic nationalism. The three-way struggle of Latvian, Estonian, and Lithuanian nationalists against their Russian rulers and German and Polish elites, respectively, which characterized and limited their nationalism before the First World War, was replaced by nationalist sentiments that evolved in conflict with the just one opponent: the USSR. The first nationalist response to annexation by the Soviet Union was armed resistance, in part by former soldiers of the Baltic units of the German military and in part by peasants opposed to collectivization, that lasted into the early 1950s. A second form of nationalism surfaced in Latvia, during Khrushchev's "Thaw," based on the use of the local Communist Party to further the national interests of the republic.

The third phase of Baltic nationalism was the establishment of alternative political forces—the Popular Fronts—during Gorbachev's *glasnost* and *perestroika* era, which led the three Baltic republics to challenge Gorbachev's authority ever more decisively and eventually be the first of the republics to break away from the USSR and catalyze and witness its ultimate breakup.[147]

The first steps of what were to become the mass movements of Baltic nationalism were inspired by Gorbachev's restructuring movement, though all the while seeking to to utilize it for increasing regional autonomy. In September 1987, four Estonian economists creatively "reinterpreted" the much-touted though still vague views of some of Gorbachev's closest advisers on *khozraschet* (self-financing) to make it suit regional rather than Soviet interest. Among their innovative suggestions were (1) transfer of enterprises and resources under the management of the central Soviet authorities to the jurisdiction of the authorities of the Estonian SSR, (2) granting the republic extensive autonomy in the management of its economic affairs by replacing centralized planning and allocation with market principles and prices in interrepublic and foreign trade. There was, however, one area which the economists declined to leave to the market, the movement of labor within the Soviet Union; they demanded that labor migration be "regulated by a special system" and (3) that taxes paid by enterprises from the Soviet authorities be redirected to the republic, which was to negotiate the size of its contribution to the central Soviet budget.[148]

The aim of the group of Estonian economists was to turn their republic into a "self-managing economic zone"[149] with a market-based economy. To allow Estonia to realize its advantage as a relatively developed region within the USSR,[150] the narrow goals of "self-financing" contemplated by Soviet economic reformers did not seem sufficient. To truly free the Baltic economies from the economic stagnation of the politically dominant USSR, the economists sought to re-create the framework of a unified, separate national market within the republic. A year later the Estonian program of economic autonomy was also adopted by representatives of Lithuania and Latvia as the "Baltic model" for Soviet restructuring.[151] The desire of relatively well-developed regions to liberate their economies from an archaic state, which in Nairn's words "had become an obstacle to their further progress," led, as Roeder noted, "the nationalities with the highest levels of educational, occupational, and often political attainment, rather than the disadvantaged or marginal ones...[to] have advanced the most ambitious agendas for change and engage... in the most extensive protest."[152] Not surprisingly, the better-off Baltic regions were accused of "nationalist selfishness" by the less-developed republics of the USSR, just as Catalonia had been in the late nineteenth and early twentieth centuries by Castile.[153]

Another significant step toward the birth of the popular phase of Baltic nationalism was taken in the meeting of the plenum of Estonia's cultural unions. On April 1–2, 1988, the unions adopted the call for regional economic self-management but added demands of their own although still keeping them within the framework of *perestroika*. The cultural elite's new demands included the making of Estonian the state language and the creation of an Estonian SSR citizenship. Together with economic self-management these represented a desire for "far-reaching economic and political autonomy."[154] The Estonian Popular Front in Support of *Perestroika* was launched by "reform-minded Communists" two weeks later to implement the cultural unions' comprehensive proposals.[155] Similar congresses and resolutions of the Latvian[156] and Lithuanian writer's unions gave the impetus to the formation, in June 1988, of the Lithuanian Restructuring Movement—the Sajudis—and subsequently of the Latvian Popular Front.

These mass movements triggered leadership changes in all three republics, as reform-oriented native-born leaders replaced Brezhnev's appointees, some of whom were Russians. In a surprisingly short period of time the demands of the new movements transformed the public agenda and by year's end were adopted by the republics' Communist Party branches, which, on their part, moved to forge alliances with the Popular Fronts. At this stage, the aim of the nationalist movements and reformed Communist Party branches was "real autonomy...usually expressed in the term 'sovereignty'"; that is, a demand for the transfer of economic and political decision making to the republics tempered by a willingness to leave foreign policy and defense in the hands of the central authorities.[157] The initial response of the Soviet authorities was not altogether negative. During a visit to Latvia and Lithuania in August, Aleksander Yakovlev, the Secretary of the CPSU's Central Committee and the leading light of the reformers, sought to harness the positive response in the Baltics to the carriage of Gorbachev's reforms and argued that "the national factor can and should become one more motive force for restructuring."[158] Gorbachev, on his part, seemed willing to make the Baltic republics the "showcase of *perestroika*" and a "laboratory" for the examination of the viability of the planned changes.[159]

Toward the end of 1988 the Popular Fronts underwent another decisive mobilizing and radicalizing experience. On October 22, 1988, the Soviet press published the drafts of the Law on Changes in and Additions to the USSR Constitution in the area of republic-center relations and the Law on the Election of USSR People's Deputies that were scheduled to be ratified at the November 29 session of the Supreme Soviet of the USSR. These proposed amendments reflected a backlash against regional autonomy movements and, therefore, sought to increase central control over the republics. This tergiversation, typical of the Gorbachev dynamic of reforms, was perceived in the Baltics as a step back from *perestroika* and the resolutions of the earlier nineteenth All-Union Communist Party Conference that already agreed to enhance republican sovereignty.[160]

The reaction in the Baltic republics to the planned legislation was fast and furious. The Popular Fronts and the Sajudis undertook a very successful campaign of signature collection, and on the ground-swell of nationalist feelings each one of the three republics introduced concrete and symbolic decisions that enhanced its distinct identity and sovereignty. The Estonian Supreme Soviet went the furthest, by proclaiming the republic's sovereignty on November 16, 1988, and its right to veto USSR laws that violate that sovereignty. It also amended the republic's constitution to allow the introduction of private property and transferred to republican ownership all natural wealth and industrial property within the republic.[161] These changes were voided by the USSR Supreme Soviet, but were subsequently reaffirmed by its Estonian counterpart.[162] Lithuania and Latvia followed the Estonian lead and declared their sovereignty and the concomitant right to veto laws of the USSR that violated it, on May 18 and November 10, 1989, respectively.

The seesaw reaction of the Kremlin to Baltic and other nationalist demands, by seeming to revoke what already appeared to have been conceded, contributed significantly to the process of national radicalization. The rapid shifts made it plain that the leaders of the restructuring drive were wavering and likely to bow to pressure if it was brought to bear on them. The Popular Fronts, born in the context of the increased democratization of the USSR, realized that their freedom of operation was closely connected with *glasnost* and *perestroika*. At the time of their appearance in the spring of 1988, the Popular Fronts adopted a reformist stance, seeking to use the new opening to foster Baltic freedom and development as part of a reformed USSR. For example, the resolutions of Latvian Writer's Union, that provided the impetus for the creation of the Latvian Popular Front, called for "making the status of the republic such that in practice Latvia would be internationally recognized as a sovereign and national state in the composition of the Soviet Federation."[163] All three Popular Fronts initially rejected the idea of independence, but the limited progress and repeated backtracking on their economic and political demands further radicalized Baltic nationalism. When independence finally came under active discussion, the Baltic Popular Fronts adopted it explicitly as their goal, in early spring 1990.[164]

I will turn now to separate discussions of the economic and political issues and the initiatives of the Popular Front movements and Baltic governments. Two key demands of the Popular Fronts, the establishment of republican citizenship apart from Soviet citizenship and the recognition of the eponymous language as the state language, were so closely intertwined with the relationship between the nationalist movements and the Russian and Slavic immigrants in the Baltic republics that I will hold them over for subsequent sections, which are focused on issues of ethnic exclusivity and conflict.

The Estonian interpretation of self-management aimed at unifying the Estonian economy and in the process subjecting it to republican control. The Latvian leadership, on its part, equated economic independence with ownership of natural wealth and the "property created or located" on its territory.[165] Not surprisingly, a major conflict between the Baltic separatists and the Moscow authorities was joined over the ownership of the all-union enterprises. In May 1989, during the first meeting of the three Baltic Popular Fronts, "the inadmissibility of economic opposition at the Union level was discussed with particular urgency."[166] In April 1988, the Politburo agreed to hand over the management of several economic sectors to Estonia but only as part of the "self-financing" program of *perestroika* and without accepting the demand for economic autonomy.[167]

Proposals and counterproposals were passed back and forth between Moscow and the Baltic reformers in which the central authorities accepted the principle of economic autonomy but kept whittling down its practical applications. A March 1989 Politburo plan, for example, still left energy, metallurgy and machine building, the chemical industry, and transportation and communication under all-union control.[168] The Baltic legislatures passed a number of constitutional amendments to transfer to republican control a variety of natural resources and industrial enterprises, and in spring 1989, the Estonian and Lithuanian supreme councils forced the hand of the Moscow authorities by onesidedly establishing economic autonomy starting in January 1, 1990.[169]

A new round of negotiations commenced and finally on November 28, 1989, the USSR Supreme Soviet adopted a compromise Law on the Economic Independence of the Baltic republics that went into effect on the same day, 1990, though it also declared invalid the Baltic laws that transferred all-union property onesidedly under their jurisdiction. The law defined "each national territory as a single and coherent entity and [gave] its administrators a frame of reference for making decisions." At the same time, central planning and management remained split between Moscow and the republican authorities. To make matters worse, basic economic laws regulating property, land, and uniform taxation under *perestroika* had not yet existed at the time Baltic economic self-management was approved and left even what was accomplished uncertain. These reforms, in short, did not ensure economic autonomy but, at most, afforded "a kind of semiautonomy."[170]

When the Baltic republics escalated their political demands by declaring their independence, the conflict over the control of the all-union enterprises assumed even more bitter tones and lead to desperate tactics, bordering on economic warfare. In July 1990, the USSR Council of Ministers approved the creation of the Integral Association, an umbrella body "which unite[d] Union-level enterprises and associations" and linked those in the Baltic republics with such enterprises in other parts of the USSR, with the aim of canceling much of Estonian economic autonomy.[171] The Estonian government viewed the creation of the Integral Association as "one more attempt to keep enterprises subordinate to the union" to hinder Estonian independence. The directors of two of the all-union enterprises in Estonia, which were among the initiators of the association, accused the Estonian authorities of wanting "to put Union enterprises under the republic's jurisdiction at any cost."[172] In short, the central authorities were willing to grant ever-growing concessions to the Baltic republics, but they steadfastly refused to accept two demands: (1) the transfer of ownership or control over the large industrial enterprises, which according to Article 73 of the USSR Constitution were centrally managed, to the republics, and (2) outright independence.

Although there was Soviet willingness to grant concessions on economic matters, in turning to an examination of the political demands of the Popular Fronts and the responses of the Soviet authorities we encounter uncompromising opposition to the Baltic independence aspirations. When the Soviet law on secession was passed on April 7, 1989, in response to nationalist stirrings, it stipulated that a two-thirds majority was required in a referendum of all USSR citizens who are residing permanently on the republic's territory (and possibly in a repeat referendum as well) and an up to five year transitional period for working out the details of the secession.[173]

The opposition to Baltic political autonomy, and later independence, came from both Moscow and particular segments of the immigrant populations. Just weeks after the formation of the Estonian Popular Front in April 1988, a counterforce calling itself the Internationalist Movement (usually referred to as Interfront) was born. Similarly, the founding congress of the Latvian Popular Front served as the impetus for the formation of the Internationalist Front of the Working People in Latvia.[174] These movements represented those sections of the Russian immigrant population that overtly opposed two central planks in the Popular Fronts' platforms: the creation of republic citizenship and making the language of its eponymous nationality into the republic's official language.[175] Their raison d'être, however, was in equal measure rooted in opposing the Popular Front's program of using the goal of economic self-management to transfer control of all-union enterprises to the republic.

The Estonian Internationalist Movement seemed to be the better organized and more articulate of the defenders of the status quo. Although the Popular Front, as we have seen, was born out of a synthesis between the Estonian economic reformers and creative unions, prominent among the leaders of the Internationalist Movement were the directors of several plants of union subordination,[176] though the leaders of the Internationalist Movement, in a time-honored Soviet fashion, claimed that theirs was a true workers' movement.[177] The Russian opposition to Estonian nationalism had some of its strongest bases in the cities with large Russian populations in northeastern Estonia, such as Narva, Kohtla-Järva, Paldiski, and Sillamae, and in the apparatus and leadership of the institutions that represented the principle of centralization and homogeneity and actively held together the USSR: the Communist Party, the KGB, and the military.[178]

Almost simultaneous with the birth of the moderate Popular Fronts and their main antagonists, the Interfronts, the organizations of radical Baltic nationalism, the National Independence Parties of Latvia and Estonia, were also founded. In contrast to the initial willingness of the Popular Fronts to operate within the Soviet political system, the Independence Parties denied the legitimacy of the Soviet regime and sought the reestablishment of Baltic independence by means of legal continuity with the prewar Estonian and Latvian republics. To accomplish that aim, in early 1989 they formed grass-roots "citizens' committees" to register those individuals who had Estonian and Latvian citizenship prior to June 1940 and their descendants as the legitimate citizens of the republics and conduct elections to alternative bodies to the republic's Supreme Soviets.

The political freedoms of the *perestroika* era, especially the relatively free elections, allowed the Popular Fronts to officially consolidate their influence in the Baltic republics and dismantle the domination of the Communist Parties. The March 1989 elections to the USSR Congress of People's Deputies and the Council of Nationalities, the December 1989 local elections, and the most important elections of all, the February–March elections to the republic's own

Supreme Councils (or Parliaments, the equivalents of the Supreme Soviets in the other republics), were fought out between the Communist Parties of the republics, the Popular Fronts, and the Interfront organizations while, officially, the Independence Parties boycotted the elections.

The elections were not yet contested by official parties, and the candidates ran as individuals affiliated with, or endorsed by, one and sometimes more different political organizations. It is difficult, therefore, to gauge the exact success of each of the forces, but the tendencies were obvious: the Popular Fronts swept election after election, and in the process adopted the independence programs of the National Independence Parties, while still acting within, and using to their advantage, the Soviet political institutions. All four seats for the USSR Congress of People's Deputies, and seventeen of the thirty-two seats for the Council of Nationalities went to Popular-Front-endorsed candidates in Estonia and six more to candidates fully acceptable to them, while the Communist Party and Interfront among them received only five seats.[179] Similarly, in Latvia 80 percent of the elected candidates were affiliated with the Popular Front.[180]

The Communist Parties of the republics were caught between a rock and a hard place. In Estonia they supported the Popular Front from early on, in Latvia after Gorbachev replaced their first secretaries. For a while the communist leaders in the republics were able to maintain part of their influence by jumping on the Popular Front's bandwagon and in rapid succession put through the supreme councils a considerable part of the moderate nationalist programs, but their poor showing in the elections to the Congress of People's Deputies demonstrated that their position was already compromised.

In December 1989, a decisive step was taken by the reformist leaders of the Lithuanian Communist Party, who, under Brazauskas, decided to split from the Communist Party of the Soviet Union (CPSU). This time the unity of the Communist Party, the major unifying organization of the Soviet Union, was at stake, and it was Gorbachev's turn to visit Lithuania. The first secretary of the new Lithuanian Community Party (LCP) did not back down following his meeting with the secretary general of the CPSU, and the CPSU's Central Committee broke relations with the LCP and recognized the splinter LCP-CPSU.[181] The Estonian and Latvian Communist Parties also split between nationalist and pro-Soviet wings and, at the same time, along ethnic lines. The uses of the alliance between the Popular Front and the republic's Communist Parties dissipated: the Communist

Parties could no longer be used as a safe shelter for the realization of nationalist aspirations, and the short flourishing of national communism was over.

The electoral campaign on the eve of the first relatively free elections to the republic's supreme councils led the Popular Fronts to close ranks with the more radical wings of the nationalist movements and declare their goal to be independence. The March 1990 elections to the Supreme Council of Latvia produced a 56 percent majority for candidates endorsed by the Latvian Popular Front. Although the directly endorsed candidates of the Estonian Popular Front received only 41 percent of the seats, in part because of a more flexible electoral system, the front had no difficulty forming the government with coalition partners.[182] Edgar Svisaar, one of the Estonian economists who created the plan for regional self-management and the person who initially conceived of forming a Popular Front in support of *perestroika* and then led it, was elected the prime minister of Estonia in April 1990. Sajudis-supported candidates won 74 percent of the seats in the new Supreme Council of Lithuania and on March 11, 1990, elected its leader, Landsbergis, chairman and proclaimed the reconstitution of the independent Lithuanian republic.

The threat of Lithuania's independence from the USSR brought the imposition of an economic blockade that halted the supply of gasoline and some food supplies. The Supreme Council of Latvia, on its part, also voted for independence, but specified an indeterminate transition period, while the Estonian leadership, initially the boldest one, took an even more cautious approach to avoid confrontation with the Soviet authorities.[183] Eventually, the Lithuanian leadership agreed to accept a moratorium on the independence declaration in return for ending the blockade. Throughout the rest of 1990 and the first half of 1991, inconclusive and frequently interrupted negotiations were held between the Soviet and Baltic leaders to determine their future relationships. In the meantime, the two sides operated two sets of institutions that produced conflicting policies and interpretations, creating, as it were, a classical revolutionary situation of "dual powers."[184]

Gorbachev's most fateful conservative turn between the fall of 1990 and late summer 1991 seemed to portend the rolling back of the power and accomplishments of the Baltic nationalist movements. The simultaneous control of the Communist Party, the KGB, Ministry of Interior, the military, and industrial planning—that is, the centralizing organizations of the USSR—by conservative appointees created the conditions for trying to rein in Baltic separatism. An internal Lithuanian crisis provided the Moscow hardliners the opportunity. A rift developed between the Prime Minister Prunskiene, who sought to break the impasse by negotiating a favorable agreement with the Soviet authorities on Lithuania's future, and the "second wave" of Sajudi leadership, elected under the radicalizing conditions of the blockade, who converged around Landsbergis's uncompromising attempt to push independence and make the necessary economic sacrifices for its sake.

The pro-Soviet Communist Party attempted to bring down the Landsbergis government by organizing mass demonstrations against its price hikes. The failure of the demonstrations to accomplish their aim, and world opinion riveted to the pending outbreak of war in the Persian Gulf, led to a military seizure of communication centers in Vilnius, on January 13, 1991. The attack on the television tower brought loss in life and condemnation from demonstrators in Moscow and around the world.[185] Much smaller scale attacks took place in Latvia as well.[186] In both Lithuania and Latvia "national salvation committees" appeared during the crackdown; in Latvia it was led by the first secretary of the Latvian Communist Party and supported by the Latvian Interfront.[187] Yeltsin traveled to Tallinn during the crisis and expressed his support for the right of the Baltic peoples to self-determination.

The Baltic crisis revealed the growing rift within the Soviet leadership, the disappearance of the rule of law, and the loss of control by Gorbachev over the course of events. Gorbachev's inability, or maybe unwillingness, to move further ahead with economic reforms and his limited progress with a new nationalities policy and the concomitant deterioration in both the economic situation and the relations between the central authorities and the leaders of a growing number of republics and other territorial units combined with the continued tolerance for illegality in the Baltic republics furnished the grounds for the abortive August 1991 coup.

The coup was centered in Moscow and the Baltic republics, where reforms and loss of power by the Soviet authorities had progressed furthest. The failure of the coup and the emergence of the Russian Federation as the heir to the USSR destroyed two of the main organizations that held the union together: the Communist Party and the KGB. On the heels of the foreign recognition of the independence of the republics of Lithuania, Estonia, and Latvia, the Soviet Union's reformist leadership granted independence on September 6, 1991. On December 31, 1991, the USSR ceased to exist. The declarations of independence by the Baltic republics was the first step in the breakup of the Soviet Union. On August 31, 1994, under U.S. and Western European prodding, the last Russian troops pulled out of Estonia and Latvia.

The first elections since independence produced new parliaments and governments in all three Baltic republics. In both Estonia and Latvia the more right-wing, culturally conservative and economically liberal, parties took the helm. The Estonian Popular Front that played an important role in the independence struggle received only 12 percent of the vote and 15 representatives in the 101 seat Riigikogu, in the September 1992 elections. The center-right Fatherland Alliance, an electoral alliance of the Christian Democratic and Conservative parties, became the largest bloc with 22 percent of the vote and formed a coalition of fifty-three seats (see Table 5.1). This turn to the right ensured a "solid mandate for continuing and even accelerating the political and economic reform processes."[188]

Similarly, the Latvian Popular Front splintered and in the June 1993 was replaced as the largest bloc by the center-of-right alliance, the Latvian Way, which received 32.4 percent of the votes (see Table 5.2) and formed a coalition government with a mandate similar to its Estonian counterpart. The electoral results directly reaffirmed the process of economic reform in both Estonia and Latvia and replaced

TABLE 5.1

Results of National Elections in Estonia in September 1992, in Percentages

Party	Votes	Seats
Fatherland Alliance	22.0	29
Secure/Safe Home	13.8	17
Popular Front	12.2	15
Moderates	9.7	12
ERPS	8.7	10
Citizens	6.8	8
Monarchists	7.1	8
Greens	2.6	1
Entrepreneurs	2.3	1
Others	14.7	—

Source: Fitzmaurice 1993, Table 1, p. 16. Reprinted by permission of the publisher, Butterworth-Heinemann Ltd.

TABLE 5.2

Results of National Elections in Latvia in June 1993, in Percentages

Party	Votes	Seats
Latvian Way	32.4	36
National Independence	13.4	15
Concord	12.0	13
Farmer's Union	10.6	12
Equality	5.8	7
Fatherland and Freedom	5.4	6
Christian Democrats	5.0	6
Democratic Center	4.8	5
Others	10.6	—

Source: *Electoral Studies* 12, no. 4 (December 1993):, p. 420. Reprinted by permission of the publisher, Butterworth-Heinemann Ltd.

the unstable coalitions that led to independence with more clearly defined political blocs.

The Lithuanian elections produced a surprising result, demonstrating that just as in the past the political and economic history of Lithuania diverged from that of Latvia and Estonia, so there is no, or only limited, convergence in the present. Lithuania, the most militant campaigner for independence from the USSR under President Landsbergis but less developed and industrialized than either Latvia or Estonia returned a part of the old, in part reformed, guard. The Sajudis, reluctant to be transformed into a political party, splintered into many parliamentary factions and the weakened Landsbergis assumed an increasingly authoritarian style. In the two-round elections in October–November 1992, the Sajudis dropped from ninety-seven to thirty-five seats and their opponents, the Democratic Labor Party led by Brazauskas, the head of the Lithuanian Communist Party that already in December 1989 split from the Soviet Communist Party and supported independence, received an absolute majority of seventy-nine seats in the Seimas. Brazauskas, who was elected president, was also supportive of economic reforms but planned to slow the process of reform and provide more protection to large factories while they underwent privatization, as well as build closer ties with Russia.[189]

Of the republics of the former USSR, Estonia and Latvia made most progress toward the adoption of a market economy. Estonia became the first former Soviet republic to introduce its own currency, the Estonian kroon, in June 1992. It was followed between March and June 1993 by Latvia, which put into circulation the lats.[190] The new Estonian and Latvian currencies were freely convertible, and they remained stable and even rose against Western currencies. The foreign reserves of Estonia more than doubled in a year.[191] The new currencies were backed mostly by gold reserves transferred to Britain when the Baltic republics were captured by the USSR in 1940 and returned after they became independent. Inflation, which topped 600 percent in 1991, fell considerably in all three republics by December 1993.[192] The contrast with the other ex-Soviet republics, still an appropriate frame of reference in measuring Baltic development, is revealing: in 1993, nine of the fifteen republics had inflation rates of more than 1,000 percent, whereas comsumer prices in Lithuania rose 410 percent, in Latvia they rose 109 percent, and in Estonia they rose 89 percent, the lowest rates in the former USSR.[193]

The signs of an early economic recovery in the Baltic economies was the result of an ambitious process of marketization of prices and privatization of enterprises. These processes have not been completed, many large-scale companies have not been disposed of yet, but their execution followed the step-by-step logic that the Soviet reformers were unwilling to follow. These included the elimination of subsidies and the liberalization of prices, over a period of three years. Initially consumer prices rose sharply the but chronic shortages and queues were eliminated as privatized production spread. The transition was compounded by the shock of world market prices for energy that the Baltic republics, which chose to stay outside the Commonwealth of Independent States, were the first to be charged by Russia. The massive decline of industrial production that lowered the GDP by about 30 percent in Estonia and Latvia in 1992 seemed to be over in mid-1993, as industry adjusted to the new energy prices.

In 1993, the GDP of fourteen of the former Soviet republics fell (Turkmenistan, a major gas exporter, was the exception) on the average by 12 percent. The decline in Latvia, Kazakhstan, and Uzbekistan was by about 10 percent and in Estonia close to 4 percent, the lowest of the fourteen.[194] Latvia and Estonia moved rapidly to reduce their dependence on Russia for trade and increase exports to the Scandinavian countries and to Germany.[195] The benefits of the Baltic economies' marketization has not been shared by all: pensioners are hard-pressed to make ends meet, homelessness emerged as a social problem, and organized crime made its appearance. But, although the same social crises exist in all the other former Soviet states to a much larger extent, the economic recovery that took shape in Latvia and Estonia eluded most of them. In comparing former Soviet economies, the developed economies of Estonia and Latvia promise to become the success stories of the former USSR.

Language Laws: Cultural Exclusion and Assimilation

The Baltic struggle for independence was waged on two fronts: on one front it was directed against the economic, political, and cultural control exerted by the central and centralizing Soviet authorities; on the other front, it was aimed against the Slavic immigrants in their midst. So far we observed the former, we will now focus on the latter.

The demographic threat of "denationalization," the dilution of the ethnic homogeneity and compactness of the native population by the influx of Slavic immigrants, was a major and persistent complaint of Estonian and Latvian nationalists.[196] It is hard to overestimate the frantic resistance to and fear of minoritization by the small Latvian and Estonian people in their republics.

Already during Khrushchev's Thaw, Latvian leaders favored industries that would employ local labor. In Misiunas and Taagepera's view, a sudden upsurge of Russian immigration into Latvia in 1956 (without comparable immigration into Estonia) was a likely reason for the "nativist" reaction in the Latvian Communist Party that brought on the severe purge in the Thaw's aftermath.[197] During *perestroika* a dramatic language was adopted to oppose the immigration to the republic, which seemed to "threaten...the existence of the Estonian nation" and "the preservation and development of the Latvian people."[198] At its most extreme a presentation by the chair of the Latvian Popular Front's Immigration Committee was titled "The Latvian Nation and the Genocide of Immigration."[199]

Russian immigration to the Baltics, which slowed down in the early 1970s, began increasing again in the early 1980s, this time into Estonia and Lithuania, where a number of large investment projects were undertaken. Though the percent of the native-born population in Lithuania has not been altered since 1940, even it saw agitation against what has been described as secret Soviet directives to reduce the native element to 60 percent of the population in the republic and 40 percent in the capital.[200]

The approach of Baltic nationalists to immigration sharply departed from their attitude to other economic issues. The 1987 call of the four Estonian economists for regional economic autonomy, later echoed by the creative unions and the Popular Fronts, already sought market-based development in all areas of the economy but demanded "strict regulation and control of the process of migration."[201] Two specific demands were raised early in the chronology of Baltic nationalism as part of the goal of restricting and, if possible, rolling back immigration: the transformation of Latvian and Estonian into their respective republic's official language, and the creation of a republic citizenship separate from Soviet citizenship. I will examine now the implementation of these demands and their potential impact on the economic position of Russian speakers, as part of the Popular Fronts' struggle under the Soviet regime and in the first three years of independent Latvia and Estonia.

The Estonian republic's creative unions meeting in April 1988 already suggested that the status of official state language be secured for Estonian, a demand taken up later that year and made into a central programmatic idea of the Estonian Popular Front. On January 18, 1989, the Law on Language cleared the still communist-dominated Estonia's Supreme Soviet. The law declared Estonian the official language of the republic, established the predominance of Estonian in the republic's territory, differentiated levels of proficiency in Estonian required of people engaged in six occupational categories (from level F, complete fluency by government and party officials and factory directors to level A, limited comprehension and speaking ability by repair people, newsstand sellers, and so on) and ordered "a virtually mandatory and universal changeover in the conduct of official business...to Estonian."[202] As part of the changes, the law mandated sessions and meetings of governmental and administrative bodies as well as all judicial proceedings to be conducted in Estonian.

The Language Law was to be implemented in stages and take final effect in four years, that is, January 1993.[203] After independence, as part of the February 1993 Law on Estonian Language Requirement for Applicants for Citizenship, a written and verbal language test, corresponding roughly to level D of the language proficiency scale, was adopted.[204]

Similar laws were passed by the Supreme Soviet of the Latvian SSR. The Latvian Law on Languages required people "employed in government agencies, retail trade, the service sector, transport, education, the judicial system, public health, culture, etc." to learn Latvian. Yet the Latvian law was less stringent than its Estonian counterpart: it accepted that government documents would be kept, for an intermediary period, in Russian, and left the choice of languages in public situations to discretion of the individuals involved.[205] At the same time, the law was expected to take effect in three years.[206] In March 1992, the Parliament of independent Latvia tightened the requirements laid down in the earlier language law. The new law made obligatory the use of Latvian in official documents, place names and signs, and so forth and specified fines for failure to use Latvian in the prescribed ways, but preserved the right to use other languages in private documents.

The transformation of the republic's eponymous nationality's language into the official language was not confined to the Baltics but was also carried out in Tadjikistan, Uzbekistan, Moldavia, and elsewhere. This aspiration was accepted by Gorbachev as legitimate because it seemed to fall within the confines of the union republics' cultural autonomy, which was already established in the early Soviet nationalities policy, even if it was frequently violated. The revised nationalities policy from August 1989 effectively recognized the republic's jurisdiction over this matter.[207]

An analyst noted as a "striking feature" of the Baltic language laws "the[ir] degree of detail and rigidity,"[208] though the original Latvian law, at least, had its share of ambiguities. The implementation of the language laws, however, was postponed or its conditions altered. In January 1991, one month before the deadline for having all sales and service personnel in Estonia speak its language at the appropriate level of profficiency, the implementation of this section in the language law was postponed by the Estonian Supreme Council.[209] A decision to amend and tighten the Latvian Language Law indicates that "four years after the passage of the 1989 law, Russian was still being used in government institutions and other organizations."[210]

In general, there is a shortage of native-born Baltic personnel in many areas where Russians predominate, and it is not very likely that the current occupiers of those positions could be replaced within the foreseeable future. Nor are Balts likely to want to take over the jobs of unskilled Russian and Slavic industrial workers. It is much likelier that, as in Catalonia, they will aspire to fill the upper echelons of their economy and leave the lower ones to immigrants. It is more than likely that the implementation of the Baltic language laws will be inconsistent and that they will be repeatedly amended. At first some categories of Russian speakers, such as Russian administrators in higher education, especially women, were fired.[211] In addition to individuals in elite positions, less protected groups, among them women, very probably will remain the other casualties of the language laws.

The time span provided for the linguistic transition was obviously too short for a successful implementation of the Baltic language laws. It is much likelier—and the concurrently passed electoral laws support this interpretation—that the aim of the law was not just to protect and promote the Estonian and Latvian languages, but to serve as a tool for the transfer of highly desirable jobs from Russian and other Slavs to native-born Balts. In fact, Lapidus observed that the campaigns to enhance the status of the republic's language at the expense of Russians were typically led by a coalition of political elites, intellectuals, and professionals whose status and career opportunities would be enhanced by the shift and by workers resentful of competition from Slavic immigrants into their republics.[212]

Under the language laws, the Estonian and Latvian authorities came close to considering Russian speakers a national minority. Estonian-language education was guaranteed under the law, and non-Estonians were granted the right to receive an education in their native languages, without correspondingly binding the republic to provide it to them.[213] The Latvian law tried to strike a balance between guaranteeing the rights on non-Latvians to be educated in private secondary and professional schools in their own languages and requiring the use of Latvian as the language of instruction in institutions of higher learning starting from the second year. The graduates of all secondary schools and above are also required to pass a Latvian language test.[214] Although the earlier version of the Latvian law made "legal provisions for Russian as the language of communication among nationalities" the Estonian law considered Russian only as "the most commonly occurring native language in the Estonian SSR after Estonian."[215]

The Russian-speaking minority then received a limited acknowledgment of its lingustic minority rights. The new policy is a far cry from the Estonian national minority policies of 1925, which allowed for the voluntary establishment of cultural self-governments and cultural councils, with the authority to tax their members and receive state funding to defray the costs of their educational cultural services, and even from the less generous Latvian policy of the interwar years. One of the reasons for the difference is that, after the First World War, members of minorities received citizenship in indepedent Estonia and Latvia, whereas after the dissolution of the USSR only a part of them did and the rest could, if they wish, apply for naturalization subject to (as we shall see in the next section) residency, language competence, and other requirements.

Indeed, the Russian speakers in the two new Baltic republics (there are fewer in Lithunia) are hybrid creatures, in between a minority and an immigrant population. Most moved to the Eastonian and Latvian SSRs when these were part of the USSR, and only with the collapse of the USSR did they find themselves a minority. At the same time, they have not constituted a national minority with a long history of being separate from the local population. Being neither fish nor fowl allows for treating them in one of two ways: as a minority, which, as we have seen, is the favored option of the Estonian and to a greater extent the Latvian governments, or as one group in a society with multicultural characteritics.

In the former case, the aim is to embark on the corporatist project of needing to defend Estonian and Latvian language and culture, respectively. In the latter case, the goal is the recognition of the nationally and ethnically mixed makeup of the two republics and the integration of the immigrant groups through the widening of the purview of the native culture to include their contributions. Viewing Russian speakers as a separate national minority, whose culture and language are to be reproduced means the rejection of the multicultural character and potential of Latvia and Estonia, which could lead to treating the Russians, Ukranians and Belorussians in the republic as immigrants who might be integrated and eventually maybe even assimilated into the Baltic cultures.

As early as 1989, Erika Dailey, a contributor to *Radio Liberty*'s publication wondered whether "perhaps the most complex problem raised by the language debates is the extent to which state status legislation coincides with the spirit of current political reform [i.e., *perestroika*]," which sought to foster "natural democratic tendencies." She pointed out that the transfer of the decision concerning language-related issues from Moscow to the republics "does not necessarily mean that the power of control is reduced."[216] Although the eponymous group was linguistically empowered by the language laws, the short time tables and the restrictions placed on language use that are part of the Baltic language laws placed nationalist interest above those of democratic or cultural pluralism or multiculturalism.

Our examination of Catalonia indicated that the culture of developed regions possess a hegemonic attraction for immigrants. Are there any indications of cultural assimilation on the part of Russians and other Slavic immigrants into the equally developed Baltic republics into the eponymous nationalities, during the years of Soviet political dominance?

According to the 1970 census, 3.7 percent of the Russian population of the USSR was reported to being fluently bilingual, and over three-quarters of this group lived outside the Russian republic. The scale of Russian bilingualism, as the Soviet sociolinguist Guboglo was quick to admit in 1987, "looks significantly modest in both static and dynamic form."[217] There is, however, significant variation in the rate of Russian bilingualism according to residence. Russians living in non-Muslim republics were more likely to learn the local language than Russians in the Muslim union republics. The Baltic republics (including Lithuania) and Armenia had some of the largest bilingual Russian populations: 12.5 percent in Estonia and 17 percent in Latvia and Armenia in 1970; and 14.1 percent in Estonia, 17.7 in Armenia, and 18.3 in Latvia in 1979.[218] Among bilingual Russians, 38.7 percent of the Russians in the Estonia were in the 11–29 age group and 44.8 in Latvia; this concentration of bilingual speakers in the younger age group points to the growth of bilingualism over time.[219] Indeed, the 1989 census showed that 21.1 percent of Russians (as well as 15.5 percent of Belorussians and 8.9 percent of Ukrainians) in Latvia reported to know Latvian, although the percentage of Russian bilinguals in Estonian had fallen slightly.[220]

Many analysts assume that "about 25 percent of the entire Russian-speaking community knows Latvian to some degree."[221] A survey taken among Russian inhabitants of Estonia in 1988 allows us to gauge the extent of their bilingualism in a more nuanced fashion. Here, 12.5 percent, almost the same as in the census, reported that they speak Estonian completely fluently. An additional 26 percent reported "adequate" knowledge of Estonian; 24 percent reported falling into the category of "understand but do not speak"; and 35 percent said that they know no Estonian at all.[222] This survey increases our confidence in the results of the census and also lays to rest the possibility that the self-reported category of fluency actually included diverse levels of bilingualism. The relatively high rates of Russian bilingualism in the Baltics again testifies to the correctness of Woolard's thesis that the state language, which in most areas of public life was Russian, imparts less prestige to a language than the region's level of relative economic development.

An examination of intermarriage rates also reveals the attraction of Baltic societies and identities for Slavic immigrants. In 1988, the rate of intermarriage between Latvians and non-Latvians was among the highest in the union republics, with the exception of the Ukraine and Belorussia, and amounted to 33.1 percent of all marriages.

The equivalent percent for Estonia was 16.1. These numbers are slightly under the 1978 rates of 34.1 and 17.4 percent, respectively, probably due to the increasing national tensions.[223]

The self-identification of the children of these mixed marriages also indicate a measure of willingness to assimilate into the Baltic nations. The Soviet internal passport system requires that children of mixed marriages choose the nationality on their passports when they reach age 16. This rigid choice is viewed as a test of assimilation by the Soviet ethnographer Bromley.[224] A study conducted in the 1960 by Terentjeva found that in Latvia and Estonia children of mixed marriages, in which one parent is Russian and the other belongs to the eponymous nationality, were more likely to chose the nationality of the Baltic parent over the Russian one. In Latvia 57 percent of the 16-year-olds and in Estonia fully 62 percent so chose. In Latvia the assimilation into the eponymous nationality was even higher among children whose other parent was Polish, Ukrainian, or Belorussian.[225] Misiunas and Taagepera found that the same trend continued through the 1980–1986 period.[226] This tendency, according to Dreifelds, continues the pattern of linguistic assimilation into Latvian society by members of minorities that existed between the two World Wars, in spite of the availability of state-supported schools for ethnic minorities in their own languages.[227]

The examination of both bilingualism and various measures of assimilation into the eponymous nationality indicate the hegemonic character of Baltics cultures. The reason for the attraction seemed to be the more developed material culture of the Baltics, which acted as the magnet for most of the immigrants at least since the mid-1950s. Another factor was the high prestige of the eponymous language of the developed region and its relatively assured status under the Soviet federal system. Two factors probably lowered the hegemonic attractiveness of the Baltic identity in comparison to Catalan. Knowledge of the native Baltic tongue was generally not required for social mobility; education at all levels was attainable in Russian and, in fact, higher education required knowledge of Russian and provided career advancement for a small percentage of non-Slavic individuals into the central power structure. Furthermore, the segmentation of the Baltic economy into two "ethnic" sectors provided alternative mobility channels to members of the two nationalities. For employment in certain high status jobs good knowledge of Russian was a sine que non, the "indigenization policy" set apart for members of the eponymous nation positions within the educational, administrative, and political systems.[228] Considering these differences, the attraction of Russian and other Slavic immigrants to the Baltic identity, without it providing stronger mobility possibilities, though lower than in the case of Catalonia, is impressive.

Citizenship Laws: Political Exclusion and Integration

The Russian and other Slavic immigrant groups in the Baltics republics are far from a homogenous entity. They are divided by a number of factors. Consequently, during the era of *perestroika* and the democratization struggle, the immigrants were pulled in opposite directions by the new reformist leadership in Moscow and the Baltic republics' Russian elites, who remained tied to the discredited forces of the ancien régime. The immigrants are also divided by economic class. Because they ran the whole gamut of occupations, some of the immigrants were part of the elites and others had blue-collar jobs; these groups were affected differently by the reforms. Finally, the immigrants to the Baltic republics were drawn from various parts of the USSR and united only by their current residence. In the views of one observer in 1990: "the Russians in the Baltic seem on the whole a fairly demoralized lot, flung together from all over the Soviet Union, a vast industrial class, without any real cultural institutions or much sense of community."[229] These observations seem even truer after Latvia and Estonia attained their independence. The Russians and other Slavs, not a well-established national minority but immigrants and their decedents who arrived in the Baltics in the post-1945 era, sought to "fill the vacuum left by the obsolescence of Soviet identity."[230]

Shortly after the formation of the Baltic Popular Fronts for *perestroika*, Yakovlev, one of *perestroika*'s architects, was sent to Latvia and Lithuania, where he met with both the local party leaders and the Baltic reformers. As a result of his report, Gorbachev replaced the first secretaries of the Latvian and Lithuanian Communist Party branches with supporters of *perestroika* and publicly hailed the Popular Fronts.[231] Gorbachev and Yakovlev chose to cooperate with Baltic nationalists because the latter shared the Moscow reformers' criticism of the centralized management of the Soviet economy. But, by siding with the Popular Fronts, Gorbachev also turned against the Russian economic, political, and military elites in the Baltics who derived their power, prestige, and privilege from their affiliation with the very centralized structures he wished to reform. This political alliance, which set the regional and national Russian leaderships against one another, had also sown confusion in the ranks of the immigrants and divided their loyalties. A survey of the political preferences and electoral choices of the immigrants demonstrates that the loss of old certainties and the struggle with the new splintering influences led a not inconsiderable number of the immigrants to identify with Baltic nationalism.

A *Christian Science Monitor* survey from October 1989 found that 79 percent Latvians and fully 64 percent of Russians in Latvia supported the Popular Front and its aims. At this time, however, these did not include breaking away from the USSR. The electoral choices of non-native-born Balts in the four electoral campaigns of the *perestroika* period—for the Soviet Congress of People's Deputies and the Council of Nationalities in March 1989, for municipal and regional Soviets in December 1989, for the Supreme Councils (or Soviets) of the Baltic republics in February–March 1990, and the plebiscite for independence in March 1991—witnessed a clear and growing measure of support not only for reform and democracy but also for Baltic nationalist aspirations. By rejecting in many cases the Russian candidates who were nominated mostly by the Moscow-based Communist Parties and Interfront, support for native-born Baltic nationalist candidates by the immigrants also meant the repudiation of the ancien régime. Consequently, in spite of the divisions between Balts and Russians, the Popular Front views and candidates (or independent candidates endorsed by them) gained the majority in all these elections.[232]

In the Supreme Council elections of early 1990, the percent of native-born Latvians elected was 70.1, while their share in the population was only 52 percent; and the respective numbers for Estonia were 76.2 out of 61.5 percent of the population.[233] The disproportionate support for representatives from the eponymous nationality resulted both from the lower electoral participation of the immigrants and from the support given by some of the immigrants to Baltic candidates. For example, although 80 percent of the residents of the Kohtla-Järve mining town in Estonia were not Estonians, they elected two Estonians in their five-seat district.[234] But the discrepancy in percentages between the population and the elected members was even larger in Latvia, where Russians made a higher portion of the republic's population, thus demonstrating that the Latvian Popular Front was particularly successful in "building bridges to non-Balts to a much larger extent than was the case in Estonia."[235]

In the March 1991 plebiscite, which was called by the Baltic Supreme Councils with the intention of preempting the Supreme

Soviet's March 17 referendum on maintaining the USSR as a "renewed federation," the turnout, in spite of calls for boycott by the Latvian Communist Party and Interfront, was as high as 87.6 percent. Among them 73.7 percent favored Latvian independence; such a high percentage of voting clearly indicates the participation and support on part of the immigrant population. Furthermore, the "yes" option carried in every district and city, including ones with Russian majorities.[236] Most surprising, the staff of the Helsinki Commission in charge of observing the counting of the votes in a neighborhood of Riga that is heavily populated by Soviet military officers, found that "the majority of voters cast ballots for independence."[237] A poll taken in December 1990 in Latvia, found that 47 percent of non-Latvians supported independence. Furthermore, the rate of approval increased with longevity of residence of Latvia: 30 percent among non-Latvians with less than twenty years of residence, 42 percent among those living in Latvia over twenty years, and 59 percent among those born in Latvia supported independence.[238]

In Estonia, 83 percent of the eligible voters participated in the plebiscite and 78.6 percent of them favored the restoration of Estonian independence.[239] According to an estimate by Taagepera based on a poll taken shortly before the plebiscite, 91 percent of Estonians and 71 percent on non-Estonians participated in the plebiscite and 96 percent of the Estonians and 40 percent on the non-Estonian voters supported independence.[240] Even according to a more conservative estimate, at least 20 percent of non-Estonians, almost all of whom were Russian, voted for Estonian independence,[241] but a comparison of successive polls in the period leading up to Estonia's independence from the USSR found that up to 37 percent of Russians residing in Estonia were supportive of Estonian independence.[242] At the same time, in the northeastern parts of Estonia where the population is overwhelmingly Russian, large margins supported in the March 17 referendum the renewal of the federation. Overall, the support given by the immigrant population to Baltic independence was somewhat higher in Latvia than in Estonia.

During both the crackdown by the Interior Ministry's contingents (the OMON) in Riga and Vilnius in January 1991 and the coup in August of that year, a portion of the Russian and Slavic immigrants came together with Baltic nationalists to defend the fledgling democracy and reforms.[243] The willingness of the Soviet authorities to allow the notorious OMON troops to continue a harassment campaign between the January crackdowns and the abortive August coup, including incidents in which civilians were killed, also "caused widespread revulsion among the non-Latvian [and, as other sources indicate, also nonEstonian] populations in the Baltic republics and throughout the rest of the Soviet Union as well."[244]

Attempts to classify the Slavic population in the Baltics according to their views of Baltic nationalism tend to divide them into three or four groups. The "old guard" of Communist Party members, all-union executives, military retirees, and in some cases workers in certain privileged branches of industry, together with Russian nationalists, were the major losers of the demise of the Soviet regime and, consequently, the most militant opponents of Baltic independence and its policies of marketization. A second category includes individuals in an ideological and, if the term may be permitted, identity limbo. Many in this category were apolitical, fearful of the deterioration of their economic status, but so far "put off defining their relationship or attitude toward their new country." The third group resembled the previous one, but it members were less parallyzed by uncertainty. Many in this group were younger, business-oriented Russians, who were critical of the flaws of the Soviet socio-economic system and, therefore, sympathized with Estonian independence but, at the same time, felt that Tallinn's demands on the Russian population were "too stringent and too hurried, given historical realities of he past fifty years." Finally, a fourth group included immigrants who had become naturalized citizens, were wishing to, or were in the process of doing so.[245]

Russians in Latvia seemed to be similarly divided, though the proportion of the groups in the extremes, the "old guard" and the petitioners and potential petitioners, were bigger than their counterparts in Estonia. It was estimated that there were about 41,000 retired KGB and Interior Ministry personnel and 20,000 retired military officers in Latvia. Because they were ineligible for naturalization, these retirees and their dependents, altogether about 200,000 strong,[246] were among the militant opponents of Latvian nationalism and independence. On the other hand, the CSCE high commissioner on national minorities, found that of the 617,443 noncitizens, who registered as part of the population registration that started in April 1992, fully 593,008 wished to acquire Latvian citizenship.[247]

Class divisions and employment patterns among the immigrant population account for much of the differentiation in the attitudes toward Baltic nationalism. The Russian and Slavic immigrants were divided between an elite that ran the all-union enterprises and the blue-collar workers employed in them and other places. In addition, the immigrant elites included those associated with the Soviet political and military organizations (the Communist Party, military, KGB and the like) that constituted the organizational hoops that held together the USSR. These bodies provided the leaders and much of the rank and file of the militant Interfront coalitions that supported abortive coup attempts in Lithuania and Latvia in January and in Latvia the failed coup of August 1991. The supporters of reform, political freedom, and Estonian and Latvian independence seem to have come mostly from two sources. First, they came from among the unskilled immigrants workers who were concerned less with loss of status and more with economic issues. For example, in a town meeting in a Russian-dominated town, Taagepera sensed "no ideo-logical or ethnic rift but negotiable bread-and-butter issues."[248]

It seems that against the economic decline that affected the USSR, life in an independent and well-developed Baltic republic appeared as relatively attractive prospects for many blue-collar workers. The second source of support came from the Westernizing segments of the Russian intelligentsia and professional stratum, harking back to its old division into Westernizers and Slavophiles. The "European" character of the Baltic republics and the repeated attempts to reform the USSR along Western patterns produced sympathy toward Baltic aspirations among the members of this group.

The support for Baltic nationalism and modernization of these two Russian groups is less surprising if we remember the results of plebiscites organized in 1918 in Eastern European regions of mixed ethnic composition. There were Poles who preferred living in Germany to living in a reborn Poland, and Slovenes who chose Austria over the new Yugoslavia for both economic and religious reasons.[249] Indeed, large percentages of Russians also voted for Ukrainian independence in the December 1991 referendum, hoping for a better future in a Ukraine rich in natural resources. In the Baltics, economic considerations alone seemed to carry much of the weight of support for Baltic independence among Russians.

In summary, a number of factors drew a segment of the immigrant population to sympathize with and actively support first the reform movement and subsequently the independence aspiration of Latvians and Estonians. First, many were critical of those aspects of Soviet life that Gorbachev sought to eradicate and, therefore, saw the Baltic reformers as their natural allies. Second, immigrants were divided among themselves and some segments of the intelligentsia as well as many unskilled workers saw the prospect of life in a relatively prosperous and "Europeanized" Baltic state appealing. Finally, as in Catalonia in 1907 and 1931, when the Solidaridad Catalana and the Esquerra Republicana de Catalunya united Catalans and Spaniards in defense of political freedom, and again in the 1970s when opposition to the Francoist dictatorship united people across ethnic and class divisions in both the Basque country and Catalonia, the struggle for reform and democracy helped build bridges between immigrants and the native born in the Baltics.[250]

It seems, however, that in contrast to Catalonia and the Basque country, the democratization struggle in the USSR was too short to bind together natives and immigrants under an umbrella of a hegemonic nationalism that was willing to integrate immigrants into the emerging independent Latvia and Estonia. Had the death agonies of the Soviet Union lasted longer and the reform movement been more protracted it is conceivable that during the period of Baltic "awakening" nationalists would have evolved a stronger hegemonic perspective within which the willingness of large cross-segments of the immigrants to be integrated into the transformed Baltics would have been viewed as outweighing past divisions.

As it was, Baltic nationalism, which upon attaining independence in 1920 evolved a strong hegemonic premise through its inclusionary minority policies, now coasted in the opposite direction and encouraged the emergence of a corporate nationalism based on the desire to protect the nation from the threat of "denationalization" seemingly posed by immigrants. The legacy of the protracted Soviet era and the alternative society and elite it brought into the Baltics loomed too large and the desire to undo it remained overwhelming. Whereas from the viewpoint of the USSR they performed a vital role in the process of Soviet state building, that is, the integration of the Baltics into the USSR, the very presence of immigrant elites, for the Baltic elites, was the result of an attempt to replace them or restrict their influence and privileged position. The Soviet authorities, during the early years of Baltic annexation went to great lengths to destroy and undermine the elites of the independent Baltic states. Not surprising, for the remaining and new economic, cultural, and political elite strata in Estonia and Latvia, the Soviet state building to which they were subjected was a manifestation of *political imperialism* and, hence, illegitimate.

The drive for establishing a privileged republican citizenship preceded Baltic independence but its evolution clearly reflects the growing influence of the radical, separatist and exclusionary, wing of Baltic nationalism. Prior to independence only the Lithuanian Supreme Council considered it wise to adopt citizenship laws, because there were fewer Slavic immigrants in Lithuania, while its Latvian and Estonian counterparts after considering various drafts settled for passing election laws, before the 1989 elections to the Baltic republic's Supreme Councils, which acted in place of citizenship laws in restricting eligibility to vote. Both the Estonian and Latvian electoral laws stipulating that candidates must be citizens (as will be defined by the Law on Citizenship once it was to be adopted) who reached 21 years of age and have lived in Estonia for at least ten years.[251] Additional Latvian laws included restrictions based on citizenship: although all residents of Latvia were to be allowed to cultivate Latvian land, only its citizens were accorded the right to own it.[252]

The Soviet reformers accepted the right of the republics to legislate their official language, but they rejected the imposition of restrictions on citizenship. Although the USSR had historically recognized the existence of republic citizenship, in practice this status was seen as overlapping with USSR citizenship and, therefore, devoid of content. Consequently, the 1989 Soviet Nationalities Policy reaffirmed that "a citizen of a Union republic is simultaneously a citizen of the USSR." In expressing its opposition to the Baltic desire to adopt a separate citizenship for some, but not all, of their residents, the new Soviet Nationalities Policy statement stated that "privileges for some Soviet citizens and the infringement of the rights of others for reasons of nationality, religion, language or length of residence are impermissible."[253]

Parallel with the incorporation of the Popular Front's citizenship policy into the election laws by the Baltic republic's Supreme Councils, and their ineffective annulment by the USSR Supreme Soviet because of their violation of "the principles of universal and equal election rights,"[254] another extralegal grassroots drive, even more dramatic and more restrictive in its methods for defining citizenship, took place in Latvia and Estonia. This was the initiave of the radical nationalist organizations: in Estonia the National Independence Party and an assortment of smaller organizations, such as the Historical Preservation Society and the Christian Union; in Latvia by the Movement for the National Independence, the Helsinki-86 group, and the Environmental Defense Club. In contrast to the Popular Fronts the alliances of these bodies declared from the outset their aspiration for renewed Baltic independence. Even when the Popular

Fronts made the goal of independence their own toward the end of 1989, tactical differences continued to divide these two wings of Baltic nationalism. The Popular Fronts used the legality of *perestroika* and the openness of its electoral process to dominate the official Soviet political institutions of their respective republic's, and the National Independence Parties viewed the Soviet regime as illegitimate and, therefore, sought the accomplishment of their aims by means of establishing legal continuity with the prewar Baltic republics.

Starting in February 1989 in Estonia and in May 1989 in Latvia, the radical wings of the nationalist movements set up its networks of Citizens Committees. These committees undertook grassroots campaigns to separate the "legitimate" citizens of Estonia and Latvia from "illegal immigrants." Individuals who had Estonian and Latvian citizenship prior to June 1940 and their descendants, even if they were emigres, were registered as legitimate citizens, whereas immigrants who so wished were registered only as applicants for citizenship. These applicants received no assurance that they would be guaranteed citizenship because "only the lawful government established after the restoration of state authority...has the right to make a final decision about the granting of citizenship." Immigrants' citizenship status, according to the radical nationalists, was to be decided only after decision concerning independence had been made.[255]

The attempt to roll back history and use the last year of Baltic independence as the chronological divide for citizenship applied an apparently civic right, the jus soli, rather than outright ethnic criterion to citizenship rights, such as the jus sanguinis. By investing a significant date with legal meaning, the Independence Parties expressed their willingness to admit prewar Russian residents into citizenship. Such approach seems to demonstrate a willingness to integrate Russian and other Slavs into the body of the Latvian and Estonian nations, that is, it appears to indicate the existence of hegemonic nationalist aspirations.

Practically, however, the particular kind of criterion chosen— the admission into citizenship of all those who had Estonian and Latvian citizenship prior to June 1940 and their descendants—did not carry the implications the choice of civic criteria has over ethnic criteria. This was a civic criterion that excluded many immigrants even if it included a small percentage of Russian speakers. The percentage of Russians, Ukrainians, and Belorussians present in the Baltic republics during years of independence was only fifth as much as it is now. In 1935, 75.5 percent of Latvia's residents were Latvian,

10.6 percent were Russian, and 1.5 percent were Belorussians or Ukrainians; of the two largest minorities, Germans (3.2 percent) left for Germany before the war and Jews (4.8 percent) were destroyed during the Holocaust, frequently with local support.[256] In Estonia in 1934 (within its then-existing borders), Estonians made up 88 percent of the state's population, and Russians 8.3 percent.[257] In addition, the Russians admitted to citizenship could be outnumbered by those citizens of Latvia and Estonia who emigrated after 1940 but were accepted as citizens though they were not present on Baltic soil. The sharp chronological dividing line of 1940, therefore, disenfranchised at one fell swoop the great majority of non-Latvian and non-Estonians and established a quasi-primordial criterion for citizenship. Jus soli in this system amounted for all practical purposes to citizenship based on jus sanguinis.

The intention of this legislation, according to George Ginzburgs's article in the *Journal of Baltic Studies*, was "to establish local citizenship criteria that would enable the titular ethnic stock to regain control of its political life in such a way as to allow a genuine test of the desire for self-determination."[258] The narrowing of the basis of political decision makers may also be presented in a more sinister light; again in Ginsburgs's words, to "shrink the political franchise at the debut in order to 'stack the deck' for a plebiscite tally that will consummate the territory's sovereign emancipation."[259]

The registered bona fide Latvian and Estonian citizens elected the Estonian and Latvian Congresses, respectively, which convened in the spring of 1990 and were, according to the organizers, the "lawful representative body" of the republics.[260] Immigrants who applied for citizenship were allowed to elect nonvoting delegates. This grassroots drive was strongly opposed by the Supreme Councils, which objected to the creation of an alternative power structure, and was either ignored or halfheartedly supported by the moderate Popular Fronts. Obviously, the Popular Fronts of Latvia and Estonia were wary of further alienating the noneponymous populations as long as it seemed that independence will be achieved through the electoral process; that is, through secession that receives the seal of the Soviet authorities. The Popular Front-dominated Baltic Supreme Councils, however, also sought to limit the voting rights of the noneponymous population, if only in a more limited and less intrusive fashion. The attainment of the Baltic self-determination "without denying the logic" of Baltic nationalist arguments, points out Ginsburgs, was "predicated on the deployment—never mind how short lived—of a discriminatory screening process."[261]

When the independence of the Baltic republics arrived as a result of the destruction of the central Soviet authorities in the wake of the failed August coup, the tactical difference between the Popular Fronts' more moderate and the more radical and exclusionary versions of the National Independence Parties and Citizens Committees lost much of their import. Because the legality of *perestroika* mattered no more, the 1940 line of demarcation emerged as the decisive test of citizenship. In the many-phased struggle over the definition of Estonian citizenship, the civic criteria, on which potentially hegemonic aspirations for the integration of immigrants could have been predicated, were pushed aside by the corporate delineation of nationhood, intolerant of the admission of most of the Russian and Slavs into citizenship within the near future.

On February 26, 1992, the Estonian legislature adopted, with the smallest possible majority, a Citizenship Law that guaranteed Estonian citizenship to those individuals who were Estonian citizens before June 16, 1940, and their descendants. Immigrants already living in Estonia who wished to become citizens were required to apply for citizenship and be naturalized. Under this law the Estonian authorities were granted only one year to approve or reject the applications and the individuals whose applications were granted would become citizens of Estonia two years later but only upon swearing a loyalty oath and passing a language test.[262] When in 1992, the first elected parliament of independent Estonia granted Estonian citizenship to persons who held such citizenship in the republic of Estonia between 1920 and 1940 and their descendants, only about 30,000 Russian citizens of prewar Estonia and their descendants received citizenship.[263]

For residents of Estonia who were left without citizenship, the Estonian parliament chose to apply the 1938 Citizenship Law's relatively lenient requirements for naturalization. The conditions for naturalization were two years of residence, language proficiency, a permanent source of income, and a loyalty oath. For the 40,000 Russians who applied for citizenship under the auspices of the Congress of Estonia, residency and language requirements were waived in February 1993. Further, citizenship was granted at birth to children with at least one parent who is a citizen or entitled to become one.[264]

It seems that these conditions of naturalization indicate a path from the corporate to the hegemonic conception of nationhood. The struggle over citizenship rights and criteria is far from over, however; and "parliamentary sessions have been dogged by a series of legislative proposals to reduce the status of non-Estonian residents."[265] On May 19, 1993, the Parliament passed the Law on Local Elections that, in violation of an earlier understanding with the Council of Europe, gave noncitizens the right to vote for local government but withheld from them the right to run as candidates.[266] Subsequently the right-wing National Independence Party proposed a "decolonization" law. But the greatest controversy ensued from the passing, on June 21, 1993, of the Law on Aliens. This law, clearly in conflict with the spirit of the revived 1938 Citizenship Law, classified all non-Estonian citizens, that is, all immigrants who arrived after 1940, as aliens and required that they apply within one year for residence.

Under the combined pressure of the Russian-speaking districts in Estonia, the decision of the Russian Parliament to suspend troop withdrawals, and the urging of the CSCE and the Council of Europe and in conformity with its specific requirements, the Estonian parliament following President Lennart Meri's lead revised some clauses of the law. The requirement that permanent residents reregister every five years was dropped as was the condition that aliens who "compromised Estonia's national interests and international reputation" would lose their alien passports.[267] But the Law on Aliens' requirement that all those defined as aliens, including many who had lived in Estonia for many years, need to apply for residence in Estonia had the unsettling effect of temporarily uniting the moderate and radical organizations of Russian speakers and led to referenda for national-territorial autonomy within Estonia in Narva and Sillamea.

The Estonian approach to the immigrant population has many traces of the integrationist approach toward immigrants I associated with hegemonic nationalism. This consists of the self-confidence of a relatively developed region that its continuous modernization underwrites the project of nationalist independence and, therefore, that the process of economic expansion will strengthen the prestige of its culture and language and make possible the absorption of newcomers. This confidence, however, is limited by the legacy of the apprehension that outside forces are a threat against which protection is required and is butressed by the association of immigrants with the former Soviet state and the all-union sector of the economy. Consequently, the hegemonic project remains incoherent and inconsistent and besieged by doubts and reversals demonstrated by the adoption of the Law on Aliens, in violation of the more liberal clauses of naturalization of the 1938 Citizenship Law ratified earlier. The general tendency in Estonia seems to resemble in some respects the Catalan example but it has not attained the solidity of the Catalan hegemonic approach and has not disposed of the shadows of the *corporate* view of Estonian society.

Latvia, with the highest percentage of non-Baltics among the three Baltic republics, was the last to adopt a citizenship law. The Latvian approach, starting with a series of guidelines that amount to a rudimentary citizenship law, remained the most restrictive of the Baltic republics. On October 15, 1991, the citizens of the republic of Latvia on June 17, 1940, and their descendents were declared citizens. Again, the criterion of membership chosen, the restoration of previous citizenship, was civic and based on the legal approach of jus soli. According to one source this has included the considerable number of 300,000–500,000 non-Latvians, a number at once imprecise and exaggerated even at its lower end, while excluding about 30,000–40,000 ethnic Latvians who were not citizens in 1940 or descendants of citizens. Simultaneously, guidelines for naturalization were laid down. As in Estonia, they include the knowledge of conversational Latvian and a loyalty oath. The law also prohibits dual citizenship and, in contrast to the Estonian practice, establishes a residency requirement of sixteen years. An alternative plan, favored by Prime Minister Godmanis from the Popular Front, called for a residency requirement of only five years. It did not command much support, and when the Popular Front was voted out of office the hopes of adopting a less restrictive law approach faded.[268]

The naturalization requirements also denied the right of citizenship to retired members of the Soviet armed or interior forces and persons accused of spreading "chauvinism, fascism, communism, and other...totalitarian ideas."[269] The internal debate was sharpened during the electoral campaign for the first parliament elected in independent Latvia. Latvia's Way, the party that received the largest number of votes in the June 1993 elections, supported the transformation of the guidelines into law. The second largest party, the National Independence Movement, wished to adopt yearly quotas for naturalization and make sure that Latvians constitute at least 75 percent of all citizens. The third party in size, Harmony for Latvia, sought a lenient citizenship and naturalization law, whereas Fatherland and Freedom supported the voluntary repatriation of immigrants.[270]

A complex and restrictive citizenship was debated by the Latvian Parliament in the summer of 1994 and adopted in early August. The law gave easy acess to immigrants who had family connections to Latvia, either through marriage or descent. Those born in Latvia, however, were not given citizenship but the option of applying for it before the end of the century. The rest, about 300,000 immigrants, following the suggestion of the National Independence Movement, were to be covered by quotas that would allow only about 2,000 individuals to be naturalized per year.[271] In combining the principles of a limited jus soli and a sweeping jus sanguinis Latvian nationalists chose the route of corporate nationalism, disenfranchising hundreds of thousands of immigrants and preventing them from owning land.

Needless to say, considerable controversy has been generated by the exclusionary practices of Baltic nationalism, from the early language and elections laws to the postindependence citizenship drafts and laws. The basic position of the Baltic radical nationalists is that the issue is one of the restoration of internationally recognized rights that were violated through an agreement between the two worst dictators of the twentieth century. The moderate proponents of the restrictions imposed through these legal measures point out that no country is expected to accept all immigrants, that most European countries have residency requirements, and many countries require loyalty oaths. The counterargument of many Russian and other Slavic minority members in effect amounts to suggesting an alternative historical and political context for determining citizenship rights. This alternative perspective, supported by Ginsburgs, is that the situation in which Baltic independence from the USSR was realized resembles the dissolution of multiethnic states, such as in the Hapsburg empire in the wake of the First World War. Under such circumstances, the legal precedent calls for providing "an opportunity to the members of the 'foreign' element caught in a secession case freely to vote in an individual capacity to retain their previous citizenship by a fixed date, failing which they [are] deemed to have acquiesced in being counted among the citizens of the fledgling entity."[272] Such policy would be built on the "zero-option" approach favored by most immigrants, who point out that since "they had immigrated into Estonia [or Latvia] under the laws in force as they understood them at the time, or since many of them had been born in Estonia [or Latvia]," they are entitled to make a choice from a clean slate.[273] The advantage of this approach, according to its proponents, is that it affirms the choice of those affected instead of imposing an unpopular solution. As its result, those individuals who elect to belong to the new state forfeit their previous citizenship and their former state simultaneously "waives all further claims to them." At the same time, a decision by the individuals involved to retain their former citizenship and "not to join the national constituency amounts to a voluntary surrender of political rights."[274] This solution would prevent statelessness as well as dual nationality.

The sociological approach adds an important dimension to this debate. By pointing out that a large cross-section of the immigrants to Latvia and Estonia, like most other relatively developed regions, have shown in various ways, through electoral support for reform and later independence, language acquisition, intermmariage, choice of nationality, and so forth, a willingness to be integrated into the host society, it indicates that the "zero option" is not inherently threatening Latvia and Estonia with "denationalization." On the contrary, it could help sort out those immigrants who prefer to remain unequivocally Russian and those who find that their ties to their residnece outweighs the import of their origins and who want to follow the course of integration on which they have already embarked.

However, the desire of large segments of the immigrant population to request citizenship and show indications of willingness to be integrated into the host society and its culture seems to be of lesser importance than the pattern of structural relations established between them and the host society in accounting for the openness of the latter to the immigrants' integration, as a comparison of Estonia and Latvia demonstrates. The percentage of bilinguals among the Russian and other Slavic immigrants was higher in Latvia than in Estonia (and the precent of Latvians speaking Russian higher than of Estonian Russian speakers) as was the percentage of immigrants supporting independence, and the Latvian Popular Front tried harder and was more successful in building bridges to the immigrants than its Estonian counterpart.[275]

But these indicators of commonality and early rapproachment were overshadowed by the far greater weight of the Russian immigrant elite in Latvian than in Estonia, as shown, for example, by the fact that heavy industrial component of the Soviet all-union sector was larger in Latvia than in Estonia, that Russians made up the majority in all the major cities in Latvia whereas the majority of the inhabitants of both Tallinn and Tartu were Estonian, and that during the January 1991 assaults on Baltic nationalists a pro-Soviet National Salvation Front appeared in Riga (and Vilnius) but not in Tallinn. Though more immigrants sympathized with Baltic nationalism, the polarization within the immigrant community was also greater in Latvia than in Estonia and their connections with and influence in Soviet institutions was more substantial. Latvian nationalists therefore, felt that they had more to fear from the immigrant elites but went about the business of limiting their influence in a greatly exaggerated fashion, by restricting the access to citizenship of large number of immigrants. Finally, the Estonian economy is recovering faster than its Latvian counterpart, and therefore, the integration of immigrants there seems be an easier task than in Latvia.

By insisting on the exclusivist, primordialist solution and the corresponding corporate view on immigration, the radical wings of the Baltic nationalist movements, stronger in Latvia than in Estonia, sought to purge the impact of the Soviet period from their respective histories and "redeem the country's national personality."[276] By doing so, the Latvian nationalist movement, and to a lesser degree its Estonian counterpart, demonstrated the difficulty, maybe even inability, to contemplate the hegemonic inclusionary approach according to the Catalan and the contemporary Basque models. What are the reasons for the choice of the radical exclusionary option, in the form of language, voting, and citizenship laws, and the lack of appeal of the Catalan and recent Basque views that defines the eponymous nationality as "everyone who lives and works in Catalonia" or "in the Basque country"?

This question takes us back to the examination of the economic relations and the difference between the Soviet and Spanish experiences.

Privatization and Its Ethnic Discontents

A major cause for the strength of the corporate attitude of Latvian nationalists toward the immigrants in their midst is the close association between the economic, political, and ethnic dimensions of the Russian immigrant community in the Baltic republics. The political context of this immigration—the Soviet project of state bulding in the newly acquired republics after the Second World War— meant that a large portion of the immigrants were connected with those institutions involved with the centralization of the USSR and, further, that they were the elite of a separate enclave of the economy, and finally, that they were associated with the economic interests threatened by decentralizing reforms. Consequently, before opposing Baltic nationalism, the traditional leadership of the immigrants also opposed Gorbachev's reforms.

In Catalonia and the Basque provinces immigrants usually voted for Spanish political parties, and this response, as *larrouxismo* demonstrated, was sometimes motivated by opposition to regional nationalism. At the same time, at critical moments when political freedom and democracy were at stake, they joined ranks with Catalan and Basque nationalists who were at the forefront of the opposition to centralizing Spanish dictatorships. There was, however, little or no regional political self-organization of Spaniards in these regions. Not so in the Baltics: in all three republics, part of the Slavic, and especially the Russian, population continued supporting the CPSU during the *perestroika* years and in addition also organized their own regional bodies to oppose Baltic nationalism. One members of the Russian elite in Estonia explained at the Congress of the USSR's People Deputies the rationale for this step: "The CPSU Central Committee and the Presidium of the Supreme Soviet are well aware of how events are developing in the Baltic republics. No attention is being given however, to the numerous appeals from labor collectives, primary Party organizations and individual citizens expressing alarm and concern about the future of Estonia. One has the impression that the rescue of those who are drowning is being left up to the drowning people themselves."[277]

The self-organization on part of the Russian immigrants in the Baltic republics was due to their opposition to the new reformist tendencies in the USSR. Although many of the Russians were willing to pay lip service to Gorbachev's restructuring movement and to his attempts to lay legal foundations for political power in the USSR, they knew that the decentralization of authority from Moscow to the republics would undermine the institutions—all-union ministries and enterprises under their control and the Communist Party—that were the bases of their power, status, and privilege. Unlimited support for economic and political reform in the Baltic republics came from the eponymous nationalities that sought to use restructuring to increase their control over regional economic resources and self-determination.

Whereas in Catalonia the division between Catalans and immigrants was horizontal, in the Basque country until the Civil War and in the Baltics it was vertical. The latter structure was obviously more prone to conflict because of competing elites well positioned to justify their privileges and status in nationalist terms. In contrast to the democratization movements in Spain that were tied only marginally to economic reform, Gorbachev's reform movement sharpened after 1988 the ethnic divisions within the Baltic republics, pitting the two elites, the eponymous and the immigrant, against each other. Those immigrants who opposed the potential benefits that the eponymous nationalities might reap from *perestroika*, as a threat on their own status, found themselves in opposition to the Gorbachev regime.

In this fashion, during the early period of the reform movement traditional alliances were reversed: the purportedly unifying ethnic bond between Russians in Moscow, Latvia, and Estonia, which also tied together the centralizing bodies in the center and the outlying republics, was abandoned in favor of a new coalition of regional nationalists and Soviet reformers.

The association between the economic and the ethnic dimensions of the Russian self-organization in the Baltics are illustrated, for example, by the close connection between the Internationalist Movement and the United Council of Estonian Labor Collectives (UCELC, formerly the United Council of Production Collectives).[278] The Baltic Russian elite, in charge of a large economic sector, organized its major oppositional activities within the all-union enterprises' labor collectives (i.e., the employees at all ranks of the enterprise).[279] The UCELC was founded by the republic's major enterprises, and leadership of both the UCELC and Interfront was recruited from among the managers of the largest all-union enterprises. By late 1988, UCELC already united over 100 enterprises "in which the majority of workers [were] Russian-speaking." In its Constituent Congress, some of the largest enterprises, employing 120,000 workers, were represented. On the eve of UCELC Congress, the Popular Front organized its corresponding Union of Estonian Republic Labor Collectives, which enlisted in addition to mostly Estonian-speaking industrial enterprises also collective farms, state farms, and institutions in the nonproduction sphere.[280] The dividing line between the two labor unions was ethnic, but these divisions overlapped in large measure with sectoral division between heavy industry and cultural institutions and farms and between the type of control under which they operated: all-union versus republican.

The Estonian Interfront was opposed above all to the weakening of the USSR's centralized power and the loosening of the ties between the USSR the Estonian SSR. In the economic sphere the Estonian Interfront rejected the path of self-financing (or self-management) for the republic[281] and declared "against the blanket elimination of all Union and Union-republic ministries and the...complete legal resubordination of all enterprises...to the Estonian Republic's leadership bodies." In defining itself in opposition to the Popular Front, "the Internationalist Movement believes that large plants and associations, especially those important to defense,...can be managed and supplied more competently only by central agencies." The Internationalist Movement also went on record as resisting encroachment on its members' privileged access to resources by stating that it could not "fully support the idea of the independent setting by the republic of prices and wage rates." Finally, Interfront categorically rejected the introduction of Estonian citizenship and language laws and demanded that both Estonian and Russian will be declared state languages.[282]

The Estonian and Latvian Internationalist Movements held a series of strikes, for example, on Estonian railroads and at the Riga commercial seaport, against legislation that affected the all-union enterprises and the immigrant population adversely.[283] Because the products of the striking all-union enterprises were usually exported to the RSSFR, the strikes simultaneously sought to pressure the central authorities to protect the Russian population in its confrontation with Baltic nationalism.[284] During the January 1991 crackdown and the August 1991 coup, all-union enterprises, labor collectives, and the Interfront movements expressed their support for the hardliners who sought to roll back Baltic economic and political accomplishments. In fact, one of the major leaders of the ancien régime's defenders in the Congress of People's Deputies was Colonel Alksenis, a Russian officer stationed in Latvia, who lambasted Gorbachev for not bringing the January coup to completion in Latvia and Lithuania and abandoning the conspirators.

The Popular Front's uncompromising opposition toward the Internationalist Movements and its labor collective organizations resulted from *two* reasons. First, the elite of the Russian and Slavic immigrant population that led these organizations enjoyed the benefits of controlling the all-union economic sector in the republic and the privileges and resources that it provided. The partial exclusion of the eponymous nationality from, and lack of control over, these enterprises was an important source of discontent among Baltic nationalists. Second, the Interfront was part of the economic and political force that stood in the way of furthering the market-driven modernization of the Baltic economy. In the process of freeing the development of the productive forces of their republic, Baltic reformers and nationalists had to break the fetters of the all-union ministry-controlled enterprises. Just as Soviet rule was part of the archaic framework that held up Baltic development so were the all-union enterprises and their managerial elites on Baltic soil. Privatization in the Baltic republics, therefore, is a tool for both reversing exclusion from the all-union sectors of the economy and economic modernization.

Privatization is an especially potent mechanisms for accomplishing both aims at once. Latvia's November 1992 law of privatization vouchers, seemingly using nonethnic criteria, establishes a bond between length of residence in the republic and the number of vouchers individuals receive. Citizens receive one voucher for each year they resided in the republic and an extra fifteen vouchers for "their forefathers' contribution to Latvia during the inter-war period." Noncitizens receive one voucher for each year they resided in Latvia but five of these vouchers are subtracted because they did not build pre-World War Two Latvia. Similarly vouchers are deducted from the noncitizens allotment for membership in the CP, the KGB, and the military.[285]

Immigrants are affected adversely in yet another way, because the marketization and privatization of the Baltic economies affects the all-union and republic-controlled economic sectors differently. The resources likely to drive future development, according to economists, are human capital, technological education, scientific research directed toward light industry, electrical engineering, and computers, which require small-scale but flexible production organization.[286] Agricultural production is also likely to expand and modernize, and educational and administrative employment will undoubtedly increase as well. In short, "Estonians and Latvians are heavily involved in activities that have good prospects in the transformed economies" and in "the new forms of entrepreneurial activity."[287] Conversely, the large-scale enterprises, many of them involved in military production and dependent on the import of their raw materials, are less likely to make a successful transition to a market economy, as the accumulated experience in both Eastern Europe and China demonstrates.

Privatization of the state economy in the industries of high Russian employment in the Baltic republics of Latvia and Estonia, such as heavy industry and transportation, "will almost surely lead to unemployment as many of Latvia's [and certainly Estonia's as well] large industries will be forced to trim excess labor in order to produce competitive goods."[288] Because Russians and other Slavs are heavily concentrated in the industries that are most likely to suffer unemployment in the process of privatization, the rates of unemployment between the eponymous nationalities and the immigrant populations are likely to vary greatly. In fact, one observer concluded that "it would be beyond the bounds of human restraints for future Estonian [and even more so the Latvian] government not to use unemployment as a means of encouraging Russians to leave, and some nationalists to whom I spoke made no secret of their hopes to do just this."[289] At the same time, the privatization of the all-union enterprises might differentiate between those immigrants, mostly members of the economic and political elite, who see their future in Russia from the blue-collar workers who prefer to say in the Baltics and might lead to an increased willingness among the hosts to grant the latter group Estonian and Latvian citizenship.

The Baltic nationalist dream, and its occasional crass and intolerant expressions, of ridding of the republics from Russian and other, mostly Slavic immigrants, relies at least on part on past experiences. In 1953, during Khrushchev's Thaw, immigration into the Baltic republics not only stopped (with the exception of the year 1956 in Latvia), but some emigration took place that, coupled with return of deportees, briefly reversed the decline of the share of ethnic Latvians and Estonians in their respective republics.[290] In addition, Russian in-migration was accompanied by considerable return migration, in some periods and areas to the tune of half or even three quarters of the immigration. Departure of immigrants indicates that at least part of the immigrant communities are made up of "guest workers," or as they are called now in the Baltic republics, *migrants*, of a transient nature.[291] Many others, however, have been in Latvia and Estonia for many years, raised families there, and are unlikely to leave.

The combined linguistic, political, and economic restrictions imposed on the immigrant populations will speed up the exclusion of the immigrant populations from the Baltic economies. Although privatization is likely to affect mostly those enterprises and their employees that were most closely related to the centralizing Soviet state and are least likely to become integral parts of a modern Baltic economy, the other forms of exclusion lump together all Russian and Slavic immigrant populations. Among those adversely affected are those Russians, Ukrainians, Belorussians, and so forth who were born in the Baltics or lived there for a long time, who have assimilated in part culturally and maybe even supported or voted for the Baltic reformist and independence movements. They are lumped together with the Interfront and labor collectives that were opposed to economic reform and political independence for the Baltics.

The economic strategy suggested as the foundation for the modernization of the Baltic economies—the "gateway strategy"[292]— that would be based on the exploitation of the location of the Baltic states at the intersection of the East-West (and to a lesser extent the North-South) lines would also be adversely affected by the corporate nationalism and exclusionary strategies of the Baltic republics. Transportation facilities, warm-water ports, telecommunications, and a technically well-qualified labor force would be used, according to this plan, for transforming a favorable location into trade and investment routes that would knot together Western and Eastern economies. There is "widespread consensus among the Baltic leaders and experts that the gateway strategy should be adopted."[293]

A gateway, notwithstanding the narrow economic foundation of this strategy, is most likely to succeed when it is also a microcosm of the poles it is tying together. A gateway strategy requires not just facilities of transshipment but is also predicated on cultural openness and served by the mixing of cultures. The Far Eastern "little tigers," for example, are not just manufacturing and trading centers but also cosmopolitan cities. Many of their residents are immigrants from the societies they trade with and serve as gateways. Some of the Baltic cities, such as Riga, Vilnius, and Tallinn, possessed sizeable German, Polish, Jewish, and Russian populations while they were part of the Romanov empire and during their independent existence between the wars. Vilnius once was the "Jerusalem of Lithuania" in Jewish perception. The creation of a class of permanent noncitizens or difficult-to-assimilate citizens who belong to one of the intended poles will limit the development of the Baltics as an economic gateway. If the cosmopolitan traditions of the culturally and ethnically mixed cities that once flourished on the Baltic shores and the liberal minority policies of independent Estonia, reflecting a hegemonic nationalism, can flourish once again, the corporate nationalist approach toward immigrants will be relaxed and the international place of the of the Baltic republics among its large neighbors will be more secure and their chances of successful economic modernization enhanced.

6

CONCLUSION

The focus of this study is the interaction of one of most potent ideological movements of our era—nationalism—and the movement of growing numbers of people in search of better and safer lives—immigration. Global migration, and even internal immigration within multinational states, intrudes upon the convenient myth of the nation-state as the shelter of a culturally homogenous citizenry. Consequently, immigrants are embedded simultaneously in two settings: the economic forces of push and pull that lead them from underdeveloped homelands to developed regions and the nationalist movements and sentiments that beget conflict and accommodation between them and their hosts. To do justice to both contexts, I sought to combine on these pages the two, usually distinct, theoretical frameworks that focus on the origins and dynamics of nationalism in developed regions and on patterns of immigrant-host relations.

In the study of immigrant-host relationships we distinguish three alternative approaches. The classical liberal theory of *push and pull* expects immigrants to seek social betterment through migration from less to more developed regions. There, in the process of social mobility, the immigrants undergo structural integration into the local economic and political organizations and cultural assimilation by learning the local language, intermarrying with local spouses, and identifying with their adopted land. Conversely, the neo-Marxist *segmentation* theory, which also considers immigration to be the result of the uneven development of the world capitalist order, expects immigrants, their descendants, and hosts to remain permanently divided economically and, therefore, to reproduce and even amplify their cultural differences.

Though there are many indications that immigrants who arrived to Catalonia and the Basque country after the Second World War are in the process of becoming integrated and assimilated into their chosen societies, there also remain questions and doubts as to how deep will this process be. Not surprising, there is a recent theory of *multiculturalism,* perched uneasily between the previous two, that expects immigrants to retain part of their distinct culture even as they are integrated into some facets of their host society and anticipates that the culture of the hosts will broaden to accommodate the diversity produced by immigration.

It is not clear, however, to what extent multiculturalism describes an empirical reality or is a political program to create it and whether the situation its proponents describe is temporary, leading to either assimilation or segmentation, or a permanent third state. But whatever measure of segregation or integration will emerge between immigrants and their hosts it seems that the goal of cultural homogeneity becomes ever more difficult and costly to uphold and justify, and the multicultural character of developed societies, almost all of which are to some extent also immigration societies, is, therefore, in the process of being acknowledged. In part, this recognition is the effect of the globalization of world economy that, in addition to its homogenizing influences, also augments regional, technological, and cultural diversity by intensifying the division of labor required to remain developed.

To examine the conflicts and accommodation between nationalists and immigrants I chose to study Catalonia and the Basque country in Spain and Estonia and Latvia while they were part of the USSR and in the three years following their independence, because they share two central characteristics: they all are relatively developed regions in comparison to the state they are, or were, part of but, at the same time, are also known as possessing distinct cultures and nationalist movements of their own. In such relatively developed regions, the native inhabitants are not very likely to be threatened by the competition of tho immigrants who elected their regions as their adopted land and, furthermore, display a distinct desire to integrate and even assimilate into the high-prestige culture they associate with high levels of development. And yet, nationalists in the Basque country between 1893 and 1936 and in Latvia and Estonia today are opposed to the integration of immigrants. In contrast, the socialist nationalists of the Basque country and Catalan nationalists are willing to accept the integration of the Spanish immigrants into their occupational frameworks and political life and into their society and culture as part of their people.

A central reason for the relative openness of nationalists in relatively developed regions toward immigrants is that their variety of nationalism, as pointed out by Nairn and Gourevich, is due to the desire to enhance the region's modernization and free it from the restrictions imposed by a backward state; separatism and modernization are viewed as two sides of the same coin. For most developed regions, the very possibility of enhanced capitalist development serves as a spur to nationalism.[1] Where modernization underlies nationalism, development and its corollaries are likely to be seen in a positive light and immigrants are accepted as necessary contributors to the prosperity of the region by increasing its labor pool; in short, not as competitors but as complements to the local effort.

The opposition to the integration of the immigrants, as I pointed out throughout this study, is not a reflection of the immigrants' lack of desire to be part of their new society and its culture; in fact, the language and culture of regions that are more developed than their neighbors are usually accorded considerable prestige. Where, in addition, the native language is a useful means of social mobility, immigrants will have added incentive to become bicultural and bilingual on the path to integration.

A brief comparative examination of the data presented in Chapters 3, 4, and 5 concerning the immigrants' willingness in relatively developed regions to integrate into the social structure of their adopted land and to assimilate into its culture and society by means of bilingualism, intermarriage, voting patterns, and self-identification.

The gap between the highest reported percent of Spaniards who speak fluent Catalan (27.3 percent) in Catalonia and the lowest percent of fluent Estonian-speaking Russians (14.1 percent) in Estonia is about half, and the lowest reported percentage of Spanish Catalan speakers is higher than of fluent Russian Latvian speakers (21.1 percent) in Latvia by about one quarter.[2] Of the many possible interpretations of this data, I would like to focus on the comparative aspects. The difference between the percentage of bilingual immigrants in Catalonia and the two Baltic republics is much smaller than one would expect from the pronouncements of nationalists, who in Catalonia repeatedly point to the immigrants' assimilation and in the Baltics decree the indifference of immigrants to the native language and culture. The relatively high rates of Russian bilingualism in the Baltics again testifies to the correctness of Woolard's thesis, which she evolved from studying Catalonia; namely, that the state language, which in many areas of public life was Russian, imparts less status to a language than the region's level of relative economic development.[3]

The Catalan and Baltic indicators of assimilation through intermarriage and national identity or language choice are even closer than were the measures of language use. In 1973, the percentage of Catalan-Spanish intermarriages in Catalonia was 34.6 percent; and between Latvian and Slavic immigrants it was 33.1 percent, though only 16.1 percent among Estonians and immigrants in 1988. The self-identification of children of mixed marriages with the eponymous nationality was 64 percent in Catalonia, slightly higher than the 62 percent in Estonia and the 57 percent in Latvia. These differences are in the 4–10 percent range, with the exception of intermarriage in Estonia, which is less than half the Catalan range.[4]

An examination of the political life of the regions under study demonstrates that nationalist parties also have a measure of attraction for immigrants. Even the socialist party (PSOE-PSC), most of whose voters are immigrants, is led by members of the educated Catalan middle class and conducts much of its campaign in Catalan.[5] In the *perestroika* era support for Baltic economic reform and up to and including Baltic independence, became manifested by segments of the Slavic immigrant population. Already in October 1989, fully 64 percent of Russians in Latvia supported the Popular Front and its, yet modest, aims. A poll taken two years later, found that 47 percent of non-Latvians supported independence, and the rate of approval increased with length of residence in Latvia. In the March 1991 plebescite, called by the Estonian authorities, 83 percent of the eligible voters participated and 78.6 percent favored the restoration of Estonian independence.[6] In this case, as in every election and plebiscite, Estonian and Latvian nationalists won by percentages for above the share of eponymous nationals in the population, obviously due to the support of immigrants. (The high participation rates indicate that immigrant abstention remained low.) Some of the Russian and Slavic immigrants in Latvia and Lithuania have even participated in the defense of installations attacked by the OMON troops of the Ministry of Interior, and others participated in demonstrations against the heavy hand of the Soviet authorities and in favor of Baltic independence.[7]

Surveys of national self-identification in the Basque Country (on which I will rely in absence of other indicators, though without being able to compare it with the Catalan and Baltic data) points in a similar direction: near half of the immigrants report that they consider themselves equally Spanish and Basque, about another quarter as more Basque than Spanish, and yet another ten percent identify exclusively as Basque (see Table 4.4).

The examination of the measures of assimilation, bilingualism, intermarriage, voting, and self-identification point to the hegemonic character of the identities and cultures of relatively developed regions, though there is a range of attraction: highest in Catalonia, somewhat lower in Latvia and Estonia, with the Basque provinces somewhere in between.

Why, then, in the face of such indicators of willingness to seek integration into the high-prestige culture of developed regions is there abundant hostility in Latvia, considerable antagonism in Estonia, and more subdued opposition in the Basque country to immigrants? Why are Basque socialist nationalists in the process of replacing their corporate nationalism with a hegemonic version and Estonian nationalists their exemplary minorities policy of the interwar years with a more exclusionary one in the 1990s? A comparison with the continuous relative openness to immigrant integration in Catalonia will help us clarify the reasons.

The nationalist movements of Catalonia, the Basque country, Latvia, and Estonia all emerged in response to the rapid modernization of their regions that set them apart from Spain and Russia, respectively. The impact of industrialization, however, varied in the four regions.

Catalan nationalists conceive of the Catalan nation's formation as a *hegemonic project* that allows the expansion of the nations' membership and boundaries. Throughout the past hundred years, the high-status, high-paying positions of the economy remained in the hands of Catalans, whereas the low-status, low-paying jobs remained the preserve of immigrants. This form of segmentation poses little or no threat to the status of the Catalan elite strata, which, from the inception of Catalan nationalism, wedded its movement to the goal of modernizing Spain and Catalonia and, hence, was never averse to the entry of Spanish immigrants to the region.

Additional factors enhanced the integration of immigrants into Catalonia. Middle class Catalan nationalism was expanded in the Second Republic from Cambó's Lliga Regionalista to Maciá's and Companys's Esquerra Republicana de Catalunya to embrace the lower middle classes and, starting in the 1960s, immigrants as well. The possibility of reviving the *lerrouxismo*, which divided socialist workers and middle class nationalists in the decade before the First World War, was decisively abandoned during the extended and combined struggle against the political, social, and national oppression of the Franco's dictatorship. As a result of the prominent role played by the Catalan nationalist movement in the struggle for Spain's democratization, the socialist party (PSC-PSOE) and its immigrant workers acquiesced in the hegemonic leadership of Catalan nationalism and embraced its demand for regional autonomy. Finally, the Catalan language was held in high esteem by Castilian, Andalusian, and other Spanish immigrants, because it was the language of the Catalan economic elite and voluntary linguistic assimilation served as a crucial mechanism of social mobility. All these processes—the expanding basis of Catalan nationalism, the drawn-out struggle for democratization, and the higher prestige of Catalan—converged to lend hegemonic influence to Catalan nationalism. Finally, Catalan nationalists employed the advantages of their extensive influence in a tolerant fashion by adopting a prolonged language normalization policy and a measure of multiculturalism to counter the effects of continuing residential and cultural segmentation of immigrants and hosts.

In contrast, the protective, corporate conceptions of the Basque nation emerged in response to the rapid modernization of the region with the loss of the foral protection after the Second Carlist War. Industrialization enhanced the centuries-old division in existence between the Hispanicized cities, that were tied to the central state, and Basque countryside and small towns. The dualistic character of modernization undermined the *traditional privilege* of the *jauntxo* (Basque notables) as well as their raison d'être, their *way of life*; and they reacted by adopting a particularly extreme form of *corporate nationalism*, frequently described as "primordial" nationalism. Given the tenuous hold of Euskera, Sabino Arana, the leader of Basque nationalism, and his political party, the PNV, relied on poorly defined racial (and putative Catholic) criteria to set Basques apart from Spaniards and Spain. He employed insulting language to denigrate the "inferiority" of Spanish worker-immigrants and justify the goal of their expulsion or exclusion. Threatened by a modern *alternative elite*, Arana wished to unify the, until then separate, Basque provinces and make them into an independent, traditionalist state.

With the disintegration of the stratum of notables and the decrease in the occupational division between immigrants and the native born during the long Franco dictatorship, except in some preserves of the traditional economy, the hostility to immigrants also subsided. The second wave of Basque nationalism gave rise to the longest surviving European terrorist movement: ETA. The various branches of ETA are divided between the contrary goals of defending the smalltown Basque way of life without concomitant privileges to protect and willingness to integrate Castilian and other Spanish immigrants while continuing to demand separation from the Spanish state. These contradictions are bridged in ETA's socialist-nationalist ideology, which, therefore, I termed *primordial socialism*. Basque nationalism has remained deeply divided and incoherent, seeking to make up for the deficiency of its conditions by violent exertions.

The integration of immigrants into Basque society, however, is reinforced by the very conditions that weaken Basque nationalism. The continued industrialization of the Basque country has diminished the occupational and sectoral barriers between Basque and other Spanish workers. The protracted Hispanicization of the Basque cities and the consequently limited knowledge of Euskera, even in the Basque population, makes the immigrants' language, Spanish, the language of communication and the industrial economy, reducing the pressure to become bilingual. Under such conditions of cultural nebulousness, immigrants can express their identification with Basque society in a variety of not very demanding ways, and the multiculturalist character of Basque society is unavoidable.

The nationalist movements of Latvia and Estonia emerged under the burden of a three-way conflict. The historical dominance of the German nobilities and the urban strata of the Hanseatic cities led the fledgling Baltic nationalist movements to seek the assistance of the tzarist government in carrying out its goals. The aims of the nationalists and the tzar, however, coincided only partially: the regime weakened the German nobility only in areas in which its own aim of administrative centralization and Russification could be put in its place. Consequently, Baltic nationalism remained relatively weak, willing to be satisfied with regional autonomy and, especially in Latvia, without hegemonic influence over the socialist faction of the militant working class. Yet, in the context of the League of Nations' minorities policy, Estonia evolved a far-reaching liberal program of self-administered cultural autonomy for its minorities and Latvia offered the more customary range of minority rights.

The energy of the recent nationalist movements of Estonia and Latvia, the Popular Fronts, was squarely focused on their single opponent, the USSR, which annexed them as part of its sinister deal with Nazi Germany. But the Soviet nationalities policy left a contradictory legacy for the Baltics. The political, military, and police institutions of the USSR were the main tools of centralization. In the cultural sphere the outcome was the opposite. In spite of attempts at Russification, cultural institutions and schools in the native languages and, therefore, their elites were preserved.

The USSR, which continued the modernization of the region as part of its attempt to tie it more strongly to the rest of the state, subjected the Baltic republics, like other parts of the USSR, to a dualistic pattern of development. Side by side with a small service and light industrial local economic sector, a large, heavy industrial sector that answered to Moscow and was managed and employed Russian speakers had been set up. The institutional division of the economy of the Latvian and Estonian republics of the USSR begot two modern elites and two systems of production and consumption, and it also reproduced the ethnic, linguistic, and cultural divisions between the employees. This division helped perpetuate the Baltic nationalist aspirations and undermine the integration of the Baltic republics into the all-Soviet institutions. The control over the all-union sector was a major bone of contention between the nationalists and the Soviet authorities during the *perestroika* years.

In both the pre-Civil War Basque country and the Estonian and Latvian SSRs, the division between hosts and immigrants differed from the Catalan pattern. Whereas in Catalonia hosts and immigrants were divided in the labor market *horizontally*, in the Basque provinces and in the Baltic republics of the USSR the division was *vertical*. Spanish immigrants, under the Hispanicized industrial elite, and Russian, Ukrainian, and Belorussian immigrants within the all-union sector of the economy, under their own immigrant elite, formed a society within a society. In both cases, the vertical segmentation of the society pitted the native-born elites against elites tied to the central state, and in the Basque country and the Baltics the elite strata evolved a *corporate* view of their societies to oppose outside intervention. In Latvia and Estonia, the Soviet state-building efforts that brought not only workers but also an elite cadre was attacked as political imperialism. Nevertheless, in the pre-Civil War Basque provinces the opposition to modernization and the integration of the immigrants was particularly strong and uncompromising because not only the traditional elite's privilege but also its customary way of life was under jeopardy; whereas in Estonia and more strongly in Latvia, where an already modern foreign elite competed with the modern local elites, the danger seemed less because political imperialism threatened the privileged status of the native-born elites but not their way of life.

Relatively few forces in the Baltics enhanced the customary desire of immigrants to adopt some of the culture of their chosen developed region. By keeping the Slavic immigrants apart from the native born to a considerable extent, the sectoral division of the Baltic economies also made their mixing largely unnecessary and hostility toward the immigrants high. The regional culture and language also seemed to be under threat from immigrants who had relatively little need to integrate for social mobility. Nevertheless, even here the attraction of the "Europeanized" Baltic cultures in economically well-developed Latvia and Estonia was reinforced by additional forces.

Whereas the Russian elites of the all-union sector and the political institutions by and large were opposed to both *perestroika* and democratization, other strata of the immigrant population, the intelligentsia, working class, and the emerging entrepreneurial stratum had closer ties with their host societies and supported its Popular Fronts. The exceptionally rapid disintegration of the USSR, however, cut short the collaboration of nationalists and immigrants, and the obstructionism of the Russian elite's Interfronts reinforced the divisions between them. The vertical segmentation of Latvia and Estonia led to adoption of a corporate nationalist attitude but one tempered, especially in Estonia, with a distinct readiness to integrate part of the immigrant population. The privatization of the all-union enterprises that is likely to differentiate between those immigrants who see their future in Russia from those who contemplate it in the Baltics might lead to an increased willingness among the hosts to grant the latter group Estonian and Latvian citizenship.

Even in Catalonia, however, it is not clear that assimilation will be more than partial, given the continued residential segregation and undetermined rate of social mobility. Consequently, *multiculturalist* practices were adopted to sustain the customary openness toward immigrants. At the same time, multiculturalist policies toward Spanish immigrants could contradict the customary assimilationist approach of Catalan nationalists. A working multiculturalism seems the most likely outcome in the Basque region, where there is only limited occupational segmentation between native born and immigrants and the weight and significance of Basque culture is relatively limited. The growing integration of Spain into the European Union might make it even easier to acquiesce in relinquishing the homogenizing tendencies associated with modern nation-states.

In the Baltic republics, multiculturalism carries a somewhat different meaning. Since "the cultural identity of Russians and Russian-speaking people living in Estonia, Latvia, and Lithuania," who were internal migrants within the USSR, "has never been based solely on their ethnic origin,"[8] there are two options in host-immigrant relations. Continued exclusionary policies are not likely to bring on the voluntary departure of many of the immigrants but its result, the continued segmentation of the two groups, is likely to "ethnicize" the Russian and other Slavic immigrants and organize them around the demand to be recognized as separate *national minorities* and, potentially, enhance their wish to be reunited with Russia. In fact, the partial recognition of the linguistic rights of the Russian speakers by the Estonian and Latvian governments indicates that they also seem more comfortable in using the categories already familiar in Eastern European history, such as national minority, in their treatment of the immigrants.

Multiculturalism, including support for Russian language schools and media, the relaxation of official language laws, combined with a policy of partial integration by further easing admission to citizenship, however, is likely to forestall irredentist desires among the immigrants and lead to mutual accommodation between them and their hosts. Those who are worried that a multiculturalist policy is divisive forget that a policy that considers the remaining disenfranchised Russians, Ukrainians, and Belorussians in Latvia and Estonia an unassimilable official, or semi-official, national minority carries far greater divisive and disruptive potential.

In none of the four societies under study has full integration, similar to that attained by pre-First World War immigrants, taken place, although there are indications, strongest in Catalonia and weakest in Latvia, that such desire exists. In all four societies, some measure of multiculturalism is an important complement to partial integration and the remaining segmentation.

Multiculturalism is still a hotly debated issue in the West but it is feared mostly by nationalists of one of two stripes: full assimilationists and full separatists. These are representatives of the old school of nationalism, which believes that the common culture of a homogenous citizenry is an essential condition of its solidarity. This form of nationalism is in odds with the contemporary recognition that cultural diversity seems better to reflect the globalized economy, which is especially typical of relatively developed regions that attract immigrants. After all, multiculturalism has been adopted into the Canadian constitution and in the policies of such dynamic Western societies as Australia, Great Britain, Sweden, and the Netherlands. It is also being appraised and adopted in many communities in the United States and elsewhere as a way of anticipating their growing diversification due to further immigration.[9]

It seems to be more appropriate to view multiculturalism as a step beyond tolerance of immigrants and the legal proscription of discrimination against them, along the path charted by liberal philosophy.[10] Multiculturalism is potentially an open-ended and dynamic framework. The legitimation of cultural diversity, associated with it, presupposes shared political institutions that lead to civic solidarity, itself a crucial element of a well-ordered political society.[11] Multiculturalism is compatible with an individualistic approach by reserving each individual's right of "exit" from his or her cultural grous.[12] Instead of viewing society as consisting of majority and minorities, multiculturalists seeks to redefine the modern state as a plurality of cultural groups in flux and with blurred borders between them. The mutual respect of cultures within each society, the fundamental tenet of multiculturalism, is likely to lead to their cross-fertilization and hence to the kind of continuous and voluntary cultural change that are of importance especially in developed societies founded on complexity. Finally, a multiculturalist approach to immigrants accepts a delay in their assimilation but anticipates it.

The multiplicity of cultures already is apparent in all developed societies; and this has been recognized by some willingly, by other grudgingly, and yet by some who wish to rid themselves of it. The internal migration that produced multiple cultures in Catalonia, the Basque country, Latvia, and Estonia are far from unique, and these societies' approaches to immigrants will be most effective when taking the widespread process of cultural diversification, whatever its origins, and its continuous growth in the future into account.

NOTES

Chapter 1. Introduction

1. Hollifield 1992, pp. 45–73.

2. Hammar 1990, pp. 12–18.

3. Marshall 1973, passim.

4. For the struggle for migrant rights, see Buechler 1987, pp. 297–99.

5. Del Campo and Navarro López 1987, Table 2.6, p. 100; Schroeder 1990, Table 1, p. 45.

6. Even in Vilnius non–Lithuanians constitute well–nigh half of the inhabitants.

7. *CDSP*: Estonia 40, no. 12, (February 8 1989): 18; Latvia 40, no. 20 (May 5 1989): 20; Lithuania 40, no. 36 (September 7 1989): 7, and (January 26 1989).

8. The first exciting, but still limited, attempt to combine these literatures I have come across is found in Castles and Miller 1993.

9. This distinction is derived from Gramsci's (1971) comparison of classes with and without the potential to lead other classes in revolutionary struggle.

10. Park and Miller 1921; Park 1950.

11. Gordon 1964, pp. 71–81.

12. Inglehart and Woodward 1972, p. 359.

13. Castels and Kosack 1973; Portes and Walton 1981.

14. Hawkins 1991, pp. 214–42; Rex.

15. Castles and Miller 1992, p. 261.

16. Rex 1994.

17. Castles and Miller 1992, p. 227.

18. C. Price 1993, pp. 21–22.

19. Rex 1994.

20. Lerner 1993, pp. 82–86.

21. Quoted in ibid., p. 88.

22. Wolfrum 1993, pp. 159–61; Lerner 1993, pp. 88–91.

23. Lerner 1993, pp. 98–99.

24. Wolfrum 1993, p. 153.

25. Ibid., p. 155.

26. Wolfrum argues that the acquisition of such rights under Article 27 by groups of migrants "cannot be excluded completely," (p. 162.) but even according to him this seems to be a farfetched possibility.

27. Hechter 1975, passim; Nairn 1977, passim.

28. Gellner 1983, pp. 52, 73.

29. Nairn 1977, pp. 185–87.

30. Gourevitch 1979, p. 306.

31. Belgium's 1830–1832 revolution was not just a Catholic protest again Calvinist Netherlands, but the impatience of an entrepreneurial bourgeois class, enjoying deposits of iron and coal and a favorable crossroads position in international trade, with the decaying Dutch mercantile empire (See Nairn 1977, p. 185).

32. Nairn includes in his category of nationalist movements in overdeveloped regions also Ibo secessionism in Nigeria and the later stages of the Kurdish demands for autonomy in Iraq on the grounds of their oil riches (Nairn 1977, p. 185). Such "gold rush" separatism, however, is either short lived or attains longevity only when linked with other factors that usually predate the discovery of the mineral or oil resources. I will not address this type of nationalism in the present context.

33. Diez Medrano.

34. Social and nationalist activists in developed regions, like their nationalist counterparts in underdeveloped regions, also seem to be predisposed to complain about the siphoning off of their resources for the benefit of less developed regions in the same state. I am not convinced, however, that this is an important cause of their disaffection because policies of interregional tax transfers are typical to most stable federal states.

The Catalan–Spanish connection certainly falls outside the colonial characterization. The Basque provinces were authorized, as part of their *concierto económico* with the Madrid authorities, to assess and levy their own taxes until their defeat in the Civil War. Da Silva calls attention to the fact that the Basque provinces and the province of Barcelona could not have been unduly burdened with taxes even under the Franco dictatorship, because their disposable per capita income remained the highest among Spain's fifty provinces in 1967. Although the province of Madrid had the highest per capita income in Spain, the per capita disposable income of its residents fall below that of Guipúzcoa, Vizcaya, Alava, and Barcelona provinces. (da Silva 1975, Tables 2 and 3, p. 240). In fact, taxation during the Franco era remained so low and regressive that it was hardly an important political issue until 1976.

The relationship between the Russian, or Slavic, core and the peripheral regions of the former USSR was fraught with internal contradictions but, even here, it seems that colonial exploitation was just one, and rarely central let alone widespread, aspect of interregional ties within the former USSR. In fact, there are strong indications of a net outflow of resources from Russia to the other republics of the USSR and that the Baltic republics used to be the largest net recipients of subsidies per person. (See *Europa World Year Book* 1990, as well as Chapter 5.)

Finally, it is very difficult to successfully measure the extent, let alone the significance, of interregional transfers and, even more important, as long as a region remains relatively developed and its economy does not stagnate it is well–nigh impossible to make its "colonial exploitation" transparent to the extent that it alone would generate sustained resistance. Hobson and David Landes, among others, argued that colonial exploitation served the interests of only small elites in the metropole and, further, that formal colonial control rarely paid off. Landes, however, disagrees with Hobson's identification of the beneficiaries of colonial exploitation as the great international bankers. (Hobson, *passim*; Landes, p. 505).

35. Nairn 1977, pp. 336–37.

36. Ibid., pp. 338–40.

37. Greenfeld 1992, p. 11. She also proposes a second criterion: individualistic–libertarian and collectivistic–authoritarian types of nationalism.

38. Brubaker 1992, p. 81.

39. Ibid., pp. 1–6, 184–87.

40. Gramsci 1971.

41. Inglehart and Woodward 1972, passim.

42. Diez Medrano 1989.

43. See the comparative study by Kimmel 1989.

44. Geertz 1963, p. 109.

45. Ibid., p. 110.

46. Ibid., p. 128.

47. Nairn 1977, p. 329. Nationalism is always Janus faced but one of its visages usually predominates. Traditional elites learn to emulate the modern ones if only to foil their modernizing designs and vice versa: modern groups will assume at least some of the potent characteristics of the pre-modern groups they struggle against.

48. Trotsky 1959, p. 4.

49. Keegan 1990, pp. 181–82.

50. Hechter 1975, p. 63.

51. Lustick 1985, p. 3.

52. Tilly 1975, pp. 38–46.

Chapter 2. Similarities Between the Regions

1. Linz 1973b, p. 99.

2. Linz 1967, p. 199.

3. Douglass 1985, p . 10; Linz 1973b, pp. 47–48.

4. Douglass 1985, p. 10.

5. Tilly 1991, p. 573; for an outline of this process from Peter the Great to Catherine the Great, see Tilly 1990, pp. 139–42. Tilly, actually contrasts Russia's "coercion–intensive" path with Spain's combined "capitalized–coercion path," which was made possible by the coincidence of military power and centers of capital in early modern Spain (Tilly 1990, pp. 127–60). Yet, this coincidence in the case of Castile did not last long.

6. A third, and in Orridge's view, less important basis is institutional autonomy (Orridge 1982, p. 49). The evolution of regional autonomy and the threats to it from modern state formation will be examined as part of the analyses of the distinct cases in Chapters 3, 4, and 5.

7. Greenwood 1977, p. 84.

8. Hobsbawm 1990, p. 54.

9. Raun 1987, p. 77.

10. Conversi 1990, p. 59.

11. Misiunas and Taagepera 1983, p. 121.

12. Arbós 1987, p. 144.

13. Douglass 1985, pp. 5–6.

14. Fundación FOESSA 1975, p. 773.

15. Carr 1980, p. 24.

16. Ibid., p. 25.

17. Zirakzadeh in Douglass 1985, p. 269.

18. Thaden 1981b, p. 18.

19. Plakans 1974, pp. 124–25; Raun 1981, p. 288.

20. Thaden 1981b, p. 19.

21. Raun 1974, pp. 137–38; Thaden 1981b, pp. 19–20.

22. Harned 1975a, p. 95.

23. Raun 1981, pp. 288–89.

24. Raun 1974, p. 137.

25. Rauch 1974, pp. 123–28.

26. Bohnet and Penkaitis 1988, p. 36.

27. Bruk 1972, Table 11, p. 353.

28. Misiunas and Taagepera 1983, p. 104. King (1965, p. 93) concurs with this assessment. And, according to Dunmore, in industrially developed areas as the Baltic areas that, furthermore, "had been relatively well treated by the Nazis," more rapid returns could be expected on investment, as renovation and adaption to production could be accomplished at a fraction of the cost of new development (Dunmore 1980, p. 51).

As far as the labor force is concerned, we need to remember that many people with skills either emigrated or were killed during or after the Second World War, and overall "the level skills remained too low for the rapid pace of forced industrialization." (See King 1965, pp. 166–69.)

29. See, for example, Adirim 1988, pp. 53, 57.

30. Bohnet and Penkaitis 1988, p. 45; Misiunas and Taagepera 1983, pp. 104,176.

31. Bohnet and Penkaitis 1988, pp. 40, 42, 43.

32. Rauch 1974, p. 123.

33. "The first major influx" of immigrants in Barcelona from outside Catalonia and Asturias took place during the years of the First World War (Payne 1970, p. 30).

34. Larronde 1980, p. 20 (he also argues for an increase, between 1900 and 1910, from 310,000 to 350,000; p. 20.)

35. Beltza 1978, p. 195.

36. Del Campo and Navarro López 1987, calculated from Table 2.6, on p. 100.

37. Núñez 1977, pp. 168–69. These numbers are for 1975.

38. King 1965, pp. 91–94; Dreifelds 1990, p. 45.

39. Levin 1990, p. 53.

40. Dreifelds 1984, pp. 66–73; Parming, pp. 53–61, 65–77; Zvidrins 1979, passim; Taagepera 1981, passim.

41. Zvidrins 1979, pp. 277–78.

42. For Latvia, see ibid., p. 278; for Estonia, see Parming, p. 54.

43. Taagepera 1981, Table 1, p. 36.

44. Parming 1972, p. 64.

45. Zunde 1965, pp. 160, 169.

46. Misiunas and Taagepera 1983, p. 104.

47. Järvesoo 1978, p. 139.

48. Grandstaff 1975, pp. 494–95.

49. Lewis and Rowland 1977, p. 23.

50. Ibid., pp. 15–16.

51. Parming 1972, p. 64.

52. Prikhodko 1973, p. 226.

53. Zaslavskaya 1984, p. 231.

54. As recently as 1989, Lewis reiterated that "the Russian 'influx' into places like Estonia and Latvia is not the result of demographic policy. Centrally planned economic development is simply proceeding too rapidly in relation to the growth of the indigenous labor force" ("Panel on Nationalism in the USSR" 1989, p. 486). And Rowland concurring in 1990, wrote that "the most fundamental point to be made about the reasons for migration in

the USSR is that, as elsewhere in the world, economic factors predominate and people generally move voluntarily. The fact that the USSR is a totalitarian state with migration policies, an internal passport and registration system, and some forced migration should not distract one from the basic similarities to universal migration factors" (Rowland 1990, p. 335).

55. Mill 1961, pp. 448–51.

56. Fredrickson 1981, p. xv.

Chapter 3. Hegemonic Nationalism in Catalonia

1. Vincens Vives 1969, p. 74.

2. Elliot 1963, pp. 6–8; Payne 1970, p. 15.

3. Linz 1973b, pp. 43–45.

4. Elliott 1963, p. 8.

5. Payne 1971, pp. 15–16; Linz 1973b, pp. 38–39.

6. Tilly 1990, p. 168.

7. Hargreaves–Mawdsley 1973, p. 8; Carr 1982, p. 63; Payne 1970, p. 16.

8. Payne 1971, p. 16.

9. Ibid., p. 16.

10. An excellent overview of Spanish state and nation formation and political life from the perspective of the historical sociologist is found in Linz 1967 and 1973b.

11. Carr 1980, pp. 1, 10–15.

12. Linz 1967, p. 200.

13. Vilar 1980, p. 559. In Linz's less class-conscious terminology "the system was controlled by professional politicians, mostly lawyers, professionals and landowners, who relied on the largely apolitical and even illiterate mass electorate of the countryside and the provincial cities and towns..." He also mentions the considerable weight wielded by the "bourgeois army officer corps overexpanded in the civil and colonial wars" within the political elite (Linz 1967, pp. 198, 204).

14. Linz 1967, pp. 198–201.

15. Payne 1971, p. 17.

16. Fundación FOESSA, p. 773; Carr 1980, p. 23.

17. Diez Medrano.

18. Vilar 1980, p. 555.

19. Ibid., p. 551.

20. Ibid., p. 559; Carr 1982, p. 554.

21. At one point, out of forty-nine provincial governors appointed by the Republican authorities thirty-two were from Catalonia (Payne 1971, p. 17).

22. Diez Medrano.

23. Salmeron's speech on June 18, 1908, quoted in Vilar 1980, p. 547.

24. Vilar 1980, pp. 546, 551.

25. Solé–Tura 1974, pp. 285–86.

26. Payne 1971, p. 18.

27. Carr 1980, p. 62.

28. Conversi 1990, passim.

29. Pi–Sunyer 1971, p. 122.

30. Balcells 1977, p. 128.

31. Diez Medrano.

32. Vilar 1980, p. 560; Diez Medrano.

33. Quoted in Vilar 1980, p. 555.

34. Carr 1980, p. 104.

35. Ibid., p. 64.

36. Payne 1971, p. 22.

37. Herr 1974, p. 127.

38. Carr 1982, pp. 549–50.

39. Ibid., pp. 551–53.

40. Ibid., p. 550.

41. Carr 1980, p. 6.

42. Payne 1971, p. 27.

43. Carr 1982, p. 553.

44. Laitin 1989, p. 301.

45. Carr 1980, pp. 53, 57.

46. Balcells 1977, p. 59.

47. Vilar 1980, p. 538.

48. DiGiacomo 1985, p. 48.

49. Carr 1980, p. 101.

50. Vilar 1980, p. 539.

51. Pi-Sunyer 1985, p. 267.

52. Carr 1982, pp. 609, 631.

53. Rizal, "El catalanismo de izquierdas," *Diario de Barcelona*, (September 7, 1977).

54. Ben-Ami 1978, p. 237.

55. Carr 1980, p. 65.

56. Carr 1982, p. 638.

57. Gramsci 1971, pp. 74, 168. Gramsci's expectation that social blocs would be without internal contradictions, however, is the result of philosophical reasoning and not political observation and, therefore, is far-fetched and unrealistic.

58. Payne 1971, pp. 40–41.

59. Carr 1982, p. 448; Ben-Ami 1978, pp. 113–14.

60. Ben-Ami 1978, pp. 113–14, 237–38.

61. Medhurst 1987, p. 4.

62. Vilar 1980, p. 538.

63. Pi-Sunyer 1980, p. 108; Llobera 1989, pp. 252–53.

64. Linz 1973a, p. 242.

65. Clark 1981, p. 93; da Silva 1975, p. 248.

66. Marsal and Roiz 1985, p. 214.

67. Medhurst 1987, p. 6.

68. Gunther, Sani, and Shabad 1988, p. 252.

69. Quoted in Arbós 1987, p. 146.

70. Shabad 1986, p. 1.

71. Ibid., p. 8; Di Giacomo 1986, pp. 76–79.

72. DiGiacomo, 1986, p. 72.

73. Medhurst 1987, p. 8.

74. DiGiacomo 1986, p. 73.

75. Estaban Pinilla de las Heras, "Resultados electorales en Cataluña," *El Correo Catalan* (June 22, 1977).

76. Medhurst 1987, p. 8.

77. Tom Burns, "Basque Elections Fragment Power," *Washington Post* (December 2, 1986).

78. Medhurst 1987, p. 8.

79. Maluquer i Sostres 1963, pp. 34–35.

80. Carr 1980, p. 62.

81. Conversi 1990, pp. 53–58.

82. Woolard 1986b, p. 56; 1989, pp. 36–37.

83. Pujol, p. 104.

84. DiGiacomo 1986, p. 72.

85. See ibid., pp. 87–88; Woolard 1986a, p. 95.

86. DiGiacomo 1985, pp. 66–67.

87. Woolard 1989, p. 31

88. One of the problems of intergenerational mobility comparisons is that they coincide, in part, with structural changes in the occupational structure, thus the margins do not stay the same.

89. Pinilla de las Heras, p. 279.

90. Beltza 1976, p. 162.

91. Woolard 1989, p. 131.

92. Another shortcoming of the study is that it is focused solely on intergeneration mobility of men, and gives no indication of woman's mobility.

93. Llobera 1989, p. 258.

94. Woolard 1989, p. 30; Llobera 1989, p. 255.

95. Maluquer i Sostres 1963, p. 39.

96. Ibid., pp. 57–58.

97. Ibid., p. 114.

98. Woolard 1989, pp. 95–121.

99. Ibid., p. 121.

100. Inglehart and Woodward 1972, p. 359.

101. Brand 1985, pp. 291–92.

102. Pi-Sunyer 1985, p. 273.

103. G. Price 1979, pp. 32–37.

104. Woolard 1989, p. 125; see also G. Price 1979, pp. 37–41; and Pi-Sunyer 1985, p. 273.

105. Hence, in contrast to the willingness of lower status immigrants to learn and speak Catalan, the Spanish middle-class civil servants who were posted to Catalonia during Franco's dictatorship show no such interest (Giner 1980, p. 48). See also Beltza 1976, p. 166.

106. Linz 1967, p. 272.

107. O'Donnell 1989.

108. Strubell i Trueta 1981, p. 153. There seems to be no significant correlation between the gender of parents and children in mixed marriages and their language preferences.

109. Ibid., pp. 154–55.

110. Ibid., p. 151.

111. See, for example, Conversi 1990, p. 63; and Linz 1967, p. 272.

112. Woolard 1989, pp. 73–74.

113. Woolard 1986a, pp. 94–97.

114. Woolard and Gahng 1990.

115. Woolard 1986a, p. 96.

116. Woolard 1986b, p. 97.

117. Woolard 1986a, p. 101.

118. Solé 1985, pp. 194–234.

119. Woolard and Gahng 1990. The original study is Woolard 1989.

120. A positive answer to any of three questions categorized a respondent as Catalan speaker: had they spoken the language as a child, do they normally used it at work, or do they speak the language. (Gunther, Sani, and Shabad 1988, p. 243.)

121. Enquesta 1990, Table 2.3, p. 56.

122. Quoted in Woolard and Ghang 1990.

123. See Pi-Sunyer 1980, pp. 111–12.

124. Pujol, p. 104

125. Ros 1993.

126. Giner 1980, p. 48.

Chapter 4. From Racism to "Primordial Socialism" in the Basque Country

1. Diez Medrano 1989.

2. Carr 1980, p. 67.

3. Medhurst 1987, pp. 3, 8.

4. Ibid., p. 9.

5. Trotsky 1959, pp. 3–4.

6. Heiberg 1989, p. 20.

7. Ibid., pp. 17–20.

8. Greenwood 1977, p. 91.

9. Heiberg 1989, pp. 13–24.

10. Ibid., p. 14.

11. Greenwood 1977, p. 96.

12. Ibid., p. 93.

13. Heiberg 1989, p. 27.

14. Payne 1971, p. 33.

15. Heiberg 1989, pp. 28–32.

16. Ibid., pp. 35–36, Diez Medrano 1989.

17. Medhurst 1982, p. 237.

18. Heiberg 1989, p. 36.

19. Payne 1975, pp. 64, 94, 103.

20. Harrison 1977, p. 372; Diez Medrano 1989.

21. Payne 1975, p. 106.

22. Diez Medrano 1989.

23. Carr 1982, p. 435; Heiberg 1989, pp. 40–41; Diez Medrano 1989; Medhurst 1987, p. 4.

24. Medhurst 1982, p. 240.

25. See, for example, Harrison 1977, pp. 75–76.

26. Da Silva 1975, p. 239.

27. Payne 1975, p. 63.

28. Heiberg 1975, p. 181.

29. Ibid.

30. Beltza 1978, p. 197.

31. Ibid., pp. 195–96; Heiberg 1989, p. 42.

32. Linz 1967, p. 272.

33. Beltza 1978, pp. 198, 208.

34. Medhurst 1982, pp. 237–38; da Silva 1975, p. 246.

35. Medhurst underestimated the survival of the religious element in Arana's nationalism. Medhurst 1982, p. 239; see also Carr 1980, p. 68; and Sullivan 1988, p. 5.

36. Diez Medrano.

37. Payne 1975, p. 93; Clark 1981, p. 99; da Silva 1975, p. 241; Medhurst 1982, p. 241; Heiberg 1975, p. 179.

38. Medhurst 1982, p. 241.

39. Ortzi 1980, p. 107.

40. Heiberg 1989, p. 47; Diez Medrano.

41. Diez Medrano.

42. Heiberg 1989, pp. 46–47; da Silva 1975, p. 230.

43. Heiberg 1989, p. 47.

44. Carr 1982, p. 556.

45. Ibid., p. 556.

46. Arana 1897, p. 71.

47. Payne 1975, p. 75.

48. Sullivan 1988, p. 5.

49. Greenwood 1977, pp. 90, 97, 102.

50. Carr 1982, p. 556.

51. Conversi 1990.

52. Linz 1980, p. 41.

53. Harrison 1977, p. 376; Beltza 1978, p. 210.

54. Heiberg 1975, pp. 184–85.

55. Harrison (1977) argues that "Arana firmly expressed the sentiments of the nationalist rank and file when he declared that he fervently detested all liberalism from the most radical to the most moderate. In the long run, however, much of the hostility of this profound anti–movement was to be transferred from the capitalists to the workers which they recruited to their mines and factories, many of them migrant laborers. Far worse than the liberalism of the employers was the atheism, socialism and internationalism of the trade union movement founded after 1888" (p. 376).

56. Sullivan 1988, p. 11; Payne 1975, p. 93; Beltza 1978, p. 231.

57. Harrison 1977, passim.

58. Diez Medrano; see also Ortzi 1975, p. 113.

59. Da Silva 1975, p. 241.

60. Diez Medrano.

61. La Granja 1986, p. 566.

62. Diez Medrano.

63. La Pasionaria, for example, was of Basque descent (Carr 1982, p. 630).

64. Payne 1971, p. 48.

65. Clark 1984, pp. 25–27; Sullivan 1988, pp. 31–36.

66. Sullivan 1988, p. 42; Clark 1984, p. 34.

67. Clark 1984, p. 145.

68. Ortzi, p. 286. He actually talks about the petty bourgeois industry, which seems to me better rendered as an artisan stratum.

69. Garmendia 1980, vol. 2, p. 142.

70. Waldman 1985, pp. 223–25.

71. Clark 1984, pp. 185–203; Garmendia also mentions the importance of the Goierri region for ETA (Garmendia 1980, vol. 2, p. 142).

72. Clark 1984, p. 196.

73. There are only five towns with a population over 100,000, and very few middle sized towns. Of the townships 70 percent have a population less than 2,000 (Clark 1981, pp. 87, 91).

74. Sullivan 1988, pp. 198–203.

75. Medhurst 1982, pp. 248–52.

76. Ibid., p. 249.

77. Ibid., p. 252.

78. Ortzi, p. 113.

79. In 1986 socialists held one more seat than PNV, because of the split between PNV and EA.

80. Douglass and Zulaika 1990, pp 246–47; Medhurst 1987, p. 7.

81. Gunther et al. 1988, pp. 342–43.

82. Douglass and Zulaika 1990, p. 247; Gunther et al. 1988, p. 342.

83. Medhurst 1987, p. 9.

84. *El País* (October 29, 1990).

85. *El País* (January 21, 1985).

86. Shabad 1986, p. 13.

87. Medhurst 1987, p. 9.

88. "Acuerdo para la normalizacion y pacificacion de Euskadi" (January 12, 1988).

89. Ortzi 1987, p. 112; Sullivan 1988, pp. 8–9.

90. Ortzi 1987, p. 112.

91. Da Silva 1975, p. 231; Sullivan 1988, p. 14.

92. Douglass and Zulaika 1990, p. 246.

93. Ibid., p. 247.

94. Shabad 1986, p. 14.

95. Heiberg 1975, p. 185.

96. Payne 1975, p. 74.

97. Quoted in ibid., p. 76.

98. Sullivan 1988, p. 10.

99. Ibid., p. 13.

100. Urla argues that "one of the striking aspects of the Basque movement since its inception is the endless discussion in popular newspapers, magazines, and books on the subject of who and what is a Basque" (Urla 1988, p. 385). It seems, however, that this "collective identity crisis" is relatively new and exploded into public consciousness only since the mid–1970s.

101. Clark 1984, pp. 32–34; Garmendia 1980, vol. 1, pp. 139–51.

102. Sullivan 1988, p. 48.

103. Ibid., p. 41.

104. Ibid., p. 50.

105. Douglass and Zulaika 1990, p. 244.

106. Sullivan 1988, p. 55.

107. Ibid., p. 39.

108. Ibid.

109. Medhurst 1982, p. 251.

110. Shabad 1986, p. 10.

111. Ibid., Table 3, p. 34.

112. This pattern did not hold in the 1982 elections that brought the Socialist Party to power in Spain.

113. Medhurst 1987, p. 7.

114. Ibid., pp. 6–7.

115. Calculated from Table 45 in Núñez 1977, p. 172.

116. Núñez 1977, pp. 173–74; Miguel 1974.

117. Beltza 1976, p. 158.

118. Linz 1980, p. 35.

119. Coverdale 1985, p. 229.

120. Clark 1981, pp. 87–91.

121. Beltza 1976, p. 33.

122. Clark 1981, p. 91.

123. Ibid., p. 97.

124. Beltza 1976, p. 162.

125. Ibid., pp. 160–61.

126. Linz 1985, p. 229.

127. Clark 1981, p. 96.

128. Llera 1986, p. 178, Table 9.

129. Ibid., p. 179, Table 11.

130. Medhurst 1987, pp. 94–95.

131. Clark 1981, p. 95.

132. Medhurst 1987, p. 10.

133. Laitin 1989, p. 313.

134. Woolard 1989, p. 121.

135. See Linz 1985.

136. Of Euskera speakers born of Basque parents In the Basque provinces, 77 percent identlfy themselves as Basque tout court, and another 13 percent as more Basque than Spanish (ibid., p. 227).

137. Ibid., Table 10.1, p. 209.

138. Ibid., pp. 209, 212.

139. Ibid., p. 212.

140. Ibid., p. 223.

141. Ibid., p. 231.

142. Ibid., p. 221. Linz prefers to call the civic criterion a territorial one.

Chapter 5. Baltic Awakening and the Lure of Exclusivity

1. Rauch 1974, pp. 1–4; Misiunas and Taagepera 1983, pp. 2–3.

2. Raun 1987, p. 38.

3. Haltzel 1981, pp. 113–14.

4. Ibid., pp. 112–13.

5. Ibid., p. 114.

6. Siilivask 1983, pp. 205–6.

7. Thaden 1981b, p. 18.

8. Plakans 1974, pp. 124–25; Raun 1981, p. 288; Raun 1987, pp. 45–56; Harned 1975a, p. 98; Taagepera 1975, p. 76.

9. Raun 1974, p. 137.

10. Jansen 1985, p. 47.

11. Hobsbawm 1990, pp. 73–74.

12. Kreindler 1988, p. 6.

13. Raun 1981, p. 293.

14. Plakans 1981, pp. 214, 231–32; Raun 1981, p. 293.

15. Raun and Plakans, p. 133; Loit 1983, p. 64.

16. Plakans 1974, p. 127; 1981, pp. 210–12.

17. Loit 1983, p. 61; Raun and Plakans, p. 133; Raun 1987, pp. 55–56.

18. Hroch 1985, pp. 80 146–47.

19. Ibid., pp. 82, 136 150–51, 157, 180.

20. Ibid., pp. 170–73; Loit 1983, p. 66.

21. Harned 1975a, p. 96; Bilmanis 1951, pp. 251–57.

22. Hroch 1985, p. 158.

23. Thaden 1981b, p. 17.

24. Raun and Plakans 1990, p. 132.

25. Haltzel 1981, pp. 126–33.

26. Haltzel 1974, p. 144.

27. Parming 1977, p. 30. Vilnius, "to a great extent, developed as a bastion against the Orthodox to the east." The Polish writer Czeslaw Milosz, who was born there, described it "almost like a Jesuit city somewhere in the middle of Latin America" (Lieven 1990, p. 61).

28. In contrast, the Lithuanian Catholic Church played a crucial role in the birth of Lithuanian nationalism, because in the hierarchy of the Church, side by side with the strong Polish presence, were many Lithuanians. Russification, therefore, threatened an quintessential "Lithuanian ethnic institution," that is, in Parming's description, "the institutional framework underlying the national identity of the Lithuanian people." So did the Russification of education, which until then remained a preserve of church-sponsored schools. In contrast, Russification in neighboring Livonia, Courland, and Estland was undermining Baltic German institutions (Parming 1977, pp. 30–31). Consequently, whereas in the Lutheran provinces, the cultural and political centralizing activities of the tzarist regime indirectly weakened the hold of the German nobility, in Lithuania they brought no such benefit.

29. Raun and Plakans 1990, pp. 138–39; Raun 1987, pp. 65–66.

30. Raun 1987, pp. 64–66; Bilmanis 1951, pp. 241; Misiunas and Taagepera 1983, p. 6.

31. Plakans 1981, pp. 229–30; Loit 1983, p. 70.

32. Bilmanis 1951, pp. 240–41, 245–47; Misiunas and Taagepera, 1983, p. 6.

33. Haltzel 1974, pp. 144–46.

34. Ibid., pp. 146–47.

35. Raun and Plakans 1990, p. 134.

36. The right–wing of the Latvian Social Democratic Party sought "autonomy and a constituent assembly for the Latvian people" side by side with an All–Russian Constituent Assembly (see Bilmanis 1951, p. 262).

37. Harned 1975a, p. 98.

38. Raun 1987, pp. 82–86; Bilmanis 1951, pp. 266–68.

39. Rutkis 1967, p. 219; Järvesoo 1974, p. 162.

40. Raun 1987, pp. 100, 104.

41. Harned 1975a, pp. 98–99; Bilmanis 1951, p. 292.

42. Raun 1987, pp. 104–5. In 1922, Russia took the official name USSR.

43. Harned 1975b, p. 122; Misiunas and Taagepera 1983, pp. 8–9.

44. Harned 1975a, p. 99.

45. Rutkis 1967, p. 219.

46. Rauch 1974, p. 135.

47. Garleff 1987, p. 81.

48. Rauch 1974, pp. 142–43; Aun 1951–1953, p. 27.

49. Aun 1951–1953, p. 29; Rauch 1974, p. 141.

50. The openness of the Estonian authorities to the "privatization" of education by different ethnic groups was in part due to the tradition of Estonian education being provided by private societies (Aun 1951–1953, pp. 32–35).

51. Rauch 1974, p. 144.

52. Ibid., p. 142.

53. The latter was especially important in view of the fierce internal divisions within the various minorities.

54. Aun 1951–1953, p. 39.

55. Rauch 1974, p. 141.

56. Levin 1990, p. 54; Rauch 1974, pp. 146–61; Garleff 1978, pp. 93–94.

57. Nodel 1974, pp. 230–31.

58. See a succinct presentation of Lenin's and Stalin's respective views in Carrère d'Encausse 1992, pp. 35–43, and an analysis of the Stalinist practices in the rest of her book.

59. Carrère d'Encausse 1992, p. 220.

60. Roeder 1991, pp. 203–4.

61. Schroeder 1990, p. 43.

62. Shanin 1989, p. 418.

63. Graham Smith 1989b, p. 230.

64. See, for example, Nove 1986, p. 57; Graham Smith 1989a, p. 324.

65. Jones and Grupp 1984, p. 159; Lapidus 1989, pp. 208–9.

66. Vardys 1965b, p. 238; Ziegler 1985, p. 23.

67. An example of the way in which national identities in the USSR were reproduced is the internal passport system. These passports, introduced in 1932 with the aim of controlling the migration of peasants from the collectivized countryside to urban areas, demarcate the bearer's national identity. The nationality of children is determined solely on the basis of their parents's nationality. Even individuals who had been assimilated into another nationality, had never learned or forgotten the language of nationality, and had resided outside of its territory could not officially change their nationality. The sole choice was afforded to children of mixed ethnic couples who had to chose the ethnic identity of one parent over the other when they reached 16 years of age (Zaslavsky 1980, pp. 46–49).

68. Slightly different formulations are found in Oliner 1976, p. 263.

69. Kreindler 1988, p. 11.

70. Graudins 1988, p. 28; Kreindler 1988, p. 13.

71. Guboglo 1990a, Table 1, p. 249. Slightly different results are reported in "Panel on Nationalism in the USSR," 1989, Table 5, p. 461.

72. Harris in "Panel on Nationalism in the USSR," 1989, p. 457; Olcott 1990, p. 236.

73. Guboglo 1990b, p. 263.

74. Guboglo 1990a, pp. 248–49.

75. Dreifelds 1990, p. 61. The percentage of Latvians who speak Russian fluently does not include those for whom Russian is a first language. I have no comparable date for Estonia and Lithuania from the 1989 census.

76. Kreindler 1988, p. 13.

77. Graham Smith 1989b, Table 9.1, p. 240.

78. Kreindler 1988, p. 14.

79. Ibid., pp. 7–8.

80. Misiunas and Taagepera 1983, p. 261.

81. Kreindler 1988, p. 16.

82. Graham Smith 1989b, p. 241; Roeder 1991, pp. 203–7.

83. Jones and Grupp 1984, pp. 159–60; Roeder 1991, p. 207.

84. Kreindler 1988, p. 10.

85. Hodnett 1978, pp. 104–5.

86. Ibid., Table 1.6, p. 40.

87. For example, among the thirteen members of the Politburo of the Latvian Communist Party in 1970, only two people had non–Latvian names, three of them, however, were born in Latvia (Zaslavsky 1980, p. 65).

88. Ziegler 1985, p. 23.

89. Zaslavsky 1980, p 53.

90. "Panel on Nationalism in the USSR" 1989, pp. 462–63.

91. Ziegler 1985, p. 28.

92. G. Smith 1989a, p. 10.

93. Dunmore 1980, p. 26.

94. Ibid., pp. 27, 46.

95. Ibid., p. 47.

96. Ibid., p. 64.

97. Ibid., p. 66.

98. Ibid., pp. 49, 66.

99. Ibid., pp. 67–68.

100. Ibid., pp. 69–71.

101. Ibid., p. 72.

102. Ibid., p. 86.

103. Grossman, pp. 75, 77, 78.

104. G. Smith 1979, p. 61; Shryock 1977, pp. 91, 95.

105. Zaslavsky 1980, pp. 64–65.

106. Nove 1986, p. 54.

107. For description of the *sovnarkhozy* system, see ibid., pp. 59–64.

108. Misiunas and Taagepera 1983, pp. 179, 218; see also Nove 1986, p. 59.

109. Misiunas and Taagepera 1983, pp. 217–18.

110. "Sovereign Economic Rights for Republics," CDSP 40, no. 45 (December 7, 1988): 1; CDSP 40, no. 49 (January 4, 1989): 28. Even Boris Pugo, a key member of the junta that organized the 1991 August putsch, argued in his previous position as the leader of Latvian Communist Party that central ministries exercised "limitless diktat" over Latvia's economy (Nahaylo and Swoboda 1990, p. 306).

111. Dreifelds 1990, p. 69.

112. "Panel on Nationalism in the USSR" 1989, p. 492.

113. Järvesoo 1978, p. 138.

114. International Monetary Fund et al. 1990, p. 26.

115. Igitkhanian 1990, Table 1, p. 7; Oxenstierna 1991, pp. 257–58.

116. Oxenstierna 1991, pp. 257–58.

117. Ibid., p. 258.

118. Misiunas and Taagepera 1983, p. 187; *CDSP* 40, no. 46 (December 14, 1988): 5, mention that outside recruitment for employment in Latvia was mainly for industry and construction.

119. Misiunas and Taagepera 1983, pp. 107–8. Smith similarly indicates that "in the late 1940's and early 1950's, the top tier of the social structure of the [Latvian] Republic had been saturated by a massive injection of loyal Russians and Ukrainians. Concurrent with this movement of non-Latvian cadres into the Republic was the immigration of large numbers of industrial workers" (G. Smith 1979, p. 54).

120. King 1965, pp. 92, 134–36, 159.

121. Misiunas and Taagepera 1983, pp. 177, 207; *CDSP* 40, no. 25 (July 20, 1988): 6.

122. King 1965, p. 165.

123. Dreifelds 1990, p. 73.

124. Ibid., Table 9, p. 72.

125. Ibid., Table 8, p. 70.

126. Oxenstierna 1991, p. 258.

127. Ostapenko and Susokolov 1990, Table 2, p. 221.

128. Ibid., p. 223.

129. King 1965, p. 187.

130. Misiunas and Taagepera 1989, p. 72.

131. Dreifelds 1990, Table 5, p. 56; Misiunas and Taagepera 1983, p. 208; "Estonia: Influx of Russians Causes Tension," in *CDSP* 40, no. 6 (March 9, 1988): 6.

132. Misiunas and Taagepera 1989, p. 72; Dreifelds 1990, p. 55; Järvesoo 1978, pp. 134–35; Oxenstierna 1991, p. 259.

133. Misiunas and Taagepera 1983, p. 110; G. Smith 1989a, p. 12; *CDSP* 40, no. 8 (March 9, 1988): 7–8.

134. Dreifelds 1988, Table 10, p. 82.

135. The preference for medicine and economics for one of the Baltic groups is probably a reflection of the institutional profile of the higher education in its republic.
    The career specialization of Latvian students, in fact, led to a shortage of skilled and technically educated laborers, and in 1984 a school reform was undertaken with the intention of increasing their supply in the republic (Graudins 1988, pp. 21–25).

136. V. Koroteyeva, L. Perepelkin, and O. Shkaratan report to the nineteenth All–Union CP Conference, "Sovereign Economic Rights for Republics?" *CDSP* 40, no. 40 (December 7, 1988): 4.

137. "Estonia: Call for Two State Languages," *CDSP* 40, no.42 (November, 16 1988): 9; Misiunas and Taagepera 1983, p. 125.

138. Misiunas and Taagepera 1983, p. 107.

139. Koroteyeva et al. 1988, "Sovereign Economic Rights for Republics?" p. 4. Shkaratan also reports, although in what seems an over-simplified fashion, that "it is typical that the Russian population of republics works in industries under central control, while the native population works in industries under local control" (ibid., p. 14).

140. G. Smith 1989a, p. 13.

141. Nove 1986, pp. 213–15.

142. International Monetary Fund et al. 1990, p. 33.

143. Misiunas and Taagepera 1983, pp. 187, 227.

144. *CDSP* 40, no. 6 (March 9, 1988): 7.

145. Järvesoo 1978, p. 172.

146. See the debate between "ethnic competition" and "ethnic segmentation" theorists; for example, in Nagel and Olzak 1982; Ragin 1979; Nielsen 1980.

147. The early influence of the Baltic Popular Fronts is documented by Pourchier and Plasseraud 1989, p. 26, and throughout Nahaylo and Swoboda 1990.

148. Miljan 1989, pp. 154–55; Lapidus 1989, pp. 220–21.

149. Nahaylo and Swoboda 1990, p. 279.

150. During 1987, modest demonstrations also took place in commemoration of the victims of Stalin's deportations and the prewar states' independence days. Some of these demonstrations were reluctantly tolerated by the authorities, others were obstructed or repressed. A history of these events is in Trapans 1991a.

151. Miljan 1989, p. 161.

152. Nairn 1977, p. 185; Roeder 1991, p. 197.

153. Miljan 1989, p. 160.

154. Misiunas 1990, p. 209; "Estonia," *RAD Baltic Republics*, no. 251 (December 30, 1988): 19. The resolution of the plenum of the Latvian Union of Writers is reproduced in Olcott 1990, pp. 515–26.

155. Toomas Ilves, "The People's Front: The Creation of a Quasi Political Party," *Radio Free Europe: Baltic Area Situation Report*, no.5 (May 20, 1988): 10.

156. Toomas Ilves, "Estonia: The Cultural Unions' Resolution to the Leaderships of the ECP and ESSR," *Radio Free Europa, Baltic Area Situation Report*, no. 6 (June 3, 1988): 7–14; and Dzintra Bungs, "Latvia: Cultural Leaders Call for Greater National Sovereignty," *Radio Free Europa, Baltic Area Situation Report*, no.7 (July 13, 1988): 15–19.

157. Misiunas 1990, p. 210; Nahaylo and Swoboda 1990, pp. 294–99.

158. Nahaylo and Swoboda 1990, p. 312.

159. Pourchier and Plasseraud 1990, p. 38.

160. Nahaylo and Swoboda 1990, p. 315; Dzintra Bungs, "Legal Experts' Views on the Proposed Amendments to the Soviet Constitution," *Radio Free Europe: Baltic Area Situation Report*, no.11 (November 22, 1988); Levits 1989, p. 406.

161. "Estonia Claims Right to Veto USSR Laws," *CDSP* 40, no. 47 (December 21, 1988): 1–3.

162. Nahaylo and Swoboda 1990, p. 317.

163. Olcott 1990, p. 517.

164. For the process of radicalization in Latvia, which is typical to its two neighbors as well, see "A Woeful Look at Latvia's Soviet Period," *CDSP* 42, no. 16 (May 23, 1990): 1. For adoption of goal of independence by Latvian and Estonian Popular Fronts, see *CDSP* 42, no. 5 (March 7, 1990): 29.

165. *CDSP* (July 26, 1989): 5.

166. "Baltic Fronts Meet, Agree to Cooperate," *CDSP* (June 14 1989): 15.

167. Miljan 1989, pp. 157–58.

168. "Panel on Nationalism in the USSR" 1989, pp. 492–93.

169. Miljan 1989, pp. 162–63.

170. *CDSP* 41, no. 46 (December 13, 1989): 5–6; no. 48 (December 27, 1989): 11; Andris Trapans 1991, pp. 97–98.

171. *CDSP* (August 29, 1990): 26–27; Commission on Security and Cooperation in Europe 1991, pp. 92–93.

172. *CDSP* (August 22, 1991): 25–26.

173. "The Law on Secession," *CDSP* 42, no. 15 (May 16, 1990): 20–21.

174. *CDSP* (December 21, 1988): 13–14; (March 15, 1989): 6–7; (March 22, 1989): 20.

175. "Ethnic Tensions Mount in Estonia," *CDSP* (September 28, 1984): 6.

176. *CDSP* (November 2, 1988): 5.

177. See, e.g., *CDSP* (December 21, 1989): 14; *Radio Free Europe Background Report: Eastern Europe in 1988* (December 30, 1988,): 20.

178. *CDSP* (April 18, 1990): 16. For example, the Latvian Interfront organized a procession during Soviet Army Day, (*CDSP*, [March 22, 1989]: 8–9).

179. Taagepera 1990a, pp. 336–37.

180. *Baltic Area Situation Report* (April 21, 1989): 23–24.

181. Senn 1991, p. 247.

182. Taagepera 1990b, Table 1, pp. 304, 308.

183. Plakans 1991, p. 261; Raun 1991, p. 255.

184. Jan Trapans 1991b, p. 41.

185. Senn 1991, p. 248; *CDSP* 43, no. 2 (February 13, 1991): 1–10.

186. O'Clery, p. 10.

187. *CDSP* 43, no. 3 (February 20, 1990): 8–9.

188. Fitzmaurice 1993, p. 168.

189. *New York Times* (October 27, 1992 and November 17, 1992).

190. Economist Intelligence Unit 1993, pp. 8, 26, 40. Lithuania's transitional currency, the talonas, stabilized only in the summer of 1993, enabling the Lithuanian authorities to introduce the litas in late June.

191 *CDRP* 45, no. 10 (April 7, 1993): 18–19.

192. William E. Schmidt, "The Baltics Can Afford to Live a Little," *New York Times* (December 5, 1993).

193. *The Economist* (August 27, 1994): 90.

194. Ibid.

195. Economist Intelligence Unit 1993, passim.

196. This term is used, for example, by Misiunas and Taagepera 1983, p. 205.

197. Ibid., pp. 134, 137–38.

198. "Latvians, Estonians Seek Greater Autonomy," *CDSP* 60, no. 25 (July 20 1988): 2; Olcott 1990, p. 517.

199. Dreifelds 1990, p. 43.

200. The reference is to an article by archeologist R. Rimantene. See *CDSP* (March 22 1983): 20.

201. Olcott 1990, p. 517.

202. *CDSP* (November 16, 1988): 9; (February 1, 1989): 28–29; (April 19 1989): 18; (November 22, 1989): 36.

203. *CDSP* (February 15, 1989): 27; Commission on Security and Cooperation in Europe 1993a, p. 11.

204. Commission on Security and Cooperation in Europe 1993a, p. 12.

205. Dailey 1989, p. 27.

206. *CDSP* (June 14, 1989): 20–21.

207. "Party's Draft Platform on Nationalities Policy," *CDSP* (September 13, 1989): 7. See also reference to *Pravda*'s article from March 6, 1989, which "explicitly supports the efforts of non–Russian republics to promote their native languages," in Dailey 1989, p. 27.

208. Erika Dailey, "Report on the Status of Non–Russian Languages in the USSR," *Report on the USSR* 1, no. 30 (July 28, 1989): 27.

209. Commission on Security and Cooperation in Europe 1991, p. 90.

210. Commission on Security and Cooperation in Europe 1993b, p. 17.

211. Oxenstierna 1991, p. 269.

212. Lapidus 1989, p. 224.

213. *CDSP* (February 1, 1989): 28–29.

214. Commission on Security and Cooperation in Europe 1993b, p. 17.

215. Dailey 1989, p. 27.

216. Ibid., p. 28.

217. Guboglo 1990b, p. 264.

218. Ibid., Table 2, p. 265.

219. Ibid., Table 1, p. 261.

220. Dreifelds 1990, p. 62; Commission on Security and Cooperation in Europe 1991, p. 87.

221. Commission on Security and Cooperation in Europe 1993b, p. 4.

222. Ilves 1991, p. 77.

223. "Data on Ethnic Intermarriages" 1990, Table 2, pp. 165–66; Dreifelds 1990, p. 65. For data from 1959 and 1970, see Hodnett 1978, Table 1.6, p. 41. There was no difference between intermarriage rates by gender.

224. Bromley 1988, pp. 3–4.

225. Terentjeva 1970, Table 4, pp. 7, 11.

226. Misiunas and Taagepera 1989, p. 71.

227. Dreifelds 1990, p. 61.

228. G. Smith 1989b, pp. 236, 238.

229. Lieven 1990, p. 66.

230. Kirch et al. 1993, p. 179.

231. Jan Trapans 1991b, p. 35.

232. For the results of the 1989 elections, see Taagepera 1990a.

233. Taagepera 1990b, Table 1, p. 304; Tishkov 1990, Table 7, p. 48. In Lithuania of 140 Supreme Council members 122 were Lithuanian, 7 were Russian, and 10 were Polish; in Latvia of 199 members 139 were Latvian, 53 were Slavic, and 7 were others; in Estonia of 104 members 80 were Estonian, 22 were Slavic, and 2 were others (Tishkov 1990, Table 6, pp. 45–46).

234. Taagepera 1990b, p. 308.

235. Ibid., p. 309.

236. Dreifelds 1990, p. 74.

237. Commission on Security and Cooperation in Europe 1993b, p. 4.

238. Dreifelds 1990, p. 68.

239. Commission on Security and Cooperation in Europe 1991, p. 91.

240. Taagepera 1991, Table 1.

241. Commission on Security and Cooperation in Europe 1991, p. 85.

242. Commission on Security and Cooperation in Europe 1992, p. 18.

243. See, for example, Dreifelds 1990, p. 78.

244. Plakans 1991, p. 263.

245. Commission on Security and Cooperation in Europe 1993a, pp. 9–10. Kirch et. al also developed a "citizen loyalty" scale that points to a similar pattern of internal division. I felt that some of the assumptions of the research, the questions used for constructing the scale, and the concept of "loyalty" are at once too naive and ideologically loaded to render their specific findings useful.

246. Commission on Security and Cooperation in Europe 1993b, pp. 16–17.

247. Ibid., pp. 4–5.

248. Taagepera 1991, p. 2.

249. Hobsbawm 1990, p. 134.

250. The eponymous and immigrant populations in the Baltic republics appear to share one more interest: they are overwhelmingly in favor of
halting further migration into the republics. A September 1989 poll found
that close to 80 percent of respondents of all nationalities supported such
policy, hoping obviously to decrease pressure on housing and other high
demand commodities (Dreifelds 1990, p. 75).

251. For Estonia, see Ginsburgs 1990, pp. 12–13; *CDSP* (November 1,
1989): 25–26. But in Taagepera's view, some provisions of the electoral law for
local councils, were undemocratic. For example, the decision over the
number of representatives to be elected from each district is left to the
discretion of the local Soviet or city council and "gives local officials the
opportunity to manipulate the electoral process in order to deprive minorities
of representation" ("Draft Law for Local Elections in Estonia is Criticized,"
Radio Free Europe Research Situation Report, Baltic Area [August 11, 1989]:
9–11).
 For Latvia, see *CDSP* (December 13, 1989): 34. "Some Republic Laws
Called Unconstitutional," (December 13, 1989): 6; (August 23, 1989): 33.

252. *CDSP* (August 8, 1990): 24.

253. "Party's Draft Platform on Nationalities Policy," *CDSP* (September
13, 1989): 7.

254. "Some Republic Laws Called Unconstitutional," *CDSP* (December
13, 1989): 6.

255. Rein Taagepera, "A Brash Nation Awaits Do-It-Yourself Election,"
Los Angeles Times (February 22, 1990); Vello Pettai, "Estonian Citizens'
Committees to Organize Congress of Estonian Citizens," *Radio Free Europe
Research Situation Report, Baltic Area* (July 7, 1989): 7–9; *CDSP* (August 9
1989): 5; (September 6, 1989): 7; (May 30, 1990): 27–28.

256. Dreifelds 1990, Table 1, p. 55.

257. Calculated from Parming 1972, Table 3, p. 61.

258. Ginsburgs 1990, p. 10.

259. Ibid., p. 14. Although the quote is taken from Ginsburgs's assessment of only the Latvian law, it is a fair summary of his view of the citizenship laws in the other two Baltic republics as well.

260. *CDSP* (April 18, 1990): 16.

261. Ginsburgs 1990, p. 15.

262. *Svenska Dagbladet* (February 27, 1992).

263. Commission on Security and Cooperation in Europe 1993a, p. 22, and n. 12.

264. Ibid., p. 11.

265. Economist Intelligence Unit 1993, p. 7.

266. Commission on Security and Cooperation in Europe 1993a, p. 13; Economist Intelligence Unit 1993, p. 7.

267. Ibid., pp. 14–16.

268. Commission on Security and Cooperation in Europe 1993b, pp. 14–15; Tamara Jones, "Latvia Playing Russian Roulette," *Los Angeles Times* (March 14, 1992).

269. Commission on Security and Cooperation in Europe 1993b, pp. 14, 24.

270. Ibid., p. 24.

271. *The Economist* (June 25 1994): "Divided Latvians Awaiting Clinton," *Los Angeles Times* (July 5 1994).

272. Ginsburgs 1990, p. 22.

273. Commission on Security and Cooperation in Europe 1993a, p. 11.

274. Ginsburgs 1990, pp. 22–23.

275. Taagepera 1990b, p. 309.

276. An expression used in another context by Ginsburg 1990, p. 11.

277. Speech by V. I. Yarovoi, the chairman of the United Council of Labor Collectives, reported in *CDSP* (August 16, 1989): 23.

278. The chairman of the presidium of the UCELC was V. I.Yarovoi, the director of the Lenin State Union Dvigatel [Engine] Plant Production Association in Tallinn (*CDSP* [August 16, 1989]: 23). A number of additional organizations form the Russian immigrant movement in Estonia: Democratic Development and For Equal Rights, were also opposed to the residence requirement of the election law (*CDSP* [December 6, 1989]: 24); The Committee for the Defense of Soviet Power and Civil Rights was organized in opposition to the meeting of the Estonian Congress and its call for Estonian independence (*CDSP* [April 18, 1990]: 16).

279. For example, see *CDSP* (April 19, 1989): 17.

280 *CDSP* (January 4, 1989): 28–29; *Radio Free Europe Background Report: Eastern Europe in 1988* (December 30, 1988): 20.

281. See also *CDSP* (June 28, 1989): 20.

282. *CDSP* (April 19, 1983): 17–18.

283. "Estonian Voting Law Sparks Russian Strikes," *CDSP* (September 6, 1989): 6–8; (June 14, 1989): 19–20.

284. Vello Pettai, "Russians Strike Against Self-Management?" *Radio Free Europe Research Situation Report, Baltic Area* (August 11, 1989): 4. When in March 1990 the Estonian Congress recommended the reestablishment of militarized self-defense organizations that existed in the independent republic of Estonia, the Committee for the Defense of Soviet Power called on the formation of workers' self-detachments (*CDSP* [April 18, 1990]: 16).

285. Commission on Security and Cooperation in Europe 1993a, p. 7; 1993b, pp. 18–19.

286. Samonis 1991, pp. 7–9.

287. Oxenstierna 1991, p. 258.

288. Dreifelds 1990, p. 69.

289. Lieven 1990, p. 64.

290. Misiunas and Taagepera 1983, p. 134.

291. Ibid., pp. 186, 206.

292. This is the recommendation of the multivolume report of the International Baltic Economic Commission of the Hudson Institute presented to the prime ministers of Latvia, Lithuania, and Estonia in the presence of Vice President Quayle in 1991. See summary of proposals in Samonis 1991.

293. Samonis 1991, p. 9.

Chapter 6. Conclusion

1. A supplement of the Lithuanian government to the November 1991 issue of *Euromoney* carries the proud title, "Independence—The First Step Towards a Free Market in Lithuania."

2. Enquesta 1990, Table 2.3, p. 56; Dreifelds 1990, p. 62; Commission on Security and Cooperation in Europe 1991, p. 87.

3. Woolard 1989, p. 121.

4. Strubel i Trueta 1981, pp. 151, 154–155; Terentjeva 1970, Table 4, pp. 7, 11; Misiunas and Taagepera 1989, p. 71.

5. Medhurst 1987, p. 8.

6. Dreifelds 1990, p. 68; Commission on Security and Cooperation in Europe 1991, p. 91.

7. Dreifelds 1990, p. 78; Tamara Jones, "Latvia Playing Russian Roulette," *Los Angeles Times* (March 24, 1992).

8. Kirch 1993, p. 179.

9. Hawkins 1988, pp. 22–23.

10. Raz 1994, pp. 68–69.

11. Ibid., p. 77.

12. Ibid., pp. 73–74.

BIBLIOGRAPHY

Adirim, Itzchok. 1988. "Realities of Economic Growth and Distribution in the Baltic States." *Journal of Baltic Studies* 19, no. 1 (Spring): 49–66.

Alcock, Anthony E., et. al. 1979. *The Future of Cultural Minorities*. London: Macmillan.

Allworth, Edward ed. 1977. *Nationality Group Survival in Multi-Ethnic States: Shifting Support Patterns in the Soviet Baltic Region*. London: Praeger.

Anderson, Benedict. 1983. *Imagined Communities: Reflections on the Origin and Spread of Nationalism*. London: Verso.

Arbós, Xavier. 1987. "Central Versus Peripheral Nationalism in Building Democracy: The Case of Spain." *Canadian Review of Studies in Nationalism* 14, no. 1: 143–60.

Aun, Karl. 1951–1953. "The Cultural Autonomy of National Minorities in Estonia." *Yearbook of the Estonian Learned Society in America* 1: 26–41.

Balcells, Albert. 1977. *Cataluña contemporánea I (sigolo XIX)*. Madrid: Siglo veintiuno editores.

Banco de Bilbao. 1967. *Renta Nacional de España y su distribución provincial*. Bilbao.

———. 1985. *Renta Nacional de España y su distribución provincial*. Bilbao.

Beltza (E. López Adán). 1976. *Nacionalismo vasco y clases sociales*. San Sebastián: Txertoa.

———. 1978. *Del Carlismo al nacionalismo burgues*. San Sebastián: Txertoa.

Ben-Ami, Shlomo. 1978. *The Origins of the Second Republic in Spain*. Oxford: Oxford University Press.

———. 1991."Basque Nationalism between Archaism and Modernity." *Journal of Contemporary History* 26, nos. 3–4 (September): 493–521.

Bidart, Pierre ed. 1980a. *La nouvelle société Basque: Ruptures et changements*. Paris: Editions l'Harmattan.

————. 1980b. "Politique, culture et science." In Pierre Bidart, ed., *La Nouvelle société Basque: ruptures et changements*, pp. 5–18. Paris: Editions l'Harmattan.

Bilmanis, Alfred. 1951. *A History of Latvia*. Westport, Conn.: Greenwood Press.

Blom, Raimo, et. al. 1991. "The Economic System and the Work Situation: A Comparison of Finland and Estonia." *International Sociology* 6, no. 3 (September): 343–60.

Blondel, J., and Hualde Eseverri. 1983. "The Spanish General Election of 1982." *Electoral Studies* 2, no. 1 (April): 72–80.

Bohnet, Armin, and Norbert Penkaitis. 1988. "A Comparison of Living Standards and Consumption Patterns Between the RSFSR and the Baltic Republics." *Journal of Baltic Studies* 19, no. 1 (Spring): 33–48.

Braithwaite, Jeanine D. 1990. "Income Distribution and Poverty in the Soviet Republics." *Journal of Soviet Nationalities* 1, no. 3 (Fall): 158–73.

Brand, Jack A. 1985. "Nationalism and the Noncolonial Periphery: A Discussion of Scotland and Catalonia." In Edward A. Tiryakian and Ronald Rogowski, eds., *New Nationalism of the Developed West*, pp. 277–93. Boston: Allen & Unwin.

Brass, Paul R. 1980. "Ethnic Groups and Nationalities: The Formation, Persistence, and Transformation of Ethnic Identities." In Peter F. Sugar, ed., *Ethnic Diversity and Conflict in Eastern Europe*. Santa Barbara, Calif.: ABC-Clio.

Brölmann, Catherine, et. al. 1993. *Peoples and Minorities in International Law*. Dordrecht: Martinus Nijhoff.

Bromley, J. V. 1988. "Present-Day Ethnic Processes in the USSR." Paper presented at the 12th International Congress of Anthropological and Ethnological Studies, Zagreb, July 24–31.

———— and Viktor Kozlov. 1989. "The Theory of Ethnos and Ethnic Processes in Soviet Social Studies." *Comparative Studies in Society and History* 31, no. 3 (July): 425–38.

Brubaker, Rogers. 1992. *Citizenship and Nationhood in France and Germany*. Cambridge, Mass.: Harvard University Press.

Bruk, S. I. 1972. "Ethnodemographic Processes in the USSR." *Soviet Sociology* 10, no. 4 (Spring): 331–74.

Buechler, Judith-Maria. 1987. "A Review—Guest, Intruder, Settler, Ethnic Minority, or Citizen: The Sense and Nonsense of Borders," in Hans

Christian Buechler and Judith-Maria Buechler, eds., *Migrants in Europe: The Role of Labor, Family, Labor, and Politics*, pp. 233–304. Westport, Conn.: Greenwood Press.

Cahm, Eric, and Vladimir Claude Fisera, eds. 1980. *Socialism and Nationalism in Contemporary Europe (1848–1945)*, vol. 3. Nottingham: Spokesman.

Calhoun, Craig. 1991. "Nationalism, Civil Society and Democracy." Paper presented at the Convention of the Hungarian Sociological Association on Hungary in the World: Central European Societies from the Perspective of Comparative Social Analysis, Budapest, June 24–28.

Candel, F. 1967. *Els altres Catalans*. Barcelona.

Carr, Raymond. 1980. *Modern Spain 1875–1980*. Oxford: Oxford University Press.

————. 1982. *Spain 1808–1975*, 2d ed. Oxford: Claredon Press.

Carrère d'Encausse, Hélène. 1980. "The Bolsheviks and the National Question (1903–1929)." in Eric Cahm and Vladimir Claude Fisera, *Socialism and Nationalism in Contemporary Europe (1848–1945)*, vol. 3, pp.113–26. Nottingham: Spokesman.

————. 1992. *The Great Challenge: Nationalities and the Bolshevik State, 1917-1930*. New York: Holmes and Meier.

Castles, S., and G. Kosack. 1973. *Immigrant Workers and Class Structure in Western Europe*. New York: Oxford University Pess.

Castles, Stephen and Mark J. Miller. 1993. *The Age of Migration*. NY: Guilford Press.

Clark, Robert P. 1980a. *The Basques: The Franco Years and Beyond*. Reno: University of Nevada Press.

————. 1980b. "Euzkadi: Basque Nationalism in Spain Since the Civil War." In Charles R. Foster, ed., *Nations Without a State: Ethnic Minorities in Western Europe*, pp.75–100. New York: Praeger.

————. 1981. "Language and Politics in Spain's Basque Provinces." *West European Politics* 4, no. 1 (January): 85–103.

————. 1984. *The Basque Insurgents: ETA, 1952–1980*. Madison: University of Wisconsin Press.

————. 1985. "Dimensions of Basque Political Culture in Post-Franco Spain." In William A. Douglass, *Basque Politics: A Case Study in Ethnic Nationalism*, pp.217–63. Reno, Nev.: Associated Faculty Press and Basque Study Programs.

Claude, Inis L., Jr. 1955. *National Minorities: An International Problem.* Cambridge: Harvard University Press.

Commission on Security and Cooperation in Europe (CSCE). 1990. *Elections in the Baltic States and Soviet Republics: A Compendium of Reports on Parliamentary Elections Held in 1990.* Washington, D.C.:

————. 1991. *Minority Rights: Problems, Parameters, and Patterns in the CSCE Context.* Washington, D.C.

————. 1992. *Ethnic Russians in the Baltic States, Implementation of the Helsinki Accords.* Washington, D.C.: U.S. Government Printing Office.

————. 1993a. *Human Rights and Democratization in Estonia.* Washington, D.C.

————. 1993b. *Human Rights and Democratization in Latvia.* Washington, D.C.

Connor, Walker. 1978. "A Nation Is a Nation, Is a State, Is an Ethnic Group, Is a..." *Ethnic and Racial Studies* 1, no. 4 (October): 377–400.

Conversi, Daniele. 1988. "L'integrazione degli immigrati a Barcellona." *Studi Emigrazione*, no. 89 (March): 67–82.

————. 1990. "Language or Race?: The Choice of Core Values in the Development of Catalan and Basque Nationalisms." *Ethnic and Racial Studies* 13, no. 1 (January): 50–70.

Corcuera, Javier. 1986. "La configuracion del nacionalismo vasco." In Francesc Hernández and Francesc Mercadé, *Estructuras sociales y cuestión en España*, pp.130–58. Barcelona: Ariel.

Coverdale, John F. 1985. "Regional Nationalism and the Elections in the Basque Country. " In Howard R. Penniman and Eusebio M. Mujal-León, eds., *Spain at the Polls 1977, 1979, 1982: A Study of the National Elections*, pp. 226–52. Durham, N.C.: Duke University Press

Crane, Keith, and Matthew J. Sagers. 1991. "Estonia, Latvia, and Lithuania: Baltic States Political Profile Overshadows Economic Clout." *Plan Econ Report* 7, nos. 47–48 (December 23).

Cullen, Robert. 1990. "Lithuania: Independence or Nothing." *The Atlantic* (July): 24–32.

Da Silva, Milton M. 1975. "Modernization and Ethnic Conflict: The Case of the Basques." *Comparative Politics* 7, no. 2(January): 227–51.

Dailey, Erika. 1989. "Report on the Status of Non-Russian Languages in the USSR." *Report on the USSR* 1, no. 30 (July 28): 26–28.

"Data on Ethnic Intermarriages." 1990. *Journal of Soviet Nationalities* 1, no. 2 (Summer): 160–71.

Del Campo, Salustiano, and Manuel Navarro López. 1987. *Nuevo Análisis de la Población Española*. Barcelona: Ariel.

Diez Medrano, Juan. 1989. "Nationalism and Independence in Spain: Basques and Catalans." Unpublished dissertation, University of Michigan.

———. Forthcoming. *Divided Nations: Class, Politics, and Nationalism in the Basque Country and Catalonia*. Ithaca, N.Y.: Cornell University Press.

DiGiacomo, Susan M. 1985. "The Politics of Identity: Nationalism in Catalonia." Unpublished dissertation, University of Massachusetts.

———. 1986. "Images of Class and Ethnicity in Catalan Politics, 1977–1980." In Gary W. McDonogh, ed., *Conflict in Catalonia: Images of an Urban Society*, pp. 72–92. Gainesville: University of Florida Press.

Doersam, Christopher. 1977. "Sovietization, Culture, and Religion." in Edward Allworth, *Nationality Group Survival in Multi-Ethnic States: Shifting Support Patterns in the Soviet Baltic Region*, pp.148–93. London: Praeger.

Douglass, William A. ed. 1985. *Basque Politics: A Case Study in Ethnic Nationalism*. Reno, Nev.: Associated Faculty Press and Basque Studies Program.

——— and Milton da Silva. 1971. "Basque Nationalism." In Oriol Pi-Sunyer, *The Limits of Integration: Ethnicity and Nationalism in Modern Europe*, pp.147–86. Amherst: University of Massachusetts, Department of Anthropology Research Report 9.

——— and Joseba Zulaika. 1990. "On the Interpretation of Terrorist Violence: ETA and the Basque Political Process." *Comparative Studies in Society and History* 32, no. 2 (April): 238–57.

Dreifelds, Juris. 1984. "Demographic Trends in Latvia." *Nationalities Papers* 12, no. 1 (Spring): 49–84.

———. 1988. "Social Inequalities in the Baltic: The Case of Occupational Hierarchy and Upward Mobility." *Journal of Baltic Studies* 19, no. 1 (Spring): 67–88.

———. 1990. "Immigration and Ethnicity in Latvia." *Journal of Soviet Nationalities* 1, no. 4 (Winter): 43–81.

Dunmore, Timothy. 1980. *The Stalinist Command Economy: The Soviet State Apparatus and Economic Policy*, 1945-1953. London: Macmillan.

Durkheim, Emile. 1965. *The Division of Labor in Society*. New York: The Free Press.

Economist Intelligence Unit (EIU). 1993. *Baltic Republics: Estonia, Latvia, Lithuania, country profile*, 1993–1994. London.

Elliott, J. H. 1963. *The Revolt of the Catalans*. Cambridge: Cambridge University Press.

Elorza Antonio. 1978. *Ideologías del nacionalismo vasco 1876–1937*. San Sebastián: Haranburu.

———. 1978. *Nacionalismo vasco 1876-1936: Temas*. San Sebastián: Haranburu.

Enquesta metropolitana 1986, Vol. 20. Transmissió i coneixement de la llengua catalana a l'àrea metropolitana de Barcelona. 1990. ed. Marina Subirats. Barcelona: Institut de Sociolingüística Catalana.

Estava Fabergat, Claudio. 1975. "Ethnicity, Social Class, and Acculturation of Immigrants in Barcelona." *Ethnologia Europaea* 8, no. 1: 23–43.

Fitzmaurice, John. 1993. "The Estonian Elections of 1992." *Electoral Studies* 12, no. 2: 168–73.

Fleming, Judith. 1977. "Political Leaders." In Edward Allworth, ed., *Nationality Group Survival in Multi-Ethnic States: Shifting Support Patterns in the Soviet Baltic Region*, pp.123–47. London: Praeger.

Foster, Charles R., ed. 1980. *Nations Without a State: Ethnic Minorities in Western Europe*. New York: Praeger.

Fratianni, Michele, et al. 1991. *Currency Reform in the Baltic Republics*. Indianapolis: Hudson Institute.

Fredrickson, George. 1981. *White Supremacy: A Comparative Study of American and South African History*. Oxford: Oxford University Press.

Fundación FOESSA. 1970. *Informe sociólogico sobra la situación social de España 1970*. Madrid.

———. 1975. *Estudios sociologicos sobre la situacion social de España*. Madrid.

Fusi, Juan Pablo. 1975. *Política obrera en al País Vasco, 1880–1923*. Madrid.

———. 1984. *El país vasco: Pluralismo y nacionalidad*. Madrid: Alianza.

Garleff, Michael. 1978. "Ethnic Minorities in the Estonian and Latvian Parliaments: The Politics of Coalition." In V. Stanley Vardys and Romuald J. Misiunas, eds., *The Baltic States in Peace and War*,

1917–1945, pp. 81–94. University Park: Pennsylvania State University Press.

Garmendia, José Mari. 1980. *Historia de ETA*, 2 vols. San Sebastián: Haranburu.

Geertz, Clifford. 1963. "The Integrative Revolution: Primordial Sentiments and Civil Politics in the New States." In Clifford Geertz, ed., *Old Societies and New States*, pp. 105–57. London: Free Press.

Gellner, Ernest. 1964. *Thought and Change*. London: Weidenfeld and Nicholson.

———. 1983. *Nations and Nationalism*. Ithaca, N.Y.: Cornell University Press.

Gerutis, Albertas, ed. 1969. *Lithuania: 700 Years*, 2d ed. New York: Manyland Books.

Gilmour, D. 1985. *The Transformation of Spain: From Franco to the Constitutional Monarchy*. London: Quartet Books.

Giner, Salvador. 1980. *The Social Structure of Catalonia*. London: Anglo-Catalan Society.

Ginsburgs, George. 1990. "The Citizenship of the Baltic States." *Journal of Baltic Studies* 21, no. 1 (Spring): 3–26.

Gordon, Milton, M. 1964. *Assimilation in American Life: The Role of Race, Religion, and National Origins*. New York: Oxford University Press

Gourevitch, Peter Alexis. 1979. "The Remergence of 'Peripheral Nationalisms:' Some Comparative Speculations on the Spatial Distribution of Political Leadership and Economic Growth." *Comparative Studies in Society and History* 21, no. 3 (July): 303–21.

Gramsci, Antonio. 1971. *Selections from the Prison Notebooks*, ed. and trans. Q. Hoare and G. N. B. Smith. New York: International Publishers.

Granberg, A. G. 1990. "The Economic Mechanism of Inter-Republic and Inter-Regional Relations." *Problems of Economics* 33, no. 3 (July): 77–93.

Grandstaff, Peter J. 1975. "Recent Soviet Experience and Western 'Laws' of Population Migration." *International Migration Review* 9, no. 4 (Winter): 479–97.

Graudins, Maris I. 1988. "The Rationale and Implementation of the 1984 Soviet School Reform in Latvia." *Journal of Baltic Studies* 19, no. 1 (Spring): 21–32.

Greenfield, Liah. 1992. *Nationalism: Five Roads to Modernity.* Cambridge, Mass.: Harvard University Press.

Greenwood, Davydd J. 1977. "Continuity in Change: Spanish Basque Ethnicity as a Historical Process." In Milton J. Esman, ed. *Ethnic Conflict in the Western World*, pp. 81–102. Ithaca, N.Y.: Cornell University Press.

Grossman, Richard. 1977. "The Kosomol Youth." In Edward Allworth, ed., *Nationality Group Survival in Multi-Ethnic States.* New York: Praeger.

Guboglu, M. N. 1990a. "The General and the Particular in the Development of the Linguistic Life of the Soviet Union." In Martha B. Olcott et al., eds., *The Soviet Multinational State: Readings and Documents*, pp. 246–51. Armonk, N.Y.: M. E. Sharpe.

———. 1990b. "Factors and Tendencies of the Development of Bilingualism Among the Russian Population Living in the Union Republics." In Martha B. Olcott et al., eds., *The Soviet Multinational State: Readings and Documents*, pp. 258–79. Armonk, N.Y.: M. E. Sharpe.

Gunther, Richard, Giacomo Sani, and Goldie Shabad. 1988. *Spain After Franco: The Making of a Competative Party System.* Berkeley: University of California Press.

Hajda, Lubomyr, and Mark Beissinger, eds. 1990. *The Nationalities Factor in Soviet Politics and Society.* Boulder, Colo.: Westview Press.

Haltzel, Michael H. 1974. "The Russification of the Baltic Germans: A Dysfunctional Aspect of Imperial Modernization." In Arvids Ziedonis Jr. et al., eds., *Baltic History*, pp. 143–52. Columbus, Ohio: Association for the Advancement of Baltic States.

———. 1981. "The Baltic Germans." In Edward C. Thaden, *Russification in the Baltic Provinces and Findland*, pp. 111–204. Princeton, N.J.: Princeton University Press.

Hammar, Tomas. 1990. *Democracy and the Nation State: Aliens, Denizens and Citizens in a World of International Migration.* Aldershot: Avebury.

Hargreaves-Mawdsley, W. N. 1973. *Spain Under the Bourbons, 1700–1833.* London: Macmillan.

Harned, Frederic T. 1975a. "Latvia and the Latvians." In Zev Katz et al., eds., *Handbook of Major Soviet Nationalities*, pp. 94–117. New York: The Free Press.

———. 1975b. "Lithuania and the Lithuanians." In Zev Katz et al., eds., *Handbook of Major Soviet Nationalities*, pp.118–40. New York: The Free Press.

Harrison, Joseph. 1977. "Big Business and the Rise of Basque Nationalism." *European Studies Review* 7: 371–91.

———. 1985. *The Spanish Economy in the Twentieth Century.* London: Croom Helm.

Hawkins, Freda. 1988. "Canadian Multiculturalism: The Policy Explained." In A. J. Fry and C. Forceville, eds., *Canadian Mosaic*, pp. 9–23. Amsterdam: Free University.

———. 1991. *Critical Years in Immigration: Canada and Australia Compared*, 2d ed. Montreal: McGill-Queens University Press.

Hechter, Michael. 1975. *Internal Colonialism: The Celtic Fringe in British National Development, 1536–1966.* London: Routledge and Kegan Paul.

Heiberg, Marianne. 1975. "Insiders/Ousiders: Basque Nationalism." *European Archives of Sociology* 16, no. 2: 169–93.

———. 1989. *The Making of the Basque Nation.* Cambridge: Cambridge University Press.

Heisler, Barbara Schmitter. 1986. "Immigrant Settlement and the Structure of Emergent Immigrant Communities in Western Europe." In Martin O. Heisler and Barbara Schmitter Heisler, *From Foreign Workers to Settlers? Transnational Migration and the Emergence of New Minorities.* The Annals of the American Academy of Political and Social Sciences 485, pp.76–86.

———. 1992. "The Future of Immigrant Incorporation: Which Models? Which Concepts?" *International Migration Review* 24, no. 2(Summer): 623–45.

Hernández, Francesc. 1986. "El nacionalismo catalán." In Francesc Hernández and Francesc Mercadé, eds., *Estructuras sociales y cuestión nacional en España*, pp. 69–90. Barcelona: Ariel.

——— and Francesc Mercadé, eds. 1986a. *Estructuras sociales y cuestión nacional en España.* Barcelona: Ariel.

———. 1986b. "Estructura social de Cataluña." In Francesc Hernández and Francesc Mercadé, eds., *Estructuras sociales y cuestión nacional en España*, pp.91–129. Barcelona: Ariel.

Herr, Richard. 1974. *An Historical Essay on Modern Spain.* Berkeley: University of California Press.

Historical Essays of Otto Hintze. 1975. Edited by Felix Gilbert, N.Y., Oxford University Press.

Hobsbawm, E.J. 1962. *The Age of Revolution, 1789–1848.* New York: New American Library.

———. 1990. *Nations and Nationalism Since 1780: Programme, Myth, Reality.* Cambridge: Cambridge University Press.

Hobson, J. A. 1968. *Imperialism,* 3d ed. London: Allen & Unwin.

Hodnett, Grey. 1978. *Leadership in the Soviety National Republics: A Quantitative Study of Recruitment Policy.* Oakville, Ontario: Mosaic Press.

Hollifield, James F. 1992. *Immigrants, Markets and States.* Cambridge, Mass.: Harvard University Press.

Horowitz, Donald L. 1981. "Patterns of Ethnic Separatism." *Comparative Studies in Society and History* 23, no. 2 (April): 165–95.

Hroch, Miroslav. 1985. *Social Preconditions of National Revival in Europe: A Comparative Analysis of the Social Composition of Patriotic Groups Among the Smaller European Nations,* trans. Ben Fowkes. Cambridge: Cambridge University Press.

Igitkhanian, E. D., et al. 1990. "Industrial Workers's Work-Teams." *Sotsiologicheskie Issledovaniya,* no. 3 (June): 3–12.

Ilves, Toomas Hendrik. 1991. "Reaction: The Intermovement in Estonia." In Jan Arveds Trapans, ed., *Toward Independence: The Baltic Popular Movements,* pp. 71–83. Boulder, Colo.: Westview Press.

Inglehart, R. F., and M. Woodward. 1972. "Language Conflicts and Political Community." In Pier Paolo Giglioli, ed., *Language and Social Context,* pp. 358–77. Baltimore: Penguin Books.

International Monetary Fund et al. 1990. *The Economy of the USSR.* Washington, D.C.: The World Bank.

Jansen, E. 1985. "On the Economic and Social Determination of the Estonian National Movements." *National Movements,* pp. 41–57.

———. n.d. "Romantic Nationalism in Estonia." Unpublished paper.

Järvesoo, Elmar. 1974. "Estonian Declaration of Independence in 1918: An Episode of Collision Between National-Revolutionary and Bolshevist Ideologies. " In Arvids Ziedonis Jr. et al., eds., *Baltic History,* pp. 161–73. Columbus, Ohio: Association for the Advancement of Baltic States.

———. 1978. "The Postwar Economic Transformation." In Tönu Parming and Elmar Järvesoo, *A Case Study of a Soviet Republic: The Estonian SSR,* pp. 131–90. Boulder, Colo.: Westview Press.

Johnston, Hank. 1992. "Religio-Nationalist Subcultures and Soviet Nationalisms: Comparisons and Conceptual Refinements." *Journal of Baltic Studies* 23, no. 2 (Summer).

Jones, Ellen, and Fred W. Grupp. 1984. "Modernization and Ethnic Equalization in the USSR." *Soviet Studies* 36, no. 2 (April): 159–84.

Jurgela, Constantine R. 1948. *History of the Lithuanian Nation.* New York: Lithuanian Cultural Institute.

Katz, Zev, et al. eds. 1975. *Handbook of Major Soviet Nationalities.* New York: The Free Press.

Keegan, John. 1990. *The Second World War.* New York: Penguin.

Kimmel, Michael. 1989. "Defensive Revolutionaries: The Moral and Political Economy of Basque, Breton and Quebecois Nationalism." *Research in Social Movements, Conflicts, and Change* 11: 109–28.

King, Gundar Julian. 1965. *Economic Policies in Occupied Latvia: A Manpower Management Study.* Pacific Lutheran University Press.

Kirch, Aksel, et al. 1993. "Russian in the Baltic States: To Be Or Not to Be?" *Journal of Baltic Studies* 24, no. 2 (Summer): 173–88.

Kreindler, Isabelle T. 1988. "Baltic Area Languages in the Soviet Union: A Sociolinguistic Perspective." *Journal of Baltic Studies* 19, no. 1 (Spring): 5–20.

Laitin, David D. 1989. "Linguistic Revival: Politics and Culture in Catalonia." *Comparative Studies in Society and History* 31, no. 2 (April): 297–317.

———. 1991. "The National Uprisings in the Soviet Union." *World Politics* 44, no. 1 (October): 139–77.

Lapidus, Gail W. 1989. "Gorbachev and the 'National Question:' Restructuring the Soviet Federation." *Soviet Economy* 5, no. 3 (July-September): 201–50.

Larronde, Jean-Claude. 1980. "Forces politiques, classes sociales en Bizkaye à la fin du XIXe siècle: Naissance du nationalism basque." In Pierre Bidart, ed., *La nouvelle société Basque: Ruptures et changements*, pp. 19–50. Paris: Editions l'Harmattan.

Lerner, N. 1993. "The Evolution of Minority Rights in International Law." In Catherine Brölmann et al., *Peoples and Minorities in International Law*, pp. 77–101. Dordrecht: Martinus Nijhoff.

Levin, Dov. 1990. "On the Relationship Between the Baltic Peoples and Their Jewish Neighbors Before, During, and After World War II." *Holocaust and Genocide Studies* 5, no. 1 (1990): 53–66.

Levits, Egil. 1981. "Die demographische Situation in der UdSSR und in den baltischen Staaten unter besonderer Berücksichtigung von nationalen und sprachsoziologischen Aspekten." *Acta Baltica* 21: 18–142.

———. 1989. "Der politische Aufbruch in den baltischen Staaten." *Europa-Archiv* 44, no. 13 (July 10): 403–12.

Lewis, Robert A. and Richard H. Rowland. 1977. "East Is West and West Is East...Population Redistribution in the USSR and Its Impact on Society," *International Migration Review* 11, no. 1 (Spring): 3–29.

Lieven, Anatol. 1990. "Baltic Notebook." *Encounter* 74, no. 4 (May): 60–66.

Linz, Juan. 1967. "The Party System in Spain: Past and Future." In Seymour M. Lipset and Stein Rokkan, eds., *Party Systems and Voter Alignments: Cross-National Perspectives*, pp. 197–282. New York: Free Press.

———. 1973a. "Opposition in and under an Authoritarian Regime: The Case of Spain." In Robert Dahl, ed., *Regimes and Oppositions*, pp. 171–259. New Haven, Conn.: Yale University Press.

———. 1973b. "Early State-Building and Late Peripheral Nationalisms Against the State: The Case of Spain." In S. N. Eisenstadt and Stein Rokkan, eds., *Building States and Nations*, vol. 2, pp. 32–116. Bevery Hills, Calif.: Sage Publications.

———. 1980. "The Basques in Spain: Nationalism and Political Conflict in a New Democracy." In W. Phillips Davison and Leon Gordenker, eds., *Resolving Nationality Conflicts: The Role of Public Opinion Research*, pp. 11–52. New York: Praeger.

———. 1985. "From Primordialism to Nationalism." In Edward A. Tiryakian and Ronald Rogowski, eds., *New Nationalisms of the Developed West*, pp. 203–53. Boston: Allen & Unwin.

——— and Amando de Miguel. 1966. "Within-Nation Differences and Comparisons: The Eight Spains." In Richard L.Meritt and Stein Rokkan, eds., *Comparing Nations: The Uses of Quantitative Data in Cross-National Research*, pp. 267–319. New Haven, Conn.: Yale University Press.

Llera, Francisco José. 1986. "Procesos estructurales de la sociedad vasca." In Francesc Hernández and Francesc Mercadé, eds., *Estructuras sociales e cuestión nacional en España*, pp. 159–85. Barcelona: Ariel.

Llobera, Josep. 1989. "Catalan National Identity: The Dialectics of Past and Present." In Elizabeth Tonkin et al., eds., *History and Ethnicity*, pp. 247–61. London: Routledge.

Loeber, Dietrich André, et al., eds. 1990. *Regional Identity Under Soviet Rule: The Case of the Baltic States*. Kiel: Institute for the Study of Law, Politics, and Society of Socialist States, University of Kiel.

Loit, Aleksander. 1983. "Die nationalen Bewegungen im Baltikum während des 19. Jahrhunderts in vergleichender Perspektive." *National Movements*: 59–81.

Lustick, Ian. 1985. *State-Building Failure in British Ireland and French Algeria*. Berkeley: Institute of International Studies.

Maluquer i Sostres, Joaquim. 1963. *L'assimilation des immigrés en Catalogne*. Geneva: Librairie Droz.

March, Michael. 1990. "Baltic Notes." *Times Literary Supplement* (April 13-19): 394–405.

Maravall, Jose M. 1978. *Dictatorship and Political Dissent: Workers and Students in Franco's Spain*. London: Tavistock.

———. 1979. "Political Cleavages in Spain and the 1979 General Elections." *Government and Opposition* 14: 299–317.

Marsal, Juan F., and Javier Roiz. 1985. "Catalan Nationalism and the Spanish Elections." In Howard R. Penniman and Eusebio M. Mujal-León, eds., *Spain at the Polls 1977, 1979, 1982: A Study of the National Elections*, pp. 206–25. Durham, N.C.: Duke University Press.

Marshall, T. H. 1973 [1949]. "Citizenship and Social Class," in *Class, Citizenship, and Social Development*, pp. 65–122. Westport, Conn.: Greenwood Press.

McAuley, Alistair. 1979. *Economic Welfare in the Soviet Union: Poverty, Living Standards, and Inequality*. Madison: University of Wisconsin Press.

McKay, James. 1982. "An Exploratory Synthesis of Primordial and Mobilizationist Approaches to Ethnic Phenomena." *Ethnic and Racial Studies* 5, no. 4 (October): 385–419.

Medhurst, Kenneth. 1982. "Basques and Basque Nationalism." In Colin H. Williams, ed., *National Separatism*, pp. 235–61. Vancouver: University of British Columbia Press.

———. 1987. *The Basques and Catalans*. London: The Minority Rights Group, Report No. 9 (revised).

Miguel, Amando de. 1974. "Estructura social e inmigracion en el Pais Vasconavarro." *Revista Papels*, no. 3: 249–73.

Miljan, Toivo. 1989. "The Proposal to Establish Economic Autonomy in Estonia." *Journal of Baltic Studies* 20, no. 2 (Summer): 149–64.

Mill, John Stuart. 1961. *A System of Logic, Ratiocinative and Inductive*. New York: Longmans.

Misiunas, Romuald J. 1990. "The Baltic Republics: Stagnation and Strivings for Sovereignty." In Lubomyr Hajda and Mark Beissinger, eds., *The Nationalities Factor in Soviet Politics and Society*, pp. 204–27. Boulder, Colo.: Westview Press.

———— and Rein Taagepera. 1983. *The Baltic States: Years of Dependence, 1940–1980*. Berkeley: University of California Press.

———— and Rein Taagepera. 1989. "The Baltic States: Years of Dependence, 1980–1986." *Journal of Baltic Studies* 20, no. 1 (Spring): 65–88.

Molins, Joaquim M., and Josep M. Vallés. 1990. "The Spanish General Election of 1989." *Electoral Studies* 9, no. 3 (September): 246–50.

Moxon-Browne, Edward. 1991. "Regionalism in Spain: The Basque Elections of 1990." *Regional Politics and Policy* 1, no. 2 (Summer): 191–96.

Myachin, Vadim, and Matthew J. Sagers. 1991. "Soviet Industrial Landscape: Planecon's Industrial Enterprises Databank." *Plan Econ Report* 7, no. 36 (October 15).

Nagel, Joane, and Susan Olzak. 1982. "Ethnic Mobilization in New and Old States: An Extension of the Competition Model." *Social Problems* 30, no. 2 (December): 127–43.

Nahaylo, Bohdan and Victor Swoboda, eds. 1990. *Soviet Disunion: A History of Nationalities Problem in the USSR*. New York: Free Press.

Nairn, Tom. 1977. *The Break-Up of Britain: Crisis and Neo-Nationalism*. London: NLB.

National Movements in the Baltic Countries During the Nineteenth Century. 1983. The Seventh Conference on Baltic Studies in Scandinavia, Studia Baltica Stockholmiensia. Stockholm: Almqvist and Wiksell.

Negre Rigol, Pedro. 1968. *El obrero y la ciudad*. Barcelona: Ariel.

Nielsen, François. 1980. "The Flemish Movement in Belgium After World War II: A Dynamic Analysis." *American Sociological Review* 45 (February): 76–94.

Nodel, Emanuel. 1974. "Life and Death of Estonian Jewry." In Arvids Ziedonis Jr. et al., eds., *Baltic History*, pp. 227–36. Columbus, Ohio: Association for the Advancement of Baltic Studies.

Nove, Alec. *The Soviet Economic System*, 3rd ed. Boston: Allen & Unwin.

Núñez, L. 1977. *Clases sociales en Euskadi*. San Sebastián: Txertoa.

O'Donnell, Paul E. 1989. "A Study of Linguistically 'Mixed' Families in Catalonia, Spain: Plurilingualism and Politics." *Romance Languages Annual*: 572–76.

————. 1990. "Linguistic Recruitment and Linguistic Defection in Catalonia: An Interdisciplinary Approach." Paper presented at the MLA Convention, Chicago, December.

Olcott, Martha B., et al., eds. 1990. *The Soviet Multinational State: Readings and Documents*. Armonk, N.Y.: M. E. Sharpe.

Oliner, Samuel P. 1976. "The Non-Russian Peoples in the USSR: An Unsolved Problem." *Ukrainian Quarterly* 32, no. 3: 261–85.

Orridge, A. W. 1981. "Uneven Development and Nationalism, Parts I and II." *Political Studies* 29, nos. 1 and 2: 1–15, 181–90.

————. 1982. "Separatism and Autonomous Nationalisms: The Structure of Regional Loyalties in the Modern State." In Colin H. Williams, ed., *National Separatism*, pp. 43–74. Vancouver: University of British Columbia Press.

Ortzi [Francisco Letamendía]. 1975. *Historia de Euskadi: El nacionalismo vasco y ETA*. Paris: Ruedo ibérico.

————. 1980. *Breve historia de Euskadi: De la prehistoria a nuestros días*. Paris: Ruedo ibérico.

Ostapenko, L. V., and A. A. Suskolov. 1990. "The Interregional Mixing and National Composition of Labor Resources." In Martha B. Olcott et al., eds., *The Soviet Multinational State: Readings and Documents*, pp. 216–28. Armonk, N.Y.: M. E. Sharpe.

Owen, Roger, and Bob Sutcliffe eds. 1972. *Studies in the Theory of Imperialism*. London: Longman.

Oxenstierna, Susanne. 1991. "Labor Market Policies in the Baltic Republics." *International Labor Review* 130, no. 2: 255–74.

Page, Stanley W. 1970. *The Formation of the Baltic States: A Study of the Effects of Great Power Politics upon the Emergence of Lithuania, Latvia, and Estonia*. New York: Howard Fertig.

"Panel on Nationalism in the USSR: Environmental and Territorial Aspects." 1989. *Soviet Geography* 30, no. 6 (June): 449–509.

Park, Robert. 1950. *Race and Culture: Essays in the Sociology of Contemporary Man*. Glencoe, Ill.: The Free Pess.

———— and H. Miller. 1921. *Old World Traits Transplanted*. Chicago: University of Chicago Society for Social Research.

Parming, Tönu. 1972. "Population Changes in Estonia, 1935–1970." *Population Studies* 26, no. 1: 53–78.

———. 1977. "The Historical Roots of Nationality Differences in the Soviet Baltic." In Edward Allworth ed., *Nationality Group Survival in Multi-Ethnic States.* New York: Praeger.

———. 1978. "Population Changes and Processes." In Tönu Parming and Elmar Järvesoo, *A Case Study of a Soviet Republic: The Estonian SSR,* pp. 21–74. Boulder, Colo.: Westview Press.

———. 1980. "Population Processes and the Nationality Issue in the Soviet Baltics." *Soviet Studies* 32, no. 3: 398–414.

——— and Elmar Järvesoo. 1978. *A Case Study of a Soviet Republic: The Estonian SSR.* Boulder, Colo.: Westview Press.

Payne, S. G. 1971. "Catalan and Basque Nationalism," *Journal of Contemporary History* 6, no. 1: 15–51.

———. 1975. *Basque Nationalism.* Reno: University of Nevada.

———. 1991. "Nationalism, Regionalism, and Micronationalism in Spain." *Journal of Contemporary History* 26, nos. 3/4 (September): 469–91.

Pearson, Raymond. 1983. *National Minorities in Eastern Europe, 1848–1945.* London: Macmillan.

Peled, Yoav, and Gershon Shafir. 1987. "Split Labor Market and the State: The Effect of Modernization on Jewish Industrial Workers in Tsarist Russia." *American Journal of Sociology* 92, no. 6(May): 1435–60.

Pennar, Jaan. 1978. "Soviet Nationality Policy and the Estonian Communist Elite." in Tönu Parming and Elmar Järvesoo, *A Case Study of a Soviet Republic: The Estonian SSR,* pp.105–27. Boulder, Colo.: Westview Press.

Penniman, Howard R., and Eusebio M. Mujal-León, eds. 1985. *Spain at the Polls 1977, 1979, 1982: A Study of the National Elections.* Durham, N.C.: Duke University Press.

Petherbridge-Hernández, Patricia. 1990. "Reconceptualizing Liberating Non-Formal Education: A Catalan Case Study." *Compare* 20, no. 1: 41–51.

Pinilla de las Heras, Estaban. 1979a. *Immigració i mobilitat social a Catalunya,* vol. 2. Barcelona: Institut Catòlic d'Estudis Socials de Barcelona.

———. 1979b. *Estudios sobre cambio social y estructuras sociales en Cataluña.* Madrid: Centro de Investigaciones Sociologicas.

Pi-Sunyer, Oriol. 1971. "The Maintenance of Ethnic Identity in Catalonia." In Oriol Pi-Sunyer, ed., *The Limits of Integration: Ethnicity and Nationalism in Modern Europe,* pp. 117–31. Amherst: University of Massachusetts, Department of Anthropology Research Report 9.

———. 1980. "Dimensions of Catalan Nationalism." In Charles R. Foster, ed., *Nations Without a State: Ethnic Minorities in Western Europe*, pp. 101–15. New York: Praeger.

———. 1985. "Catalan Nationalism: Some Theoretical and Historical Considerations." In Edward A. Tiryakian and Ronald Rogowski, eds., *New Nationalisms of the Developed West*, pp.254–76. Boston: Allen & Unwin.

Plakans, Andrejs. 1974. "Modernization and the Latvians in Nineteenth-Century Baltikum." In Arvids Ziedonis et al., eds., *Baltic History*, pp. 123–34. Columbus, Ohio: Association for the Advancement of Baltic Studies.

———. 1981. "The Latvians." In Edward C. Thaden, *Russification in the Baltic Provinces and Finalnd, 1855–1914*, pp. 207–84. Princeton, N.J.: Princeton University Press.

———. 1991. "Latvia's Return to Independence." *Journal of Baltic Studies* 22, no. 3 (Fall): 259–66.

Portes, Alejandro, and J. Walton. 1981. *Labor, Class, and the Immigration System*. New York: Academic Press.

Pourchier, Suzanne, and Yves Plasseraud. 1989. "Retour à Riga." *Esprit*, no. 156 (November): 24–33.

———. 1990. "Vers l'indépendance des pays baltes?" *Esprit*, no. 160 (March–April): 33–39.

Prazauskas, Algis. 1991. "Ethnic Conflicts in the Context of Democratizing Political Systems." *Theory and Society* 20, no. 5 (October): 581–602.

Price, Charles. 1993. "Australia: A New Multicultural Country?" In Daniel Kubat, ed., *The Politics of Migration Policies: Settlement and Integration-The First World into the 1990's*, 2d ed., pp. 3–22. New York: Center for Migration Studies.

Price, Glanville. 1979. "The Present Position and Viability of Minority Languages." In Anthony E. Alcock et al., *The Future of Cultural Minorities*, pp. 30–43. London: Macmillan.

Prikhodko, Y. A. 1973. *Vosstanovlenie Industrii 1942–50*. Moscow: Mysl'.

Prunskiene, Kazimiera. 1990. "On Economic Independence of the Baltic Republics." *Problems of Economics* 33, no. 5 (September): 71–83.

Pullerits, Albert. 1935. *Estonia: Population, Cultural and Economic Life*. Tallinn: Stiramm.

Ra'anan, Uri. 1990. "The Nation-State Fallacy." In Joseph V. Montville, ed., *Conflict and Peacemaking in Multiethnic Societies*, pp. 5–20. Lexington, Mass.: D. C. Heath.

Ragin, Charles C. 1979. "Ethnic Political Mobilization: The Welsh Case." *American Sociological Review* 44 (August): 619–35.

Rauch, George von. 1974. *The Baltic States: The Years of Independence, Estonia, Latvia, Lithuania, 1917–1940*, trans. Gerald Onn. London: C. Hurst.

Raun, Toivo U. 1974. "Modernization and the Estonians, 1860–1914." In Arvids Ziedonis et al., eds., *Baltic History*, pp. 135–41. Columbus, Ohio: Association for the Advancement of Baltic Studies.

———. 1981. "The Estonians." In Edward C. Thaden, *Russification in the Baltic Provinces and Finland, 1855–1914*, pp. 287–354. Princeton, N.J.: Princeton University Press.

———. 1987. *Estonia and the Estonians*. Stanford, Calif.: Hoover Institution Press.

———. 1991. "The Re-Establishment of Estonian Independence." *Journal of Baltic Studies* 22, no. 3 (Fall): 251–58.

Raun, Toivo U., and Andrejs Plakans. 1990. "The Estonian and Latvian National Movements: An Assessment of Miroslav Hroch's Model. *Journal of Baltic Studies* 21, no. 2: 131–44.

Raz, Joseph. 1994. "Multiculturalism: A Liberal Perspective." *Dissent* (Winter): 67–79.

Remeikis, Thomas. 1977. "Modernization and National Identity in the Baltic Republics." In Ihor Kamenetsky, *Nationalism and Human Rights: Process of Modernization in the USSR*, pp. 115–38. Littletown, Co.: Association for the Study of Nationalities.

Rex, John. 1994. "Conceptual and Practical Problems of Multi-Culturalism in Europe." Paper delivered in a symposium on Multi-Cultural Society, organized by the Swedish Ministry of Culture, Vasteras, Sweden.

Rocket, Rocky L. 1980. "Ethnic Stratification in the Soviet Union: A Preliminary Analysis." *Ethnic Groups* 2: 327–41.

Roeder, Philip G. 1991. "Soviet Federalism and Ethnic Mobilization." *World Politics* 43, no. 2 (January): 196–232.

Ros, Adela. 1993. "State and Ethnicity: The Celebration of Andalusia in Catalonia." Unpublished seminar paper, University of California, San Diego.

Rowland, Richard H. 1990. "The Soviet Union." In Charles B. Nam et al., eds., *International Handbook on Internal Migration*, pp. 323–43. New York: Greenwood.

Rutkis, J., ed. 1967. *Latvia: Country and People*. Stockholm: Latvian National Foundation.

Sabaliunas, Leonas. 1990. *Lithuanian Social Democracy in Perspective, 1893–1914*. Durham, N.C.: Duke University Press.

Sáez, Armand. 1980. "Catalunya, gresol o explotadora? Notes sobre immigracio i creixement." In *Immigració i reconstrucció nacional a Catalunya*, pp. 25–35. Barcelona: Editorial Blume.

Sagers, Matthew. 1991. "Regional Aspects of the Soviet Economy." *Plan Econ Report* 7, nos. 1–2 (January 15).

Samonis, Valdas. 1991. *From Dependence to Interdependence: Transforming Baltic Foreign Economic Relations*. Indianapolis: Hudson Institute.

Schiffer, Jonathan R. 1990. "Soviet Territorial Pricing and Emerging Republican Politics." *Journal of Soviet Nationalities* 1, no. 3 (Fall): 67–111.

Schroeder, Gertrude E. 1990. "Nationalities and the Soviet Economy." In Lybomyr Hajda and Mark Beissinger, eds., *The Nationalities Factor in Soviet Politics and Society*, pp. 43–71. Boulder, Colo.: Westview Press.

Senn, Alfred Erich. 1990. *Lithuania Awakening*. Berkeley:University of California Press.

———. 1991. "Lithuania's Path to Independence." *Journal of Baltic Studies* 22, no. 3 (Fall): 245–50.

Shabad, Goldie. 1986. "After Autonomy: The Dynamics of Regionalism in Spain." Working Paper No. 1 of the Spanish Studies Round Table, University of Illinois at Chicago.

Shafir, Gershon. 1992. "Relative Overdevelopment and Alternative Paths of Nationalism: A Comparison of Catalonia and the Baltic Republics." *Journal of Baltic Studies* 23, no. 2 (Summer): 105–20.

Shanin, Teodor. 1989. "Ethnicity in the Soviet Union: Analytic Perceptions and Political Strategies." *Comparative Studies in Society and History* 31, no. 3 (July): 409–24.

Sharpe, L. J. 1984. "The Market, the State, and Regional Peripherality in Western Europe." In M. Hebbert and H. Machin, eds., *Regionalization in France, Italy, and Spain*, pp. 55–65. London: London School of Economy.

Shils, Edward. 1957. "Primordial, Personal, Sacred and Civil Ties: Some Particular Observations on the Relationship of Sociological Research and Theory." *British Journal of Sociology* 8, no. 2 (June): 130–45.

———. 1959–1960. "Political Development in New States, Parts I and II." *Comparative Studies in Society and History* 2: 265–92, 379–411.

———. 1963. "On the Comparative Study of the New States." In Clifford Geertz, ed., *Old Societies and New States*, pp. 1–26. London: The Free Press.

Shryock, Richard. 1977. "Indigenous Economic Managers." In Edward Allworth, ed., *National Group Survival in Multi-Ethnic States: Shifting Support Patterns in the Soviet Baltic Region*, pp. 83–122. London: Praeger.

Siilivask, K. 1983. "Some of the Main Features of the Socio-Economic Development of Estonia in the Nineteenth Century." in *National Movements*, pp.205–14.

Simon, Gerhard. 1986. *Nationalismus und Nationalitätenpolitik in der Sowjetunion*. Baden-Baden: Nomos.

Smith, Anthony D. 1971. *Theories of Nationalism*. New York: Harper and Row.

Smith, Graham E. 1979. "The Impact of Modernisation on the Latvian Soviet Republic." *Co-existence* 16: 45–64.

———. 1981."Die Probleme des Nationalismus in den drei baltischen Sowjetrepubliken Estland, Lettland und Litauen." *Acta Baltica* 21: 143–77.

———. 1989a. "Gorbachev's Greatest Challenge: Perestroika and the National Question." *Political Geography Quarterly* 8, no. 1 (January): 7–20.

———. 1989b. "Administering Ethnoregional Stability: The Soviet State and the Nationalities Question." In Colin H. William and Eleonore Kofman, eds., *Community Conflict, Partition and Nationalism*, pp. 224–51. New York: Routledge.

Smyth, Terence M. 1980. "Left Responses to Nationalism in Spain: Federal Republicanism, Anarcho-Collectivism, and the Marxist Parties." In Eric Cahm and Vladimir Claude Fisera, eds., *Socialism and Nationalism in Contemporary Europe (1848–1945)*, pp.14–27. Nottingham: Spokesman.

Solé, Carlota. 1982. *Los inmigrantes en la sociedad y en la cultura catalanas*. Barcelona: Ediciones Península.

————. 1985. "Cambios en la vision de los inmigrantes sobre las instituciones, simbolos y partidos politicos de Cataluña." *Revista Española de Investigaciones Sociologices*, no. 32 (October–December): 194–234.

Solé-Tura, Jordi 1974. *Catalanismo y revolución burguesa*. Madrid: EDICUSA.

Starr, S.Frederick. 1990. "Soviet Nationalities in Crisis." *Journal of Soviet Nationalities* 1, no. 1 (Spring): 76–90.

Strubell i Trueta, Miquel. 1981. *Llengua i població a Catalunya*. Barcelona: La Magrana.

Stukas, Jack J. 1966. *Awakening Lithuania: A Study on the Rise of Modern Lithuanian Nationalism*. Madison, Wisc.: Florham Park Press.

Sullivan, John. 1988. *ETA and Basque Nationalism: The Fight for Euskadi 1890–1986*. London: Routledge.

Taagepera, Rein. 1973. "Dissimilarities Between the Northwestern Soviet Republics." In Arvids Ziedonis Jr. et al., eds., *Problems of Mininations: Baltic Perspectives*, pp. 69–88. San José, Calif.: Association for the Advancement of Baltic Studies.

————. 1975. "Estonia and the Estonians." in Zev Katz et al., eds., *Handbook of Major Soviet Nationalities*, pp.75–93. New York: The Free Press.

————. 1981. "Baltic Population Changes, 1950–1980." *Journal of Baltic Studies* 12, no. 1: 35–57.

————. 1990a. "A Note on the March 1989 Elections in Estonia." *Soviet Studies* 42, no. 2 (April): 329–39.

————. 1990b. "The Baltic States." *Electoral Studies* 9, no. 4 (December): 303–11.

————. 1991. "Building Democracy in Estonia." *PS: Political Science and Politics* 24, no. 3 (September): 478–81.

————. 1992. "Ethnic Relations in Estonia." *Journal of Baltic Studies* 23, no. 2 (Summer): 121–32.

————. 1993. *Estonia: Return to Independence*. Boulder, Colo.: Westview Press.

Tamames, R., & T. Clegg. 1984. "Spain: Regional Autonomy and the Democratic Transition." In M. Hebbert and H. Machin, eds., *Regionalization in France, Italy and Spain*, pp. 31–54. London: London School of Economics.

Terentjeva, Ludmila. 1970. "How Do Youths from Bi-National Families Determine Their Nationality?" *Bulletin of Baltic Studies*, no. 4 (December): 5–11.

Termes, Josep. 1984. "La immigració a Catalunya: política i cultura." In Josep Termes, *La immigració a Catalunya i altres estudis d'història del nacionalisme català*, pp. 127–93. Barcelona: Empúries.

Thaden, Edward C. 1981a. *Russification in the Baltic Provinces and Finland, 1855-1914*. Princeton, N.J.: Princeton University Press.

———. 1981b. "The Russian Government." In Edward C. Thaden, *Russification in the Baltic Provinces and Finland, 1855–1914*, pp. 15–108. Princeton, N.J.: Princeton University Press.

Thornberry, Patrick. 1994. "International and European Standards on Minority Rights." In Hugh Mail, ed., *Minority Rights in Europe: The Scope for a Transnational Regime*, pp. 14–21. London: Royal Institute of International Affairs.

Tilly, Charles ed. 1975. *The Formation of National States in Western Europe*. Princeton, N.J.: Princeton University Press.

———. 1990. *Coercion, Capital, and European States, AD 990–1990*. Cambridge: Basil Blackwell.

———. 1991. "Ethnic Conflict in the Soviet Union." *Theory and Society* 20, no. 5 (October): 569–80.

Tiryakian, Edward A., and Ronald Rogowski eds. 1985. *New Nationalisms of the Developed West*. Boston: Allen & Unwin.

Tishkov, Valerii. 1990. "Ethnicity and Power in the Republics of the USSR." *Journal of Soviet Nationalities* 1, no. 3 (Fall): 33–65.

Trapans, Andris. 1991. "Moscow, Economic, and the Baltic Republics." In Jan Arveds Trapans, ed., *Toward Independence: The Baltic Popular Movements*, pp. 85–98. Boulder, Colo.: Westview Press.

Trapans, Jan Arveds, ed. 1991a. *Toward Independence: The Baltic Popular Movements*. Boulder, Colo.: Westview Press.

———. 1991b. "The Sources of Latvia's Popular Movement." In Jan Arveds Trapans, ed., *Toward Independence: The Baltic Popular Movements*, pp. 25–41. Boulder, Colo.: Westview Press.

Trotsky, Leon. 1959. *The Russian Revolution*, Selected and edited by F. W. Dupee. Garden City, N.Y.: Doubleday.

Urla, Jacqueline. 1988. "Ethnic Protest and Social Planning: A Look at Basque Language Revival." *Cultural Anthropology* 3, no. 4 (November): 379–94.

Van Arkadie, Brian, and Mats Karlsson. 1992. *Economic Survey of the Baltic States.* London: Pinter.

Vardys, V. Stanley. 1965a. *Lithuania Under the Soviets: Portrait of a Nation, 1940–65.* London: Praeger.

———. 1965b. "Soviet Social Engineering in Lithuania: An Appraisal. " In V. Stanley Vardys, *Lithuania Under the Soviets: Portrait of a Nation, 1940–65,* pp. 237–59. London: Praeger.

———. 1978. "The Rise of Authoritarian Rule in the Baltic States," In Stanley Vardys and Romuald J. Misiunas, eds., *The Baltic States in Peace and War, 1917–1945,* pp. 65–80. University Park: Pennsylvania State University Press.

——— and Romuald J. Misiunas, eds. 1978. *The Baltic States in Peace and War, 1917-1945.* University Park: Pennsylvania State University Press.

Viladot i Presas, M. Angels. 1990. "Identitat ètnica: I pluralisme cultural i lingüístic." *Revista de Catalunya* 47 (December): 26–40.

Vilar, Pierre. 1962. *La Catalogne dans l'Espagne moderne,* vol. 1. Paris: Flammarion.

———. 1980. "Spain and Catalonia." *Review* 3, no. 4: 527–77.

Vincens Vivens, Jaime. 1969. *An Economic History of Spain.* Princeton, N.J.: Princeton University Press.

Waldmann, Peter. 1985. "Gewaltsamer Separatismus: Am Beispiel der Basken, Franco-Kanadier und Nordiren." *Kölner Zeitschrift für Soziologie und Sozialpsychologie* 37: 203–29.

Wallerstein, Immanuel. 1974. *The Modern World System,* vol. 1. *Capitalist Agriculture and the Origins of the European World-Economy in the Sixteenth Century.* New York: Academic Press.

Weingard, Joan T. 1975. "Language and Literature in Estonia: Kulturpolitik or Natural Evolution?" In Ralph S.Clem, ed., *The Soviet West: Interplay between Nationality and Social Organization,* pp. 10–29. New York: Praeger.

Wolfrum, R. 1993. "The Emergence of 'New Minorities' as a Result of Migration." In Catherine Brölmann et al., *Peoples and Minorities in International Law,* pp. 153–66. Dordrecht: Martinus Nijhoff.

Woolard, Kathryn A. 1986a. "The Politics of Language Status Planning: 'Normalization' in Catalonia." In Nancy Schweda-Nicholson, ed., *Languages in the International Perspective,* pp. 91–102. Norwood, N.J.: Ablex.

———. 1986b. "The 'Crisis in the Concept of Identity' in Contemporary Catalonia, 1976–1982." In Gary W. McDonogh, ed., *Conflict in Catalonia: Images of an Urban Society*, pp. 54–71. Gainesville: University Presses of Florida.

———. 1989. *Double Talk: Bilingualism and the Politics of Ethnicity in Catalonia.* Stanford, Calif.: Stanford University Press.

——— and Tae-Joong Gahng. 1990. "Changing Language Policies and Attitudes in Autonomous Catalonia." *Language and Society* 19 (September): 311–30.

World Bank. 1993a. *Estonia: The Transition to a Market Economy.* Washington, D.C.

———. 1993b. *Latvia: The Transition to a Market Economy.* Washington, D.C.

———. 1993. *Lithuania: The Transition to a Market Economy.* Washington, D.C.

Xenos, Nicholas. 1990. "The State, Rights, and the Homogenous Nation," Paper presented at the Second International Conference of the ISSEI on Comparative History of European Nationalism: Towards Europe 1992, Louvain, Belgium.

Zaslavskaya, T. I., and L. V. Korel. 1984. "Rural-Urban Migration in the USSR: Problems and Prospects." *Sociologia Ruralis* 24, nos. 3/4: 229–41.

Zaslavsky, Victor. 1980. "The Ethnic Question in the USSR." *Telos*, no. 45 (Fall): 44–76.

Ziedonis, Arvids, Jr. et al., eds. 1974. *Baltic History.* Columbus, Ohio: Association for the Advancement of Baltic Studies.

Ziegler, Charles E. 1985. "Nationalism, Religion and Equality among Ethnic Minorities: Some Observations on the Soviet Case." *Journal of Ethnic Studies* 13, no. 2 (Summer): 19–32.

Zirakzadeh, Cyrus Ernesto. 1989. "Economic Changes and Surges in Micro-Nationalist Voting in Scotland and the Basque Region of Spain." *Comparative Studies in Society and History* 31, no. 2 (April): 318–39.

Zunde, Pranas. 1965. "Lithuania's Economy: Introduction of the Soviet Pattern." In V. Stanlye Vardys, *Lithuania Under the Soviets: Portrait of a Nation, 1940–65*, pp. 141–69. London: Praeger.

Zvidrins, Peter 1979. "The Dynamics of Fertility in Latvia." *Population Studies* 33, no. 2 (July): 277–82.

INDEX

DATE DUE

APR 0 4 1996		
MAR 2 5 1996		
MAY 1 2 1997		
NOV 1 2 1997		
APR 2 1 1998		
MAY 2 1 1998		
FEB 2 5 2000		
FEB 1 4 2000		
NOV 2 3 2010		

Demco, Inc. 38-293